A CULTURAL HISTORY OF CHILDHOOD AND FAMILY

VOLUME 5

A Cultural History of Childhood and Family
General Editors: Elizabeth Foyster and James Marten

Volume 1
A Cultural History of Childhood and Family in Antiquity
Edited by Mary Harlow and Ray Laurence

Volume 2
A Cultural History of Childhood and Family in the Middle Ages
Edited by Louise J. Wilkinson

Volume 3
A Cultural History of Childhood and Family in the Early Modern Age
Edited by Sandra Cavallo and Silvia Evangelisti

Volume 4
A Cultural History of Childhood and Family in the Age of Enlightenment
Edited by Elizabeth Foyster and James Marten

Volume 5
A Cultural History of Childhood and Family in the Age of Empire
Edited by Colin Heywood

Volume 6
A Cultural History of Childhood and Family in the Modern Age
Edited by Joseph M. Hawes and N. Ray Hiner

A CULTURAL HISTORY OF
CHILDHOOD AND FAMILY

IN THE AGE
OF EMPIRE

Edited by Colin Heywood

B L O O M S B U R Y
LONDON • NEW DELHI • NEW YORK • SYDNEY

Bloomsbury Academic
An imprint of Bloomsbury Publishing Plc

50 Bedford Square
London
WC1B 3DP
UK

1385 Broadway
New York
NY 10018
USA

www.bloomsbury.com

Hardback edition first published in 2010 by Berg Publishers, an imprint of
Bloomsbury Academic
Paperback edition first published by Bloomsbury Academic 2014

British Library Cataloguing-in-Publication Data
A catalogue record for this book is available from the British Library.

ISBN: HB: 978-1-84788-798-6
PB: 978-1-4725-5471-0
HB Set: 978-1-84520-826-4
PB Set: 978-1-4725-5474-1

Library of Congress Cataloging-in-Publication Data
A catalog record for this book is available from the Library of Congress.

Typeset by Apex CoVantage, LLC, Madison, WI, USA

CONTENTS

ILLUSTRATIONS

CHAPTER 10

GENERAL EDITORS' PREFACE

The literature on the histories of children and the family has reached a critical mass. The proliferation of encyclopedia, conferences, and professional associations reflects the vitality of these closely related but independent fields. The two subjects are naturally linked; Western conceptions of the family have virtually always included children, and children and youth are irrevocably shaped by their time growing up in families.

The *Cultural History of Childhood and Family* aims to bring order to these sometimes disparate histories and historiographical traditions with original material written especially for these volumes. More than six dozen editors and authors from five continents and thirteen countries were commissioned to take a comprehensive look at the subject from a Western perspective with more than casual glances at the world beyond. Based on deep readings of the secondary literature and on representative primary sources, each of the chapters is an original work of synthesis and interpretation.

It is our hope that imposing a standard table of contents on a project covering literally thousands of years and hundreds of ethnicities, religious faiths, and communities will help us find otherwise hidden patterns and rich contrasts in the experiences of children and families and in humankind's attitudes about them. There is inevitably a bit of overlap; issues related to children and the family do not form and develop according to convenient beginning and ending dates. But there is also a variety of viewpoints, even on similar topics. Indeed, as general editors we embrace the divergence of interpretations, emphases, and even writing and organizational styles that emerge from these five dozen chapters. Some of the diversity follows naturally from the vastly different conditions facing children and their families in different eras, while in other cases it is inspired by the authors' expertise and personal approaches to the field.

There have always been many childhoods and many families in the West. The purpose of these volumes is not only to look at the constructions of childhood and the family, particularly as they reflect evolving ethnic, gender, religious, national, and class assumptions, but also the lived experiences of children and of the families in which they spend so much of their lives. The symbiotic relationship between child and parent, between brother and sister, and between the individual and the family to which he or she belongs is reflected in the intertwined historical literature on children and families. By studying both, we can learn more about each.

Elizabeth Foyster
Clare College, University of Cambridge

James Marten
Marquette University

Introduction

COLIN HEYWOOD

Children brought up in the great maritime powers of Europe during the nineteenth century basked in the reflected glory of Empire. It was as if they were at the very center of the universe. Their countries boasted of a commercial and industrial lead over others, outstanding inventiveness, and unparalleled military strength. History textbooks, for example, fed English schoolchildren a grandiose vision of their place in the world. Typical of the period around 1900 was the assertion that the British Empire "embraces people of almost every race, colour and religion, all living peacefully and prospering under the British flag." Across the channel, an aristocrat born on the eve of the First World War recalled later in life that he had considered France "the foremost country in the world, the only civilized and civilizing one."[1] There were, of course, dissenting voices at the time, anticipating our current inclination to mock such egregious claims. These did not stop the imperial powers, including aspiring new ones such as Germany and the United States, from attempting to mold colonial societies in their own interests. Children in the colonies inevitably felt some of the weight of this so-called civilizing mission. Missionary schools, for example, initiated them into the Western culture of their rulers, while European administrations turned them into wage laborers for commercial farmers and plantation owners. Such uneven relationships continue into the twenty-first century, with powerful nations in the West determined to export their vision of childhood to the rest of the world. Most children in Europe and the United States now enjoy a relatively sheltered existence, protected within their families for as long as possible from the supposedly harsh realities of the adult world. Yet this modern form of childhood, and the modern child-centered family that goes with it, only emerged after a long series of debates over such issues as to whether children should work, what they should learn at school, and whether they should have any sort of sex life. Westerners are today open to the accusation of ill-informed interference with similar debates over the nature of childhood and the role of the family in very different economic, social, and cultural contexts.

The chapters in this volume are concerned with those same nineteenth-century debates over how childhood and the family should evolve. They invite reflection on the form of childhood that people in the West now take for granted. Is it worth defending, or, in the words of the historian Paula Fass, "has it ever been more than a romanticized notion and a means to assimilate the less fortunate to the more powerful?"[2] This introduction provides the context in three ways. First, it will place nineteenth-century developments in the broader context of the long-term history of childhood and the family. Second, it will home in on some of the ideas and social changes that produced the modern conception of childhood in the West and beyond during this period. Finally, it will consider the advantages and disadvantages of the newfound desire to protect the young.

THE NINETEENTH-CENTURY CHILDHOOD AND FAMILY IN LONG-TERM PERSPECTIVE

The emergence of a modern form of childhood was a long, drawn-out process. The early modern period brought a number of changes in the ideas and experiences of childhood that would reverberate throughout the nineteenth century and beyond. Historians have debated vigorously when the decisive period for change occurred. Philippe Ariès went back as far as the fifteenth, sixteenth, and seventeenth centuries to locate the most important turning point, with his famous assertion that they witnessed the "discovery of childhood." Few historians would now accept his stark contrast between the medieval and the modern worlds in the conception of childhood. Yet a number of them have argued for the first signs of a long childhood, so characteristic of our contemporary world, during the early modern period. Certainly, the steady movement toward mass education, much in evidence during the nineteenth century in Western nations, had its origins in the fierce theological and pedagogical debates of the sixteenth and seventeenth centuries.[3] For Hugh Cunningham, among others, a more convincing case emerges for the eighteenth century as the period of decisive change—as contributions to volume 4 of this series document in more detail. It was above all in ideas about childhood that change occurred. To quote Cunningham, "Framed by the writings of John Locke at its beginning and the Romantic poets at the end, and with the strident figure of Rousseau at center stage, there seems in the eighteenth century to be a degree of sensitivity to childhood and to children lacking in previous centuries." Among the Romantics, for example, such luminaries as Goethe in Germany, Wordsworth and Blake in England, and Victor Hugo in France insisted that the child was distinct from the adult, and in some ways superior. This was an essential underpinning to the increased interest in protecting the supposedly innocent child during the nineteenth century.[4]

When it comes to the nineteenth century, historians have made further ambitious claims for its impact on childhood in the West. There are considerable variations in their approach, depending on how they have defined a modern childhood and the particular mix of social and cultural forces brought into play. Almost invariably, however, their starting point is the Industrial Revolution. In the words of Peter Stearns, "the clearest transformation in childhood's world history involves the replacement of agricultural with industrial societies." Industrialization had wide-ranging effects on such institutions as the labor market, the family, and the school. Stearns noted its early impact in West Europe and the United States during the eighteenth and nineteenth centuries. His model of a modern childhood took a largely material form, with its three fundamental characteristics of the triumph of school over work, the shift to small families, and the decline of infant mortality.

Other historians have focused more narrowly on the significance of the period for the history of the family. They note that, among the middle classes at least, economic activity steadily moved away from the household. The upshot was an upheaval in family relations. With the home now a purely domestic area, mothers took a more prominent role in the upbringing of children. Freed from the need to work, children were also readily perceived as innocent creatures requiring great care and attention. John Gillis, for example, identified a revolution in family life during the second half of the nineteenth century, at least among the Protestant classes of northwestern Europe and the United States. In the maturing industrial society of the late nineteenth century, he reasoned, families no longer sought their ideal of the good family from their religious beliefs or from the local community. Instead, they turned inward and set about creating their own symbolic universe. Mothers and children became the icons of family life; baptisms became a family rather than a communal affair; children's birthdays assumed an importance hitherto unknown in the family routine. In this way, the meaning of motherhood, fatherhood, and childhood took a radical new direction.[5]

The majority of children in Europe and the United States, brought up in the villages and popular quarters of the towns, were barely affected by these changes for much of the nineteenth century. They continued to work in some way from an early stage in life; they had little formal education; they suffered from high infant mortality rates; and their families remained open to the local community rather than in cozy domesticity. However, families in the West faced pressures from within and without to adopt a more modern form of childhood. Industrialization eventually led to a sustained rise in living standards for the masses, and demands from organized labor for a "family wage" for men workers that would allow mothers and children to remain at home. Working-class families became increasingly interested in sending their children to school for a variety of reasons linked to the rise of a more mobile, urbanized society. There was also a determined assault on established practices in the treatment of children by middle-class reformers. An influential take on this process came in 1985 from the work by the sociologist Viviana Zelizer on the change in the valuation of children in the United States between the 1870s and the 1930s. By the middle of the nineteenth century, she argued, the urban middle classes had come to accept that children would be better off in school rather than at work: their offspring had become economically "worthless." For the working class, by contrast, nineteenth-century industrialization brought more opportunities for the employment of children. As a result, the late nineteenth and early twentieth centuries saw a protracted campaign by middle-class reformers to impose their vision of childhood, pitching the moral value of an economically useless child against the price of a useful, wage-earning one. Their main weapon was the persuasiveness of the argument that childhood was "sacred." By the 1930s, the cause was effectively won, with the only work considered acceptable for children being that with some moral or instructional value. In the oft-quoted phrase from Zelizer, the "economically 'worthless' but emotionally 'priceless' child" had emerged to form the basis for contemporary childhood.[6]

The corollary of this victory of the middle-class conception of childhood and the family, with the emphasis on the dependence and infantilization of the young, was a tendency toward uniformity at this stage of life at all levels of society. The bureaucratic influence of the state during the nineteenth and twentieth centuries made a significant difference here. Families from the less "respectable" elements of society, reluctant to follow the new ideal, found themselves compelled to do so by law. During earlier periods, most people outside the elite had only a vague idea of their age. Popular usage was very loose in its use of terms such as child, adolescent, and youth. The civil registration of births, marriages, and deaths, imposed in France by the 1789 Revolution and in England by an act of 1837, for example, tightened procedures. Child labor legislation in effect defined the various ages of childhood very precisely. It invariably stipulated a minimum age for employment in a factory, mine, or workshop; regulated working hours according to age; prohibited night work for certain groups according to age and gender; and insisted on some part-time schooling for a number of years. It was the British state that provided the model for this. It first put a marker down in 1788 by banning children younger than eight from working as apprentices to chimney sweeps. The 1819 Factory Act considered children under nine too young to work in a cotton mill and limited working hours for those under sixteen. The 1842 Mines Act excluded boys under ten and all females from work underground. By 1901, the minimum working age in factories and workshops was twelve. Welfare institutions, in their turn, had to decide when their charges were old enough to look after themselves: for the *Assistance publique* in France, this was twelve; for the Poor Law in England, sixteen. Criminal responsibility was another indicator of the end of childhood, with sixteen an important age in many systems. In Russia, the 1900 Civil Code set the three ages of childhood at zero to fourteen, fourteen to seventeen, and eighteen to twenty. Above all, the shift to mass schooling led to a more uniform age grading of society. Eventually, nearly all children would start school around the age of five or six, and most would leave during their early teens. The 1876 Education Act in England defined a child as someone aged between five and fourteen. Gaining some kind of leaving certificate from a primary school marked the end of childhood for most young people well into the twentieth century—that tiny elite drawn mainly from the upper middle classes excepted.[7]

If the nineteenth century did much to consolidate and continue the transformation of childhood, it is also worth emphasizing that the modern conception is still evolving during the twenty-first century. Writing in the U.S. context in the year 2000, Paula Fass and Mary Ann Mason had the feeling that a new invention of childhood was emerging around them, in response to such changes as the massive expansion of the entertainment industry and the increasing demand for the teaching of work-related skills in the schools. Representatives of the state have come to see children as young adults, ready to take on certain responsibilities, rather than as "tender innocents." In retrospect, then, the overall effect between the eighteenth and the twentieth centuries was a transition from the "useful" to the "protected" childhood.[8] The nineteenth century, in particular, brought a decisive shift from theoretical discussion to practical initiatives. As Barbara Finkelstein observed, nineteenth-century Americans did not discover the vulnerability of childhood, nor invent the notion that children need supervision. Where they innovated was in "a disposition to define, build and organize learning communities for the young," including numerous types of schools, orphanages, and refuges.[9] From the brief outline above, it is possible to sense that historians have in their various ways settled on a few key themes. Most importantly, in the nineteenth century, children moved from the workplace to the school bench; they grew up in smaller families, with at least the ideal of a nurturing and attentive mother and father; and their welfare became a concern of the state, with intervention in such areas as health, parental abuse, crime and punishment, and sexual behavior. They were even supposed to be happy. These themes will run through this volume. It will also discuss other, related themes that specialists in the modern period have only begun to explore, such as the religious beliefs of children, their changing physical environment, and the colonial dimension.

CONTINUITY AND CHANGE DURING
THE NINETEENTH CENTURY

People in the Western nations faced an exhilarating prospect of change during the early nineteenth century, in the wake of the American and French Revolutions and with the first stirrings of the Industrial Revolution. They could dream of subjects becoming citizens, of constitutional and representative forms of government, of new sources of wealth and military strength. Yet there were also fears that the human costs of such a rapid subversion of the old order would outweigh the benefits. The revolution of 1789 brought the Declaration of the Rights of Man and the Citizen but also the pikes and scaffolds of the Reign of Terror; the new industrial centers like Manchester bristled with complex machinery and a thrusting entrepreneurial class but also the downtrodden "new barbarians" seething with discontent in the slums. Conservatives followed Edmund Burke in worrying about efforts to impose abstract principles on a society, as the French Revolutionaries had attempted during the 1790s, thereby flying in the face of experience. The old elites pondered the threats to their authority and the established social order from the subversive new forces. Ideas about the family, childhood, and children themselves could hardly avoid being caught up in this often febrile atmosphere. There were the same contradictory yearnings for change and stability, the same tensions between sources of innovation and those of inertia and resistance. Indeed, as the embodiment of the future for successive generations, children were an obvious battleground for competing ideological forces. Were the young children working in the mills on the new textile machinery heralds of an unheard-of prosperity or of a "degeneration of the race," contemporaries wondered? Would providing mass education risk subverting established authority, or would it lead to a more dynamic and competitive economy? Was the decline in religious observance among the young part of a new scientific and rationalist spirit or a threat to the very foundations of society? One can trace these ambiguous attitudes to change, and the accompanying elements of continuity and change, in various spheres. Here we will focus on two influences: competing conceptions of childhood and industrialization.

CONCEPTIONS OF CHILDHOOD

From the Olympian perspective of world history, Peter Stearns identified an idealization of the child as a peculiar feature of modern Western culture—one that might or might not appear in the modern model elsewhere.[10] As noted, debates over the nature of the child began well before the nineteenth century, and even before the transformation of the economy brought about by the Industrial Revolution. It is easy to assume that our contemporary views on childhood, thinking of children as "wondrous innocents," or as vulnerable creatures in need of protection for a long period of their lives, is a natural or universal one. There is no disputing that human infants do remain dependent on their parents and other adults for food and shelter for several years. They also evolve such abilities as the acquisition of language, walking, and self-awareness at the same age in all societies across the globe. However, different cultures attach contrasting meanings to these underlying biological realities. Childhood, in other words, is partly a social construction. For centuries, the dominant view in Christian thinking was that children were evil beings, born with the taint of original sin.[11] To quote the uncompromising view of the seventeenth-century cleric Pierre de Bérulle, "Childhood is the most vile and abject state of human nature, after that of death." For Catholics, it required the sacraments of baptism and confirmation to redeem the young; for Protestants, an inner calling to the true faith.[12] The early stages of life appeared neither interesting nor significant for the future of the individual. Most of the population did in fact have a relatively short childhood, as they slowly drifted into the world of adults from around the age of seven.

The notion of infant depravity gradually yielded ground, though not without a struggle, to another strand in Christian thinking: that of childhood innocence. Jean-Jacques Rousseau was one of the earliest and most persuasive exponents of this idea. His celebrated work *Émile* (1762) asserted that "there is no original perversity in the human heart" and invited people to respect the "amiable instinct" of the young. The idealization of children gathered pace in the nineteenth century, notably with the Romantics. They often ventured beyond attributing mere innocence to children by investing them with divine origins. Barbara Garlitz has shown how the idea that "Heaven lies about us in our infancy," from the *Immortality Ode* (1807) by William Wordsworth, struck a chord with people in the English-speaking world throughout the period. Poems, sermons, and tracts on the rights of children borrowed shamelessly from the ode. Wordsworth was a firm believer in the idea that the early years provided the individual with a reservoir of experience that could be drawn on for strength and inspiration later in life. His autobiographical poem *The Prelude* observed, in a passage written in 1799:

> There are in our existence spots of time
> Which with distinct preeminence retain
> A fructifying virtue, whence, depressed
> By trivial occupations and the round
> Of ordinary intercourse, our minds—
> Especially the imaginative power—
> Are nourished and invisibly repaired.
> Such moments chiefly seem to have their date
> In our first childhood.

The French poet Charles Baudelaire expressed a similar idea more pithily in claiming that "genius is merely *childhood regained.*"[13] The "Romantic child" depicted by various painters provided striking visual images of this delight in the young. The German Philip Otto Runge, for example, attempted to depict the divine origins and mystical beauty of the child, a splendid example being the portrait of his son Otto Sigismund that he painted in 1805. This was perhaps the first time in history that an artist had confronted the viewer with a real baby. As art historian Dorothy Johnson comments, borrowing in part from folk art style, Runge managed to express "the primitive energy and life force of the child."[14] Childhood, from this perspective, became a stage to be enjoyed and prolonged for as long as possible.

The Romantic vision of childhood appealed most to the middle classes, and perhaps to the men in particular, given that they were further removed than

FIGURE 0.1: Philipp Otto Runge (1777–1810), *Otto Sigismund, the artist's son*, 1805. Hamburg, Hamburger Kunsthalle. Oil on canvas, 16 × 14 inches (40 × 35.5 centimeters). Photo: Elke Walford. © 2005. Photo Scala, Florence/BPK, Bildagentur fuer Kunst, Kultur und Geschichte, Berlin.

most from the messy business of raising a child. The middle-class retreat into a cosseted domesticity, aided by the presence of servants, and their determination to keep their offspring away from the hoi polloi in the streets, set them up for the Romantic vision admirably. From the early 1800s, in the English case, they could expect children to display "innocence, vulnerability, ignorance and asexuality." Later in the Russian Empire, around 1900, it was again those with a good education and a secure economic position who could afford to think in terms of children having the right to leisure and imaginative self-expression.[15] Yet the vogue for reading Rousseau in the educated elites of the West and all that followed by no means eradicated older orthodoxies on the corrupt nature of childhood. Most commentators, from all parts of the political spectrum, ended up blending what might appear as contradictory views. The Methodists and the Evangelicals of the late eighteenth and early nineteenth centuries in Britain and the United States revived older orthodoxies. Hannah More wrote in 1799 that children "bring into the world a corrupt nature and evil disposi- tions." The Wesley family also proclaimed in one of their hymns that children are born in sin, but in another they wrote of childlike innocence. Best-selling authors for the Religious Tract Society in England such as Mrs. Sherwood and Hesba Stretton were "Romantic Evangelicals" for one literary critic. Among the radicals, even Wordsworth veered between describing children as naturally innocent and innately sinful. Similarly in France, after 1870, staunch Republi- cans occasionally betrayed a belief in the evil child more characteristic of their rivals in the Catholic Church.[16]

A further complication was the persistent influence of the English philoso- pher John Locke and his vision of the newborn child as a tabula rasa, or wax to be molded at will by adults. His *Some Thoughts Concerning Education* (1693) was widely read, including in translation into several languages, and the logic of its position was to emphasize the importance of early experience and education in the formation of the individual. Rousseau reacted vigorously to Locke's emphasis on developing reason in the young, preferring a "nega- tive education" that left the young to their own devices, in harmony with nature, until around the age of twelve. Unfortunately, children brought up on this principle invariably turned out disastrously. Hence, for a more practi- cal guide to education, in and out of the schoolroom, Locke was the more favored authority. Even Wordsworth eventually shifted from poetic musings on the benefits of a natural education in the Lake District, à la Jean-Jacques, to support for the monitorial school system promoted by Andrew Bell and the Anglican Church.[17] Many authorities, then, revealed a certain ambiguity in their thinking about the nature of the child.

Most people in the West, working in the villages and popular neighbor- hoods of the towns, probably took a more down-to-earth view of the nature of the child than the educated elite. As late as the mid-twentieth century, a U.S. scholar living in a French village in southern France observed, "People in Pey- rane do not believe that man is naturally good. They are more like little animals which must be domesticated at home and in the school."[18] Nonetheless, it was what those who were in power considered a proper childhood that mattered. Reformers campaigned to have parents treat their sons and daughters gently, instead of trying to beat the old Adam out of them. By the end of the century, states were beginning to pass laws to protect children from excessively harsh punishments within the family. Some raised the age of consent for girls, which lengthened the period of an asexual childhood. Above all, they all came around to insisting that all children spend a long period in school, separated as far as possible from the world of work.

Meanwhile, the terms of debate on the nature of the child moved on in the light of new intellectual currents. Belief in original sin gradually faded away over the course of the nineteenth century. So too did enthusiasm for the idea of the heavenliness of infancy. The "sacralization" of childhood doubtless took a sentimental rather than a religious form for many families. The Romantic child, in its various forms, often descended into mawkishness, and later the theories of Sigmund Freud would dent faith in the innocence of childhood. All the same, armies of psychologists, doctors, lawyers, pedagogues, and self-styled experts on child rearing testified to the seriousness with which Western societies treated childhood. And the precious child that emerged from the Enlightenment needed to be preserved as long as possible, to give him or her time to grow up: to quote Zelizer, "properly loved children, regardless of social class, belonged in a domesticated, nonproductive world of lessons, games, and token money."[19]

THE IMPACT OF INDUSTRIALIZATION

Economic development would eventually create the wealth without which in practice a modern childhood was hardly achievable. Rising real wages during the latter part of the century permitted the laboring population to follow in the footsteps of the middle classes—either willingly or unwillingly. Where there was a high enough family wage for the men, giving mothers and children the opportunity to give up industrial work, a more child-centered family could emerge. Improved standards of housing, public health measures to provide clean drinking water and effective sewerage, and moves toward a more balanced diet contributed further to the ideal of "home as nest." No less importantly, the increased wealth permitted national and local governments to construct the infrastructure necessary for a protected childhood. Building or upgrading schools, clinics, orphanages, juvenile courts, reformatories, playgrounds, and so forth required a huge investment. Of course, Rome was not built in a day: industrialization was a gradual process, transforming some regions more quickly than others. It was also a double-edged weapon as far as child welfare was concerned.

The popular view of the Industrial Revolution is that it brought riches for the few and misery for the majority. Certainly the early phases of industrialization in Europe and the United States were hugely disruptive for the poor. There is plenty of evidence of extra burdens on children employed in the "sweated" trades and in the new textile mills, squalid housing conditions, and inadequate school facilities. It was not until a relatively advanced stage in the process that the factories, mines, and sweatshops shed their child workers and compulsory schooling took over.[20] What stood out during the nineteenth century, outweighing the drift to standardization mentioned above, was the persisting diversity of childhoods in early industrial society. Class, gender, and ethnicity affected children as much as adults. Parents on small peasant farms expected their offspring to help them with their daily work routines long after their counterparts in the city had given up any such idea. Native-born Americans balked at the willingness of immigrant Irish and Italian families to put their children out to work in industry. Girls often seethed at the advantages enjoyed by brothers or male cousins in the school system.

In the first place, then, the shift from an agricultural to an industrial society may now appear a salient feature of the nineteenth century in the West, and it undoubtedly preoccupied many observers at the time, but its impact was uneven. Even in Britain, the undisputed pioneer of modern industrialization, economic growth was steady rather than explosive during the classic period of change during the late eighteenth and early nineteenth centuries. The new industrial centers in areas such as Lancashire and Yorkshire remained small islands of modernity in a sea of traditional agrarian society. Other countries took their own path to industrialization, and in places like France and Austria, this was particularly gradual and "unobtrusive." There was, in addition, a developmental gradient in Europe, running from the north and west of the continent to the south and east. The United States, in its turn, began with a markedly dualistic character to its economy, as industrial development began largely within the confines of the northeast.

It follows that, at midcentury, child labor, in the conventional sense of young people working for wages in factories and mines, was the exception rather than the rule. Beside the stock character of the little mill hand or the child sent down a coal mine, one should keep in mind their rural counterparts working on the land. The existence of peasant children was far from idyllic. They faced a Spartan regime as far as their material conditions were concerned, with very basic living conditions, a monotonous and sometimes inadequate diet, long hours working at such tasks as looking after livestock, and little or no time for school.[21] Although factory children were a minority among child workers, they remain significant in the history of childhood. Contemporaries were naturally fascinated by the spectacle of *l'ouvrier de huit ans* (the eight-year-old worker), pictured with banks of powerful machinery in the regimented conditions of a mill. For some, notably entrepreneurs such as the British industrialist Robert Owen, the factory provided a vision for the industrial society of the future. For reformers, it was a nightmare, threatening the health, the schooling, and the moral welfare of the young. In the end, of course, a template for modern childhood revolving around the factory would not last the course anywhere in the West. Victory went to the school and its supporters.

In sum, the link between industrialization and the evolution of a modern childhood is well documented, but there were numerous whirls and eddies along the way. The child employed, say, assisting a handloom weaver or a framework knitter in the protoindustrial workshops of the countryside in northern Europe came and went during the seventeenth, eighteenth, and nineteenth centuries, and so too did the factory child in the latter part of the period. The new working classes in the towns edged toward a long childhood for their offspring during the nineteenth century. At the same time, a combination of poverty and an attachment to the custom of starting work relatively early (around twelve or thirteen) held them back. The latter influence should not be underestimated. Per Bolin-Hort has pointed to the case of Lancashire cotton workers, a relatively affluent group who outraged fellow trade unionists during the 1890s by their support for the continuation of child labor through the half-time system.[22] Meanwhile, children working the land, particularly on small family farms, continued much as before on the margins of industrial society, even resisting its pressure for mass schooling. The sons and daughters of wealthy landowning and professional families in Europe continued to lead a privileged and sheltered existence. They remained aloof from the rest of society in a tight social circle maintained by their families and only gradually fused with business interests into a wealthy elite.[23] They anticipated many of the features of a modern childhood, though relations with parents might remain formal. This left a very diverse middle class in the towns to champion a modern childhood. They were certainly a product of a developing economy and wedded to the ideals of individual freedom in a competitive society. Hence they tended to devote a considerable amount of time and money to giving their children a good start in life. They were also active in channeling private and public resources into the cause, especially in the more affluent regions. They began with such institutions as Sunday schools and homes for abandoned children, and later in the century moved on to others such as primary schools, reformatories for juvenile delinquents, and organized youth movements.[24]

THE "MODERN" CHILDHOOD RECONSIDERED

The nineteenth century emerges with hindsight as a period when people in the West took strategic decisions on the paths that childhood and the family should and should not take, as the new industrial society emerged around them. These had some indisputably positive outcomes. There may indeed be no better time than the present to be brought up as a child. The evidence for Western countries is incontrovertible in such dimensions as child and infant mortality, literacy, and the general standard of living. There is a consensus that children should be given time to play, to attend school, and to develop physically. We look back with horror at the harsh physical punishments meted out to children in the past and such practices as infanticide, abandonment, and child labor. The modern family now stands as a supposed "haven in a heartless world." As it gradually withdrew from some of its earlier functions, as an economic unit or as a source of support for the aged, it focused its efforts on providing for the emotional needs of its members. A wealthy society, a culture that expects parents to devote themselves to the interests of their children, and an advanced welfare state might be thought to have taken care of many past iniquities. And yet the doubts remain. There are well-aired concerns over such issues as dysfunctional families, shortcomings in public education systems, violence on the streets, covert child labor in sweatshops and on farms, and a loss of innocence. It is therefore of interest to reflect on developments at this particular turning point in the history of young people and the family.

First, there was the concern to ease the burden of child labor and eventually to remove children entirely from the world of work. This was one of the first campaigns of reformers interested in child welfare and one whose outcomes remain unchallenged in the West today—a little casual work excepted. The reformers were surely right to highlight such hazards for children employed in industry as unhealthy working conditions, sleep deprivation, heavy lifting, sexual exploitation, and limited time for schooling. Around 1900, it was still the case that children of peasants and workers were limited to a rudimentary education, while those from middle- and upper-class backgrounds could master the classical or the modern scientific culture. Ruling elites in Europe during the nineteenth century were, in fact, quite open in providing a school for the people, leading to menial occupations, and a school for the middle classes, leading to the liberal professions and other positions of power and influence.[25]

Nonetheless, a tightening of child labor legislation combined with compulsory schooling ensured that the balance between work and school shifted decisively in a succession of Western countries. Moving children from the fields and the workshops to the school benches therefore stands out as fundamental to the creation of a modern childhood and one of the most admirable achievements of philanthropists, politicians, and public servants during the nineteenth and twentieth centuries.

The disadvantage of compulsory mass schooling was the disjunction that emerged between what was learned in school and what was needed for the world of work. Impatience with the school was perhaps most in evidence in rural areas. The state-run primary schools or public schools of the nineteenth century were largely alien intruders from the towns, bringing a literate culture to rival the oral and visual one of the villages and demanding allegiance to the nation state rather than the local community. They might have had some success in encouraging new agricultural methods or aspirations to a career in the towns, but there was a countercurrent from farm children to leave early and learn on the job. Pierre-Jakez Hélias recalled spending five days a week shut away in his primary school in rural Brittany, learning things that had nothing to do with everyday life.[26] Towns provided a more congenial climate for the schools, with the printed word all around, a more politicized atmosphere, and easier access. All the same, the strategy of concentrating on an academic curriculum at the expense of manual skills was off-putting. There was also a tension between the desire to emancipate children from their background and the opposing one of teaching them to respect the existing social hierarchy. Generally, in the nineteenth century, it was the latter, "herdsman's viewpoint" that prevailed in government circles in the West. This is not to say that an early start to work was the best way to learn a trade. Many young people in early modern times went through a series of jobs before ending up in a lifetime of unskilled labor. The apprenticeship system inherited from the medieval guilds also declined during the eighteenth and nineteenth centuries, amid a welter of abuses from masters and apprentices alike, combined with a feeling that it was being undermined by a deskilling of labor. Yet industrial societies have struggled to replace the custom of steeping young people in the skills and the culture of an occupation by gradually immersing them in it. The question of the relevance of education to adult life still lingers. The greater separation between adult and child life, according to Stearns, "could complicate children's efforts to find meaning in their own lives, encouraging new kinds of stress and disorientation."[27]

Second, there were the consequences of thinking of children as being by nature sweet, innocent creatures—when patently they are not. On the one hand, as noted above, the idealization of children was a powerful driving force behind a whole raft of measures to promote their welfare and the basis for a new, more informal type of relationship between parents and their offspring in the modern family. Indeed, it lay at the very heart of the new conception of childhood. On the other hand, this particular construction of childhood risked tensions between its high-flown ideal of innocence and a more earthy reality in everyday life. It tended to treat the child as an asexual being, which was a pleasing contrast to some of the extreme accusations of depravity leveled by Puritans, but no less of a distortion of reality for all that. Boys in Protestant countries in particular endured a barrage of warnings on the dangers to their health and sanity from the vice of masturbation. Presumably, most of this ran like water off a duck's back, but letters to the author of one of the best-known treatises on the subject during the eighteenth century revealed deep anxiety among some young people. For girls, the notorious double standard in sexual matters meant that they had to cope with particularly high expectations of purity and innocence. A reluctance to discuss "the facts of life" within families meant that young women often came to their wedding night unprepared for sexual relations with their husband. The supposedly innocent and ignorant child was deemed unfit for any political activity. The young were generally excluded from voting, and their views scoffed at by adults. Only at the end of the century did youth become an asset in political discourse. No less importantly, the middle-class ideal of dependency clashed with the more popular view, partly enforced by necessity, that children should be self-reliant from an early stage. Evidently, the strategy of prolonging childhood (and adolescence) won the day, but it came at the cost of a certain infantilization of the young. Juvenile delinquents, including the gangs of young hooligans in London and Apaches in Paris around 1900, were a worrying embodiment of resistance for the authorities.

A third, and related, source of tension generated by the shift to a modern childhood was the compulsion to protect the innocent and vulnerable child from harm. Again, there is no disputing the humanitarian motives of reformers and the benefits of measures taken by philanthropists and the state to shield the young from unscrupulous employers or hardened criminals. The nineteenth century witnessed a number of initiatives to promote the health and education of the young. The emergence of the child-centered family and institutions designed to prolong childhood still look like positive developments for the young. At the same time, they involved a colonization of childhood by adults, including teachers, clergymen, doctors, nurses, psychologists, police officers, scoutmasters, and social workers. This phalanx was the child-orientated wing of the "disciplinary society" that Michel Foucault saw emerging during the eighteenth and nineteenth centuries.

Ariès noted the paradox of the "obsessive love" of children in enlightened bourgeois circles, which encouraged a better education but also deprived the young of their liberty, inflicting on them the humiliations of the birch and the prison cell. Later, during the nineteenth century, such families would discourage their offspring from mixing with other children in their neighborhood and confine them to the potentially stifling home and garden. In a similar vein, the historian Anthony Fletcher makes clear that the affectionate relations that he discerns between parents and children among English upper-class families were accompanied by the grueling demands of a rigidly hierarchical society. It threw boys into the ordeal of a public school education—at Eton or Wellington, for example—and the girls into a patriarchal system that trained them "to live under obedience." The elementary schools of the nineteenth century could open the minds of the popular classes to a wider world but risked a tedious and often painful few years in the hands of a hard-pressed teacher. "Thank God I never was sent to school," wrote William Blake, reflecting the standpoint of the self-taught artisan.[28] The growing influence of doctors during the nineteenth century brought a certain medicalization of childhood. Doctors, professional midwives, and health visitors succeeded in reducing the hazards of childbearing and infancy, notably by making mothers aware of the benefits of personal hygiene. There remained the possibility of conflict between the easy-going child-rearing methods of the popular culture and the more regimented version promoted at this period by the medical profession. An unfamiliar emphasis on strictly regulated feeding times for babies, early potty training, and a special diet, imposed by outsiders, might provoke resentment in the villages or the poorer neighborhoods of towns. Similarly, the efforts of penal reformers to establish agricultural colonies or reformatory schools spared juvenile delinquents the harsh conditions of the prison system. Yet the well-meaning efforts of reformers also had the effect of replacing informal methods of dealing with children who made a nuisance of themselves with the full force of the criminal justice system. Instead of instant justice from a neighbor, the child risked a court appearance and a criminal record for such offences as begging, vagrancy, and petty theft. In short, from the start, the elaborate apparatus of child protection showed signs of heavy-handedness.

CONCLUSION

The nineteenth century was a pivotal period for the emergence of what we have conveniently, if imprecisely, called a modern childhood in the West.

The chapters in this volume will reveal the assorted debates, initiatives, and resistances involved. They challenge the reader to think about the costs and the benefits of a form of childhood that people in the West now take for granted. By the 1900s, for example, the little factory hand was fast disappearing from Western countries, girls were fast closing their gap in literacy rates behind boys, and infant mortality rates were finally starting to decline. The child-centered family was an influential ideal, though not one that was easy to realize, and child welfare was accepted as an important objective for the state. Yet there were pointers to the drawbacks of a childhood in an urban and industrial society. The long-running struggle between an "enlightened" and in some ways arrogant elite pushing for a protected childhood and a mass of peasants and workers still often wedded to a useful one indicated two sides to the argument. Children themselves took a hand in their own fate by struggling to pursue their school careers or playing truant, for example, or by weighing up whether to join a scout troop or go off with a street gang.

CHAPTER ONE

Family Relationships

JAMES MARTEN

Most family structures and relationships that prevailed in the West in the nineteenth century had developed long before 1800 and would survive well past 1900. But the century witnessed the emergence of a new form of family, shaped by affection, based on companionate marriage, and centered on the nurturing of children. Although it would never include most families in the West, the new model became a paradigm against which all other families would be compared. According to historians Steven Mintz and Susan Kellogg, distinguishing between "economics, religion, law, and politics and family life" would have been "unimaginable" to previous generations of Americans. Although the specifics and the pace of change varied from culture to culture, the nineteenth century would see sweeping changes in the family's functions throughout the West. The family's economic role declined, and governments, private agencies, corporations, hospitals, and schools assumed virtually all of its former educational, health care, poor relief, and economic responsibilities. The modern family, argue Mintz and Kellogg, "ceased to be a largely autonomous, independent, self-contained, and self-sufficient unit" and turned inward to "the socialization of children and the provision of emotional support and affection."[1] Inevitably, the new conception of the family would lead to a dramatic reconception of childhood.

DEMOGRAPHIC CHANGE, 1800–1900

Paradoxically, despite a dramatic increase in population in Western Europe and the United States in the late eighteenth and nineteenth centuries, families in the West generally grew smaller. Birth control practices, marriage patterns, and canon law had limited pregnancies among some segments of the population in Western Europe prior to this period. But a real decline in the average size of families set in during the nineteenth century. The gradual fall in child mortality apparently caused some parents to limit the size of their families in order to match the rising expectations for the education and material comfort that the middle-class ideal would establish. Working-class families, at least by the end of the nineteenth century, found fewer outlets for children's work outside the home and eventually began to limit the sizes of their families as well.[2]

The decline in family size varied from country to country, although all Western nations saw a dramatic change. In the United States, for instance, where the decline began in earnest in the 1820s and 1830s, the average number of children born to married women dropped from 6.4 in the late eighteenth century to 2.8 by 1900. Although these statistics are especially true of middle-class Americans, and although larger families still prevailed among some immigrant populations, the birth rate throughout the United States fell by half between 1800 and 1900. In much of Europe, the downtown began about two generations later. And in England and Wales, a serious decline did not set in until the 1890s. Still, the average size of a British family fell from six in the 1860s to three just after 1900. The age at which women began having children came later, while the age at which they stopped having children came earlier. This trend, combined with the lengthening period of dependence on the part of their children, meant that child *rearing* rather than child*bearing* came to dominate the lives of women.[3]

Many factors contributed to the decline in family size, including a number of economic impetuses. But the availability and promotion of family-planning techniques (by such organizations as the British Malthusian League), the emphasis on self-control by religious evangelicals, and feminism also led middle-class mothers to choose to stop having babies at an earlier age than women of two or three generations earlier.[4]

Even before families began shrinking, most households in northwestern Europe and North America consisted of simple, nuclear families. By 1800, for instance, only 10 percent to 20 percent of households were multigenerational. However, in southern and East Europe, the latter were more common. In the more rural areas of central and southern France, for instance, as many as 25 percent to 40 percent of households were complex, as mortality drove families to pool their resources and expanding production made it possible to support multiple generations.[5]

CREATING THE MODERN FAMILY

The decline in family size was the result of—and, in turn, encouraged—the rise of the child-centered, companionate family. A related factor, at least in European families, was the increasing stability of family structure. Fewer children, lower mortality rates, compulsory education, and improved living conditions meant less "coming or going," according to Michael Mitterauer and Richard Sieder. That predictability contributed to the development of the new conception of family. Although historians have found plentiful evidence of familial affection in the sixteenth and seventeenth centuries and earlier, the notion of family relationships revolving around emotional attachments became a given in the nineteenth century, especially in public discourse on the model family. Where traditional family structure had been marked by patriarchy and the imperatives of economic survival, the family structure that developed during the nineteenth century was more private, more democratic (at least relative to earlier forms), and characterized more by emotional attachments. According to Mintz and Kellogg, marriage was no longer an "economic transaction between families" but "an emotional bond between two individuals." Gender roles settled into separate spheres; women were expected to manage the household, raise children, and maintain their families' moral standards, while men became the primary breadwinners. Relationships between husbands and wives were increasingly based on mutual affection, while parents applied greater material and emotional resources to nurturing their children, who were expected to live with their parents longer than earlier generations. This new construction of family life substituted the principles that guided public life—ambition, independence, competition, materialism—with love, generosity, selflessness, and devotion. Modern families provided a counterpoint and, in an oft-used phrase, a "haven" from the bustle and corruption of the public world.[6]

As Western families, especially the middle class, came to rely less on outside influences such as the church or socioeconomic class to determine family routines, they created, in the words of John Gillis, "imagined families" revolving around new rituals and assumptions. They increasingly emphasized privacy in their personal and family lives. Newlyweds adopted the practice of taking honeymoons away from friends and family. Servants' living and dining spaces were separated from those of their employers, while eating meals together became a sacrosanct part of middle-class life and Sunday dinner became an important family tradition. Family-oriented Christmas and birthday celebrations—complete with commercially produced cards and gifts—replaced for middle- and upper-class families the boisterous public celebrations of the past.[7]

Although the transition to a conception of family as a source of love and contentment seems like a positive development, it was not without its costs. The same economic forces that encouraged the turning in of the family from the public sphere also provided greater opportunities for independence among young men and women. Chances for young single women to work outside the home in factories, shops, and as teachers grew slowly throughout the century. As a result, even though the relationship into which a young woman would enter when getting married was more loving than it had been in previous centuries, it also required a greater sacrifice, because a young woman had to give up her public role and submit to a much more circumscribed life as homemaker and mother. And the emphasis on emotional support and effective child rearing that helped to create the middle-class family created its own pressures. Deciding to marry became a more difficult and much more deliberate choice for middle-class women than it had been in the past, and the number of men and women who remained single rose throughout the nineteenth century. Coontz argues that Victorian marriages worked only because husbands and wives both accepted the basic inequality of opportunity between men and women and women's innate purity. Both made it difficult to establish deep emotional attachments and physical intimacy.[8]

The evolving notion of marriage as an emotional rather than an economic partnership also led to major changes in family law, including at least limited property rights for married women and child custody rights for mothers. In countries influenced by the Catholic Church and in Britain, divorce remained virtually impossible, and few marriages were legally dissolved. But in other secular and Protestant countries and in France after 1884, divorces generally became easier to obtain. The United States led the way. After 1800, U.S. states increasingly allowed courts to grant divorces and steadily expanded the grounds for dissolving marriages from impotence, abandonment, and adultery to physical cruelty, desertion, drunkenness, and "temperamental incompatibility." Early in the century, fathers had enjoyed virtually complete control over the custody of their children, but, by midcentury, some states had begun awarding custody of at least the youngest children to mothers—a step toward the twentieth-century practice of awarding mothers primary custody of children. The influence of patriarchy in the United States declined dramatically. By 1880, two-thirds of the states had allowed divorce for abusive behavior, 87 percent had made it difficult for a husband to claim his wife's property over her objections, 60 percent had strengthened the power of courts to decide child custody cases, and 96 percent had removed one of the father's traditional sources of power by creating free public schools and compulsory education laws.[9]

THE POLITICAL ECONOMY
OF THE MODERN FAMILY

At the core of the development of the ideal middle-class family were the economic changes that swept through the West in the nineteenth century. An ever-declining percentage of families earned their livelihood from the land, and even those tended to specialize in cash crops or livestock. Families became less self-sufficient, and fewer wives and children had direct roles in the economic survival of their families.

A growing number of fathers worked outside the home, limiting contact with their children and changing forever their parental duties. Prior to the nineteenth century, fathers played important roles in decisions regarding the education and discipline of their sons and daughters. This was still possible for families in small communities or on farms during the nineteenth century. But when the Industrial Revolution imposed clock time on the lives of the men working in the factories and mines and on the men serving as managers, clerks, and shopkeepers, it also removed them from their families for most hours of the day. It should be noted that some professions allowed men to work near their families; many clergymen and physicians maintained offices and surgeries in their homes.

The Industrial Revolution also affected the political economy of the nuclear family. Economic dependence on fathers traditionally stemmed from their control of the family's primary economic resource: land. The extent to which fathers could retain their patriarchal dominance in a family corresponded to the extent to which the family relied for their subsistence on landowning and farming. As a result, on the plantations of the U.S. South, among the gentry and large landholding classes in England, and in the Nordic countries, where industrialization started much later than in England, France, and the United States, fathers retained at least some of their traditional patriarchal control. But the economic support for the patriarchal system broke down whenever the Industrial Revolution developed in a given country. Unlike farmers, fathers working in factories or offices could not use the possibility of future employment or landownership as opportunities or as threats. Sons were forced to look elsewhere for work—in other shops or factories or other cities or countries, for that matter—and even daughters could find employment outside the home if necessary or if they desired. Even those children who did go to work while living at home were more independent than in the past. In effect, the transition of the father's source of income from the private to the public sphere reduced his power within the household, at least over issues related to daily child rearing and household management. In the United States, the emergence of the anti-slavery and the temperance movements in the 1820s and 1830s, both of which were directly related to the industrialization of the North, further undermined the patriarchal prerogatives of husbands and fathers.[10]

One segment of the population in which marriage and the family remained important economic axes was the *petite bourgeoisie*—the shopkeepers and artisans whose wives and children helped staff the small retail shops and, in some instances, inherited the skills or shops from their fathers. Marriage was a vital factor in the economic success of shopkeepers and artisans, who were much more likely to be married than other men in Western Europe. For instance, in the 1850s, only 12 percent of men London shopkeepers were unmarried, compared to 31 percent of men as whole, while German master craftsmen in the 1880s married at far greater rates than their peers. For this segment of the population—unlike the civil servants and white-collar workers of the middle class—homes and businesses remained closely linked. In some ways, then, the patriarchal structure of traditional families survived for the *petite bourgeoisie*. However, the gender hierarchy was undermined by the egalitarianism inherent in operating a small business and by the fact that most wives of trades-men and shop owners were fairly well educated. The importance of women's labor to these enterprises also led the *petite bourgeoisie* to reduce family size in advance of most other West Europeans.[11]

The broader economic opportunities available in the United States meant that the patriarchal family structure that characterized the early modern period no doubt vanished more quickly in the New World than in the Old. European commentators on U.S. life noticed that fathers seemed to have less power and fewer prerogatives within the family than their European coun-terparts. Although the father's roles as a kind of court of appeal for family squabbles and as the decision maker for economic matters remained more or less unchallenged, his status and authority as head of family were clearly in decline. Indeed, as the century progressed, U.S. advice books on raising children came to be aimed almost exclusively at mothers, and women's magazines devoted countless pages to the topic of child rearing.

Siblings also played an important role in poor families, as parents relied on their older children to care for the younger ones. The often dangerous sur-roundings in which most children were raised, with open fireplaces, livestock, and harsh weather conditions, required that young children be supervised constantly. Even as the percentage of families living on farms declined in the nineteenth century, city life provided its own set of threats, from vehicular traffic on crowded streets to anonymous neighbors to dangerous alleys, sewers, and abandoned buildings. Older siblings were absolutely vital to the safety of the youngest children, especially in families crowding into the industrializing cities of the West. The "little mothers," as they were called in the United States, became a fixture in working-class communities.[12]

The availability of low-paid servants in nineteenth-century cities—often recruited from among the girls who had spent their preadolescence as "little mothers"—meant that even middle-class families could hire servants. Paid cooks freed up time for mothers to care for their children, while nursemaids allowed mothers to devote even more time to managing the household or to philanthropic and social activities outside the home. The insertion of a non–family member into the family dynamic lessened the need for brothers and sisters to contribute to the functioning of the household or to watch their younger siblings. Middle- and upper-class girls were obviously less likely to serve a kind of domestic apprenticeship, which led them to enjoy a great deal of freedom before the age of twelve, with few responsibilities and many opportunities for play and leisure activities. Once they entered preadolescence, however, that freedom vanished, as they were trained to be "good" girls: under control, calm, and disciplined.

The power of Western assumptions about family can be measured, ironically, in the complicated dynamic that led U.S. slave owners to encourage slaves to form families and in slaves' insistence on maintaining even the most tenuous family ties. Although slave codes did not, in effect, recognize marriages or kinship—slave owners had complete control over the life, death, and all other facets of a slave's existence—masters and slaves alike assumed that slaves would, in fact, live in family units. Although a surprisingly large percentage of slave marriages remained intact, early death or the sale of family members sundered many slave families, and, even if families were allowed to remain together, they were constantly haunted by the possibility of a future separation. Furthermore, slave marriages were often characterized by wives and husbands living on separate plantations, allowed to see one another once or twice a month. But the presence of at least one parent and, frequently, of aunts, uncles, and other relatives, allowed members of the slave community to maintain a semblance of the responsibilities, assumptions, and privileges attached to a functioning family. Indeed, the use of the term *family* by many slave owners to describe their enslaved men, women, and children offers not only a tragic irony

FIGURE 1.1: In this photograph from the 1860s, five generations of former slaves gather in front of their quarters on Smith's Plantation near Beaufort, South Carolina. On large plantations such as those along the South Carolina coast, slave families might remain more or less intact. Civil War Photograph Collection, Prints and Photographs Division, Library of Congress.

but evidence of the power of the family metaphor, even when applied to people whose families were not legally bound. An epilogue to the determination with which slaves clung to their families came after the Civil War, when U.S. army chaplains married thousands of freed couples who wanted their unions and children to be legitimized, and by the heart-breaking advertisements published in African American newspapers seeking long-lost children and parents.

CHILDHOOD AND THE IDEAL FAMILY

The rise of the middle-class family led to a similarly dramatic reconstruction of the ideal childhood. Setting the stage for the nineteenth-century conceptions of childhood and of children's place in the family were John Locke and Jean-Jacques Rousseau, who rejected both the traditional view of child depravity and the idea that a child's character was the product of *nature*—certain innate traits with which a baby was born. They helped pioneer the notion of *nurture,* that a child could be shaped by creating an environment that instilled appropriate values and behaviors. Locke and Rousseau helped lead the charge against the old notion of children as repositories of original sin and prefigured the more extreme sympathies of the Romantic movement of the late eighteenth and early nineteenth centuries.

Seizing on the importance of a child's environment—in this case, the family—the Romantics celebrated childhood as a time of innocence and argued that children must be protected from growing up too fast. This notion of an extended childhood had emerged in colleges, universities, and boarding schools in the early modern period; the isolation and strict rules of those institutions protected students even as they limited their freedom. The Romantics of the nineteenth century took a different route to extending childhood; they believed, in Colin Heywood's phrase, that childhood was a "blessed period" and that children should be allowed to explore the world on their own terms, to revel in their natural innocence, and to enjoy the nurturing and protection that they deserved simply because they were children. Hopeful and idealized portrayals of children in paintings and literature celebrated their immaturity and suggested that their innocence and natural goodness could serve as inspirations for adults. In the hands of other educators and authors, the romanticization of childhood led to maudlin, didactic literary stereotypes and narrowly conceived books and magazines for children and youth.[13]

This radical reshaping of childhood inspired Western societies to make child rearing into the family's most important function. In some countries, the family also became central to the creation of responsible citizens. In the United States, for instance, the political values and democratization of society that followed the United States' successful war for independence from Britain created greater economic and political opportunities for all classes, made the proper rearing of children a patriotic as well as a moral duty, and

FIGURE 1.2: This masthead from an 1870s children's magazine shows the importance of specific values—including piety, the importance of education, and parental affection—in the construction of middle-class family life in the nineteenth century.

led to the creation of what historians have called "republican motherhood." The revolution in U.S. politics and society inspired, according to Jacqueline S. Reinier, "the staggering notion that one could mold the human personality in a desired direction." The "general revolt against tyranny and patriarchy," Reinier writes, lent itself to the celebration of "the affectionate nuclear family," which, in republican America, became "a kind of school for citizenship." Combined with the new construction of childhood as a time of malleability and nurturing, the republican family would help create and sustain the republican experiment in government.[14] A similar cult of motherhood emerged in France during this time, but without the political impulse contained in the U.S. version. Yet French republicans also promoted egalitarianism by advocating a less patriarchal and more affectionate style of fatherhood. Moreover, the breakdown of the old social order in France by industrialization and urbanization encouraged mobility and individualism, leading to a more dynamic, more democratic society, which carried over into families, especially within the middle class.

   A number of emotional ramifications accompanied the political developments in modern families. By the end of the nineteenth century, middle-class families had settled into a straightforward set of characteristics. Aside from the man breadwinner, members of middle-class families were seen less as sources of economic security and more as sources of emotional satisfaction. This extended to sibling relationships, which stressed love and affection rather than rivalry. Intense relationships developed between middle-class sisters, and their brothers took on the role of protectors, especially of unmarried or widowed sisters. The unmarried sister living with her brother's family or with a widower brother became something of a stereotype in Victorian literature. Of course, poor immigrant and working-class families and farm families of virtually every socioeconomic group still required the contributions of children to sustain the family economy—and would until well into the twentieth century—but children were less likely to be regarded as economic assets than they had been a century before.

Indeed, as Viviana Zelizer has asserted, by 1900 the urban middle class in the United States was well on its way to completing the "sacralization" of childhood, in which youngsters became economically "worthless" but emotionally priceless. This process revealed itself when insurance companies and the juries in wrongful death lawsuits alike began deciding claims and making awards in wrongful death lawsuits on the basis of the emotional pain caused by the loss of a child rather than on the loss of future economic contributions to the family.[15]

FAMILY AND THE LIFE COURSE: INFANCY AND EARLY CHILDHOOD

Within and without the middle class, children passed inexorably through a number of steps on their ways to adulthood. Infancy remained the most dangerous period for Western children during this time. Although the infant mortality rate declined slowly throughout the nineteenth century, it remained astonishingly high to modern sensibilities: between 150 and 300 deaths per thousand throughout much of the century. Industrialization and urbanization pushed it higher among certain groups, with the mortality rate among the working classes remaining stubbornly high. In England and Wales early in the twentieth century, for example, the infant mortality rate among the middle and upper classes was 77 per thousand live births; it soared to 152 per thousand among the working classes.[16]

Not all parents or families welcomed the birth of an infant. Illegitimacy and sparse resources were just two of the conditions some parents found impossible to overcome. Some killed their babies. Britain made infanticide a felony in the early seventeenth century, and, by the nineteenth century, the previously ambiguous practice was considered a crime as well as a sin in most countries. Although high infant mortality rates made it difficult, if not impossible, to determine accurate statistics, contemporary observers believed that most infanticides were committed by prostitutes and other poor, single young women. U.S. slaves sometimes committed infanticide to spare their children from a life of bondage. Although, once again due to the frequency of natural deaths among slave children, it is difficult to measure the extent of infanticide among slave mothers, it was clearly a concern to masters who benefited economically from the births of slave infants.

While infanticide likely receded as the nineteenth century progressed, child abandonment continued and even increased in some places. Perhaps one-fifth of all babies born in Paris early in the nineteenth century were abandoned, while the figure soared to as many as thirty percent to forty percent in Milan. Most abandoned infants lived in cities and large towns; some were born with physical disabilities or into desperate poverty; a sizeable minority were the illegitimate children of professional men who rejected their paternal responsibilities. In fact, the percentage of foundlings of legitimate birth increased in many parts of Europe in the nineteenth century—to 15 percent in Paris and, in parts of Portugal, to over 30 percent.[17]

Of course, few children were literally abandoned. By the nineteenth century, the Catholic Church had taken the lead in establishing institutions to care for foundlings, who could be left anonymously via "turning cradles." Some municipalities hired wet nurses to care for foundlings. In New York City, Chicago, and other major U.S. cities, notorious "baby farms"—some operated by individuals for a few infants, others large operations with dozens of babies—provided only the most basic care. Not surprisingly, death rates at the baby farms were horrific, although difficult to establish with confidence. Some were clearly intended to dispose of unwanted babies. The outrage over these lethal institutions helped inspire the formation of the Society for the Prevention of Cruelty to Children in the United States and the Infant Life Protection Society in Britain. Nevertheless, the practice survived in some places until well into the twentieth century.

Despite its reputation as a choice made by callous upper-class parents, wet-nursing remained fairly common among the middle classes as well, especially in urban areas in Western Europe. Although churchmen and others had railed against the custom since the Middle Ages, there were some arguments in favor of the practice. Rural wet nurses may have been physically stronger than the urban women who could afford to hire them, and the health of people living in the country certainly exceeded that of city dwellers. Working women could not afford to spend the time away from family businesses or shops, and some women were unable to breast-feed their own children. Wet-nursing was common enough in nineteenth-century France to inspire government regulation. The practice declined during the early twentieth century as more women left the workforce, as pasteurized milk became available, and, as in the Scandinavian countries, states created programs to encourage and train new mothers to breast-feed.

Such traditional practices as wet-nursing survived throughout the nineteenth century even as new methods and ideas emerged in the outpouring of advice books. Although such books had been available for centuries, the nineteenth century witnessed, as one historian has put it, "a barrage of advice from doctors and others eager to pontificate on child-rearing." Inspired by religious and political concerns early in the century, by the 1860s and beyond, as the books expanded in length and scope, they were taken over by experts, especially medical doctors from the developing specialty of pediatrics, telling mothers exactly how to feed, clothe, discipline, and care for their children.[18]

The vast majority of infants who remained with their families were embraced by their families and communities through baptisms and naming rituals, which were not only important religious practices but also gave families the opportunity to express gratitude for their children's safe arrival, to honor saints or family members, and to recognize and honor friends or relatives by making them godparents. Although these practices remained an important first stage in most infants' lives, their popularity varied by place and denomination. For instance, by the turn of the twentieth century, the vast majority of English babies were baptized (about two-thirds in the Anglican Church), but only two-thirds of Parisian babies were baptized.[19] Anabaptists in Europe and Baptists in the United States baptized their children only when they had reached the age of reason. Well into the nineteenth century, Catholics regularly named their children after saints, while Protestants chose names from the Bible or names that reflected Christian qualities. Boys were more likely than girls to be named after a relative. Another tradition that slowly died during the century was the practice of naming newborns after deceased siblings. Generally speaking, the core of acceptable names expanded throughout the West in the late nineteenth and twentieth centuries.

Framing family relationships throughout every phase of the life cycle was discipline. In the United States, Philip Greven has divided approaches to discipline into three categories: the evangelical, the moderate, and the genteel. Although all three groups originated during the colonial period, they continued to flourish in the nineteenth century and into the twentieth and are useful constructions of the ways in which parents thought about children. The evangelical approach to child rearing, originating in colonial Puritanism, was by far the sternest. Based on the Calvinist doctrine of original sin, children's wills were to be broken and their behavior to be ordered in a

FIGURE 1.3: Although taken just after the turn of the twentieth century, this photograph of a young couple and their baby on christening day illustrates the romanticized view of childhood and the family that developed during the 1800s. Prints and Photographs Division, Library of Congress.

way pleasing to God. The genteel approach, originating among the relatively small population of wealthy planters in the South, occupied the opposite end of the spectrum. Parents in this system, although still insistent on sons' and daughters' obedience and appropriate behavior, had different notions about what form that behavior should take. Sons, especially, were expected to sustain their families' honor; most behavior could be excused as long as it did not affect the boy's and the family's standing in the community. Children in these families, like those in wealthy families virtually everywhere, tended to enjoy much longer childhoods, with private tutors and, for many, college. The moderate approach, by definition, combined some of both extremes and became by far the most common approach in the nineteenth century. The differences should not be exaggerated. Despite the disapproval of many child advice books by the nineteenth century, three-fourths of U.S. children experienced some form of corporal punishment. And even in nonevangelical families, obedience would instill in children self-control, a secular virtue prized by virtually every middle- and upper-class family.[20]

FAMILY AND THE LIFE COURSE: GROWING UP

Children who survived early childhood were led by their families and a growing number of institutions outside the family through a series of coming-of-age rituals, which not only provided markers of a child's maturation but also celebrated the centrality of children to the institution of the family. These rites of passage became more standardized and were attached to specific ages as life expectancy increased, schooling became more regular, and life generally became more predictable.

Families guided or at least accompanied children and youth through subsequent coming-of-age experiences. Many coming-of-age rituals were religious in nature, as Roman Catholic and Protestant denominations established steps toward full membership in religious communities. Celebrations of first communion and confirmation, for instance, which, in the Roman Catholic Church, took place at the ages of seven and sixteen, respectively, became family as well as community events. Orthodox Jewish boys celebrated their bar mitzvahs at age thirteen, and girls celebrated their bat mitzvahs at twelve—although in Germany and the United States, most nineteenth-century Reform synagogues celebrated confirmation in groups rather than as individuals.

Some family rituals began the process of socialization to appropriate gender roles. Little boys, who commonly wore the same style of dresses and loose-fitting clothes as their sisters, were "breeched" when they were about seven. At about the same age, parents began to give their children toys related to traditional male and female roles: dolls and all their paraphernalia, of course, for girls and military toys, pony whips, and sporting equipment for boys. Boys were also given increasingly greater amounts of freedom to roam, to form friendships, and, among the working classes, to find jobs outside the home. Girls, on the other hand, were prepared for their roles as adults by staying close to home, helping with housework or younger siblings, reading, and generally remaining quiet. Propriety guided the restrictions on middle-class girls' freedom, while, for working-class girls, the need for them to help at home limited their capacity to get outside the house.

The nineteenth century saw the reinvention of Christmas as a child-centered family celebration as opposed to a strictly religious occasion (in the United States, the lingering Puritan influence had restricted the commemoration of Christmas in many regions until well into the nineteenth century). Middle-class families also began to host elaborate birthday celebrations for their children and their friends. The gift giving associated with Christmas and birthdays also reflected the emerging concern for and indulgence of children, especially among the middle classes, as toys meant to train children (blocks, didactic reading material) gave way to fantasy and adventure books, sporting toys, expensive dolls, and candy.

Those few young men lucky enough to attend universities could try out semi-independence without taking on a full set of adult responsibilities. In the politically volatile period between the 1790s and the 1840s, students participated in the mostly failed revolutions that exploded across Europe. But the final steps for most youths' coming of age, of course, were entering the workforce and leaving their parents' homes. Although most Western countries began setting the age at which children could engage in industrial labor between the 1830s and the first two decades of the twentieth century—twelve was a typical minimum—children living on farms still started working as soon as they could be useful. In almost all agricultural communities, boys as young as seven or eight herded sheep or watched cattle, and even the youngest children could plant seeds, pull weeds, and clear brush. Even slave children in the United States went to work in phases; they were not considered "full hands" until they reached the age of ten or twelve, when they could do a complete day's work without wearing down and becoming useless.

Taking a job did not mean leaving home for most young workers, especially working-class children. Many remained in their parents' homes through their teenage years and into their twenties, and at least part of their wage was turned over to their parents until they turned twenty-one. In the last part of the nineteenth century, children in West Europe and the United States contributed as much as thirty percent of their families' incomes.[21] Boys and girls often followed their fathers or, in some circumstances, their mothers into factories or mines. In addition, in the urban ghettoes of all industrialized economies by the late nineteenth century, children joined their parents in doing home work: stringing cheap rosaries, cutting cardboard shirt collars, rolling cigars, or assembling artificial flowers. Others became street traders, selling newspapers, fruit, pencils, and other cheap objects. However, a not-insignificant minority of youngsters did leave home to work as servants.

Work and school—and the choice about which was most appropriate or even possible for each child—provided one of the most potentially divisive facets in family dynamics. Parents in all but the most affluent families had to weigh carefully the benefits of education versus its costs. In Britain and France before the 1880s, and in most of the United States prior to 1900, families were often required to pay fees or provide their children's textbooks and sometimes pitch in to help with teachers' housing costs. In the United States, Jewish parents, coming out of a tradition that honored scholarship, tended to push their sons toward as much education as possible. By contrast, Italian and Polish families, often originating in rural areas of Europe where learning was a luxury and need a harsh reality—conditions that they also discovered in the cities to which they migrated—often required their children to work rather than attend school. Teenage boys often preferred work to school, especially in cities where opportunities abounded throughout much of the nineteenth century. They enjoyed freedom from the classroom, and also welcomed the chance to contribute to their families' well-being and to earn a little money for themselves. Poor girls, or girls from families still loyal to traditional religious or gender roles, were often not allowed to attend upper grades and especially high school. In any event, family choices about work and education could often lead to confrontations in these vital stages in the coming-of-age process.

OBSTACLES TO THE MIDDLE-CLASS IDEAL

Despite its coherence and the power it almost immediately exerted on thinking about family relationships and childhood, the middle-class ideal provided just one version of family life and just one construction of childhood. Many westerners only slowly accepted the largely middle-class and urban assumptions upon which it was based. Many more, even if they had wanted to espouse the values explicitly and implicitly contained in the paradigm, did not have the economic means to apply them to their own lives.

Wealth and poverty both proved to be obstacles to the child-centered, middle-class family. Rich parents could surround their children with toys and provide the finest educations to their sons and, later in the century, daughters. Yet the inevitable layers of servants, nurses, and tutors; the continuation of traditional means of maintaining family holdings, such as favoring the eldest son; keeping a tight rein on young adult offspring through allowances; and arranging marriages also placed the interests of the family above those of the individual.

Peasant and working-class families, which comprised a large majority of the population in most Western countries, faced the most serious obstacles. Even in the United States, where economic opportunity drew millions of immigrants from western, eastern, and southern Europe from the 1840s through the First World War, most families remained mired in the uncertainties of the working-class existence. The boom and bust nature of capitalist economies and the absence until well into the twentieth century of any sort of government safety net, meant that even skilled workers were only a major injury or sudden business downtown away from insolvency and homelessness. As a result, poor families could not afford the material possessions and private space that would ultimately be the surface hallmarks of the ideal, nor could they afford to keep their children out of the workforce. Urban workers also lacked the residential stability implied by the ideal. Working families moved frequently, relying on cheap rents in tawdry tenements. Families made ends meet by taking in boarders; families of two parents with a half dozen children living in two-room cold water flats regularly took in two or three boarders. Perhaps 15 percent to 20 percent of working-class families took in nonrelatives as boarders.[22] Clearly, the moral and material assumptions that shaped the middle-class family ideal could not apply to these children. Not only were children in such families forced to give up school to work on the streets or in sweatshops, they were also exposed to the coarse language, rough manners, sexual improprieties, and possible abuse that were simply not meant to be a part of "modern" childhood. Moreover, the increased opportunities for women to work outside the home offered desperately needed income but also created obstacles to the intensive mothering held up as necessary and "normal."

Observers were acutely aware of the failure or refusal of many families to fulfill the new ideal, which, along with the reform impulse originating out of the rising middle class and new concepts of religious responsibility, led to myriad movements intended to improve and discipline working-class and immigrant families, provide asylums for orphans and other dependents, and expose more children to formal education for longer periods of time. Victorian reformers in the United States and Britain feared that the instability, poor health, and moral disorder of the "disorganized families" of the working class would cause "degeneracy" among the urban poor. Virtually every country in the West saw the creation of private reform organizations to combat juvenile delinquency—which was often blamed on poor parenting—and to reform, even "civilize" the working poor and immigrants whose family relationships seemed to encourage corruption and poverty rather than nurturing and re-spectability. German Protestants established dozens of "houses of salvation" to house children from failed families; beginning in 1853, the Children's Aid Society of New York began placing out to western and Midwestern families orphans and children whose parents were apparently unable to take care of them; eventually sixty thousand were sent to largely western states, while over eighty thousand were sent to Canada. The National Society for the Prevention of Cruelty to Children, founded in England but duplicated elsewhere, inserted itself into the lives of poor families who failed to live up to the middle-class ideal. By the end of the nineteenth century, local and federal governments in the West had begun to pass laws mandating the removal of children from the worst situations, prosecuting parents who abused their children or committed them to prostitution and other criminal acts, and establishing separate court systems for the juvenile delinquents. Placing out was a direct rejection of the orphanages and other institutions that continued to house dependent children throughout the century. The practice aimed to recreate the middle-class family for children whose own families had been broken up by death or poverty. Nevertheless, the lack of confidence in the ability of hard-pressed families to sustain acceptable childhoods led to an increase in the number of young people living in institutions for paupers and dependent children, which, in the United States, rose from 1.8 percent in 1860 to 3.6 percent in 1900.[23]

EPILOGUE: INCORPORATING THE "OTHER"

That a fundamental change had occurred in Western conceptions of childhood and the family can be further demonstrated in the ways that Americans and Europeans insisted that the "others" living in the American West and in Asia and Africa adopt similar assumptions. U.S. and European commentary on the peoples they encountered, and the policies they pursued while conquering or enslaving them, simply confirmed their own ideas and led to the imposition of those ideas on the cultures with which they interacted.

Two of the hallmarks of United States Indian policy in the nineteenth century were to convert Native Americans into farmers and to destroy their distinctive cultures. Reformers, missionaries, and policymakers targeted such practices as plural marriages, the puzzling work roles of male and female Indians, and the seemingly disorganized and lenient child rearing practices of most tribes. Boarding schools—like the famous institutions at Carlisle Barracks in

Pennsylvania and at Hampton Institute in Virginia—separated Indian children from their families, forced them to take on Western dress and hairstyles and to speak English, and sought to inculcate so-called American values and skills. Americanizing meant, in many ways, imposing the new middle-class familial ideal on Native Americans.

A similar confidence in the superiority of the middle-class family helped to influence British responses to and policies in India. Civil servants, army officers, East India Company bureaucrats, and other expatriates maintained at least tenuous ties to England because they feared that the climate and other health issues, interaction with Indians, and a lack of contact with familiar institutions would jeopardize their families' ability to sustain the value and standards created by the middle-class ideal. At the same time, English missionaries and, eventually, policymakers insisted that Christianization and the extension of at least some of the features of the middle-class family would not only improve the lives of Indians, but ease the burden of governing the colony. As a result, certain traditional practices in India related to patriarchal authority within families were criminalized or regulated by the British Raj, including one of the most absolute and, to British eyes, repugnant practices in India: female infanticide. The success of the Americans, the British, and other Western nations to impose their family values on other regions and races was mixed at best. But that they attempted to do so at all suggests the power of the family model that emerged in the West in the nineteenth century.

CHAPTER TWO

Community

MARILYN IRVIN HOLT

At the age of twelve, Servetus Holt left Lancashire, England, for a new life in the United States. The year was 1842, and the boy traveled only with his maternal grandmother. As was typical of immigrants, these two new arrivals sought out and settled near a group of families from their own background. In this case, they found other Lancashire immigrants living in Illinois. In later years, Holt became a U.S. citizen, fought in the American Civil War, and then joined the migration to settle the American West.[1]

Holt's experience was not unusual in the saga of immigration and western settlement, but the reasons behind his initial journey to the United States is unknown. Perhaps it was the family's plan for others in England to follow, although that did not happen. One certainty is that the boy's home community in Lancashire was being dramatically altered by the Industrial Revolution. The Holts were millers; waterwheels provided the power. Many of their neighbors were weavers, producing cloth with hand looms. By the mid-1840s, that way of life was rapidly changing. The valley in which the Holts lived saw the introduction of steam power. Factories and their machinery reconfigured production methods, moving families away from cottage industries to factory employment. In Lancashire and other parts of Great Britain, one-time agricultural workers joined the workforce, and new workers arrived from Ireland to escape the potato famine. Towns and villages became industrial centers, and farmland gave way to urbanization.[2]

By definition, communities are not only made up of people living in close proximity to one another, but they revolve around shared interests and values, work, and social and religious institutions. When Servetus Holt left England, he abandoned the familiar and became a member of other communities. His story is one of millions that could be told by people who were uprooted by social, political, and economic forces during the nineteenth century. His personal tale is, however, representative of changes that influenced communities and the place of children's experiences. Many factors were at play, but, for this chapter, the emphasis will be on the impact of social and cultural change on communities in Europe and the United States, the mass emigration that took place across the Atlantic, the nature of western settlement and rural life, and the shift from local and informal sources of support for children and their families to state agencies.

THE WORKING-CLASS FAMILY
AND THE COMMUNITY

An influx of new workers and changing economic patterns of established populations influenced local communities. In turn, industrialization and urbanization affected not only community development but also the ways in which communities regarded children. Communities were in transition. The Industrial Revolution transformed methods of production. At the same time, it gradually changed the physical environment and social landscape of communities. For children and their families, particularly those living in the new manufacturing areas of the early nineteenth century, the onslaught of mechanization and the associated organizational changes were abrupt. They saw the old ways of doing things destroyed while they tried to adapt. Using the British textile industry as an important example of the early stages of mechanization, one writer has noted: "Historians have described industrialization as a cataclysm for workers' families."[3] For most, however, the demand that workers and the methods of production change with the times was less wrenching and reflected the gradual process of mechanization in trades and manufacturing.

There has been a debate, particularly among British historians, about whether industrialization forced more children into the labor force. One argument points out that child labor existed long before the introduction of mechanization: in the preindustrial world, children worked with their parents and outside their homes in a number of capacities. Most agree, however, that the numbers increased with industrialization, and, while employers often argued "that the new machinery had taken over the physical effort of work," children were expected to work longer hours in physically demanding work.[4]

In both Europe and the United States, workers clustered around the proliferating workshops, factories, and mines. New towns sprang up, and, in established towns and cities, working-class families crowded into the poorer sections. The working class grew in number, in such areas as Lancashire, Alsace, and (later) the Ruhr, as the demand for labor continued to rise. An apparent result was the number of children employed in mines and factories increased; British records for 1835, as one example, reported forty-one thousand children under the age of thirteen employed in cloth-producing mills.[5]

Youngsters at work were members of a community that focused on the job in the workshop or the mine. They spent more time with people at work than they did with their families at home, at church, or in social gatherings. For most of the time, children were not under parental control, but that of an employer. At the same time, fewer children were learning a skill or trade from parents, diluting the "production relationship." The number of apprentices learning a skilled trade from a master craftsman also decreased, and, by the 1850s—particularly in the United States, where the practice of apprenticeships had never been as structured or controlled as in Europe—the apprentice–master relationship was in steep decline. On both continents, social networks that once bound craftsmen and their apprentices into their own unique communities shrank when factories produced such items as shoes and furniture in greater quantity and at a cheaper price. By the end of the century, social reformers and public officials expressed nostalgia for apprenticeships "as a lost form of 'good' work."[6]

Youngsters entered the labor force at an early age. They were an economic asset for their families and for the industrial community in which they lived. A family's circumstances and those of children could quickly change, however, when accidents on the job, illness, or the death of a primary wage earner upended workers' lives. It was a short step from the working class to being unemployed and destitute. The community's responsibility to the poverty stricken was much discussed during the century, with an emphasis on saving children. By tradition and law, poor relief was up to the local unit of government; in Britain, for instance, this was the parish, and, in the United States (with the exception of Louisiana's parish system), it was the county. Larger urban centers established their own relief efforts, sometimes in conjunction with parish or county governments. As might be assumed, some relief systems were more generous than others, but, for many, the burden on local governments intensified with industrialization. Town and city governments especially grappled with what seemed an out-of-control problem. In 1849, for instance, an estimated ten thousand vagrant children roamed New York City. Some supported themselves by selling newspapers or flowers. A number turned to prostitution. An untold number resorted to theft, most of it petty. Others "in the dark and dreary alleys, barefooted and ragged" picked through garbage looking for anything of value.[7]

More dangerous and potentially disruptive to the social order were the gangs formed by children and adolescents. These groups, hanging around on streets and periodically fighting one another to protect their territory from outsiders, could be found in any urban environment. In Britain, notorious and dangerous gangs included the Peaky Blinders in Birmingham and the Redskins in Glasgow.[8] In New York City, reformer Charles Loring Brace noted: "They [the gangs] are much banded together, in associations, such as 'Dead Rabbit,' 'Plugugly,' and various target companies."[9] Brace described these groups as the "dangerous classes." They followed no laws but their own. Brace and others warned that if these gangs, these juvenile delinquents, were left unchecked, they would undermine the very foundations of society. They were not to be confused with children and adolescents who grouped themselves to play together or roam the streets of their neighborhoods. There was nothing malicious, for instance, in Kate Simon's admission that she "was always running wild in the street"; she and the neighborhood kids were just playing street games.[10]

Youngsters like Kate also knew that adults in the community looked out for her and her friends, whether from front stoops, backyards, or shop windows. When they misbehaved, their parents would hear about it. Youngsters may not always have appreciated watchful eyes or the implied social control, but there was a sense of collective security too. Among neighborhood friends and peer groups, children and adolescents created their own communities. Often youngsters grouped themselves according to age and/or gender, as well as the unwritten, but understood, code that decided who did or did not belong. Most of these child communities were harmless, but the ones for which laws and rules meant little were largely unaffected by reformers or a justice system.

Civil authorities were bound by law to deal with problems of the poor, and both public policy and private charity offered solutions. During the nineteenth century, the community response to poverty and delinquency was institutionalization. There were industrial schools, orphanages, almshouses, and poor farms. There is no doubt that many replicated the British workhouse, an institution mandated by the English Poor Law of 1834 and described in Charles Dickens's *Oliver Twist*. Many, however, attempted to provide job training, secular education, and religious instruction. Of the many institutions, the general public demonstrated the most interest in the orphanage. This institution could be found in urban and rural communities. As a general rule, in the United States, racial prejudices of the time dictated that nonwhite children be segregated in institutions meant just for them. And a number of orphanages were established by religious or fraternal organizations for a specific group only, maintaining a connection between the children and their religious or ethnic identities and communities. This was especially true in the United States, where a multiplicity of immigrant groups sought to retain cultural traditions and languages. There were, for example, orphanages exclusively for Catholic, Jewish, and German Protestant children.

During the nineteenth century, orphanages became the most accepted form of institutional care, and, although the word *orphan* suggested that child inmates had no living parents, the reality was quite different. At a time when there were few welfare services that enabled parents and children to remain together at home during times of family crises, orphanages became, in today's terminology, "community resources." Lost wages, the death of a family member, and other domestic upheavals were common reasons for parents to place children in a nearby orphanage. The children would have room and board, adult super-vision, and classroom instruction. In return, parents often paid a small sum to the institution. When, or if, family fortunes improved, parents reclaimed their children. An orphanage stay might last for a few weeks or months. For many youngsters, however, the ups and downs of family stability meant childhoods that fluctuated between living at home amid a community of neighbors and living in an institutional setting in the company of other orphans.

THE MIDDLE-CLASS FAMILY
AND THE COMMUNITY

Industrialization and urbanization created new workplaces and transformed others. Divisions within communities became more pronounced between the working class and a middle class that, by the mid-1800s, increasingly shaped social attitudes and standards for family and community life. It was a mark of the middle class that women and children did not enter the labor force. Women devoted themselves to projects that would benefit both their children and com-munities, such as organizing libraries and Sunday schools. In the home, women focused on achieving the middle-class household ideal. Mothers were to direct child training, encouraging deference to the father, who, as breadwinner and head of the family, had the final word in decision making. Children were to be nurtured and steered toward becoming responsible adults.[11] They learned a work ethic by doing chores at home or for their neighbors. "A child who never learns manual occupation besides play can have no solidity of character," warned one contemporary publication.[12] Work built character, but the middle class made a distinction between work as integral to child development and work as an economic necessity for family survival.

The protection of innocence and an emerging belief that childhood was a period of stages lengthened the time that children were sheltered at home before going out into the world. Attitudes concerning children, what constituted childhood, and the nature of the child were transitional during the nineteenth century. Enlightenment writers of the eighteenth century had repudiated the long-held belief that children came into the world tainted by original sin. Jean-Jacques Rousseau, one of the most influential philosophers of the period, argued that children were not sinners but innocents. Nevertheless, remnants of the child-as-sinner attitude persisted early in the 1800s, and child-rearing practices focused on repressing what was believed to be a natural inclination toward wickedness. By the mid-1800s, however, a noticeable shift occurred. The once-accepted premise that children were "not too little to die ... not too little to go to hell" was replaced with a belief that children were born innocent babes. When, for instance, Catharine Beecher's *Religious Training of Children*

FIGURE 2.1: Youngsters found a sense of community in many settings, including church and Sunday school. Pictured here is an 1886 gathering of a Sunday school in West Union, Nebraska. Nebraska State Historical Society.

appeared in midcentury, she emphatically denied the possibility that children bore original sin.[13]

By the close of the nineteenth century, the purity of children was a powerful theme that shaped ideas about child rearing and developmental stages of childhood. In concert were middle-class attitudes that turned inward toward the interior life of family. The nuclear family increasingly regarded home as a refuge from the world of urban growth, industrialization, and social ills. Parents were primary figures in their children's lives, but when children went out into the larger community of school, neighbors, or church, it was expected that they would be protected and surrounded by adults who had the children's best interests at heart.[14]

Traditionally, women learned methods of child rearing from their mothers, relatives, and friends. They relied on custom and age-old advice offered by a community of women. By midcentury, however, middle-class women more often turned to "expert" strangers for help. Their pursuit of the ideal of home and community life was influenced by sermons (both from the pulpit and in print) and advice literature from doctors and self-proclaimed experts in child care. Among the latter and most popular book publications in the United States was Mrs. Lydia Child's 1831 *The Mother's Book*. It supported the idea that childhood occurred in stages, and among its warnings to overzealous mothers who might push children too quickly from one step of childhood to another was the caution that too much early reading produced a dangerous "intellectual intoxication."[15] Women's magazines also offered a steady diet of advice and counseling. Some might seem ridiculous by today's standards, but others, particularly those that offered sound medical explanations for treating illness and enforcing hygiene, were important in the nineteenth-century effort to reduce child mortality.

These offerings for women sometimes suggested the dilemma of nonconformity to middle-class standards. Working-class families were unable to have all mothers stay at home and all children out of work. At the other end of the scale, the aristocracy, landed gentry, wealthy industrialists, and financiers did not necessarily embrace each particular of the middle-class ideal. Mothers often managed child rearing and education as an overseer, but daily routines and education were left in the hands of nannies, tutors, and boarding schools. Youngsters were both physically and emotionally distanced from their parents. When it ignored middle-class expectations, the upper class was criticized, particularly for what appeared to be a lack of interest in mother-directed child rearing and for its apparent obsession with dressing children to display family wealth. Time and again, critics warned that children who were "overloaded with finery or decked with jeweled ornaments" learned the wrong life lessons and, as adults, would contribute little of value to the community and larger society.[16]

MIGRATION, THE COMMUNITY, AND THE CHILD

Urban populations rapidly increased when rural residents migrated to industrial centers and when people left their home country to settle in another. England's population, as one example, was fifty-four percent urban by 1851. An influx of immigrants was partly the reason. In the 1820s, Irish artisans and textile workers, with their families, arrived, and thousands more Irish migrated during the years of the potato feminine. By the 1870s, at least thirty thousand Irish school-age children lived in England. Later in the century, England's new immigrants were Jewish, fleeing persecution in Russia, Poland, Galicia, and Romania. Generally, migrants to England tended to settle in urban environments, with people of similar ethnic and/or religious backgrounds, and near places of employment.[17]

In the United States, immigration also boosted population numbers. Economic, political, and social unrest and upheavals forced people out of their homelands, and some came for the adventure or the promise of greater opportunities than those available at home. British subjects came to the United States. A number of settlements were founded in rural locations, and most residents of these colonies were members of the landed gentry and aristocracy. Some were genuinely interested in agriculture; others spent considerable time in the leisurely pursuits of hunting and cricket. Immigration was a voluntary choice for these migrants, but the British also had a system of enforced migration, known as "transportation." Under this plan, the less desirable members of the population were sent to North America, Australia, and Cape Town. Begun in the early 1700s (when France also sent child "recruits" to its Louisiana colony in North America), British transportation was originally meant as punishment for crimes committed. The system evolved by the mid-1800s to include people whose only crime was being poor. With government approval, indigent women and children were sent to Canada and Australia under the auspices of the British Female Emigrant Society. And, on at least one occasion, in 1869, teenage boys were removed from London's Home and Refuge for Destitute Children and sent to a British farming community in the United States, where they "received a hearty English welcome."[18]

FIGURE 2.2: Immigrants often traveled to the United States in family and village groups; somewhat atypical was a group of adolescent boys sent to the United States from the Home and Refuge for Destitute Children in London. *Frank Leslie's Illustrated Newspaper*, December 25, 1869, courtesy of the Kansas State Historical Society, Topeka, Kansas.

Joining British arrivals in the United States were immigrants from all of Western Europe; by the latter half of the century, immigrants from eastern and southern Europe added to the number of foreign-born in the United States. Immigrants arrived in family groups, but it was not unusual for an individual to leave family behind. When Julia Goniprow left Lithuania, her mother saw her off at the railroad station; "when we said good-bye," remembered Julia, "she said it was just like seeing me go into my casket."[19] The break with family and home could be wrenching, and once in the United States, many immigrant groups congregated in neighborhoods that became identifiable as ethnic enclaves. In part, this allowed groups to retain a sense of belonging and identity, but it was also a response to U.S. prejudices against some groups, such as the Irish and Italians. Ethnic and religious communities replicated the social, educational, and religious institutions familiar to the new arrivals. (The same could be said of immigrant communities in England and other countries in

Western Europe.) Many had their own native-language newspapers and theaters, and most carried on the traditions of choral, instrumental, and sports groups. These elements fostered a feeling of belonging in what was an unfamiliar, and sometimes frightening, place. Children defined themselves in terms of those around them. They sang the old songs, celebrated religious days, and continued familiar customs. National, ethnic, and religious identities bound youngsters to a common past and cohesive present.

Despite the close-knit nature of immigrant communities, the mainstream culture managed to intrude. The mass media of newspapers, popular magazines, and books (many of the cheap, pulp fiction variety) widened youngsters' view of what lay outside their homes and neighborhoods. So did Americanized secular education and organizations that worked with immigrants. Hilda Satt was a Jewish girl of fourteen working in a Chicago knitting factory at the end of the century. She felt a financial responsibility to her family, but she found community at Hull House, a "settlement house" that provided language classes, job training, and structured recreation to the surrounding immigrant neighborhoods. Hilda became Americanized and struggled with the question of allegiance to the old ways and fulfilling her "individual potential." Loyalty to group values battled with individualism.[20]

U.S. culture's emphasis on personal independence and individual achievement threatened traditions that fostered group solidarity and community stability. When children internalized the message that their chances for self-improvement rose with acculturation, the obvious result was a break, or at least a partial one, with family and community. Discord also came when youngsters expressed shame, rather than pride, in their customs and traditions. It was not easy to ignore the mainstream chorus that all things American were better than anything immigrants might offer. Charles Driscoll and his siblings, as one example, experienced the split of Americanization firsthand. The Driscoll children had little interest in their father's tales of Ireland and his sufferings there. They regarded themselves as Americans, and "father," said Charles, was "destined to remain an alien in this incomprehensible country.... He was intelligent enough to know that he was considered an odd one, perhaps even by his own family."[21]

Community conformity and continuity were also influenced by mobility. British writer E. A. Wrigley, for instance, has argued that English poor laws and other forms of relief for the orphaned and aged encouraged mobility, because individuals could risk losing "intimate contact with kin" and leave home, without guilt, for more distant employment.[22] In the United States, mobility was an accepted means for achieving personal success, but mobility of some groups in both Britain and the United States was heightened by industrialization. When a mine closed or factories moved to another location, workers followed. They also tended to move within the confines of their neighborhoods, even when the workplace was permanently located. One British commentator observed that, in many districts of London, "the people are always on the move; they shift from one part of it to another, 'like fish in a river.'" A better place to live, a cheaper one, or lodging closer to work drove the impulse. Mobility and the erratic nature of some jobs resulted in disrupted family life and weakened bonds to a community. Abrupt breaks also occurred when an individual or family decided to strike out on their own. Grace Russell's family in the United States was one example. Her father moved the family out of a coal-mining town in Pennsylvania to a farm in Kansas. He wanted to be his own boss; Grace's mother wanted to live in a place where her children would never be called "coal miner's brats."[23] Breaking ties to a place and its people was worth the price, and parents like the Russells often framed their reasons for relocating as something they did more for their children than for themselves.

WESTERN SETTLEMENT

Christine Hinderlie celebrated her tenth birthday aboard the ship transporting her and her family from Norway to the United States. Rather than taking up residence in a metropolitan center, the Hinderlie family moved to a farm in what Christine described as "deathly scary" South Dakota.[24] Migration out of Europe played a large role in peopling the Great Plains and the American West. In some western mining camps, for instance, the number of foreign-born far outnumbered American-born, and "the West was the most cosmopolitan part of the nation, with between a fourth and a third of its people born outside the United States." By the end of the century, in fact, some western mining towns could claim a larger percentage of foreign populations than some sections of New York City and Chicago.[25] Settlers from within the United States and foreign-born immigrants moved into the vast region of the West in the 1850s. By the 1870s and 1880s, the numbers dramatically increased when rail lines were completed and homestead laws offered the lure of cheap land. People came to establish farms, to mine coal and minerals, and to create towns. New communities sprang up along railroad lines, near mines, military posts, and waterways. The population of the West's evolving rural and urban landscape represented multiple national and ethnic backgrounds. Said a boy settler in western Nebraska of community and neighbors: "[They were] a motley population from almost every nation in the world."[26]

The foreign population came from England, Ireland, Scotland, Wales, the German states, Belgium, and Scandinavia. There were Russians, Germans from Russia, Czechs, Dutch, French, Canadians, and Italians. Some had been influenced in their choices for relocation by U.S. railroad companies that had millions of acres of land to sell in the West. Company agents traveled through Europe, distributed pamphlets promoting the American West, and facilitated immigration by directing people to specific ports and ships. Agents arranged for the transport of family possessions and ensured that rail accommodations were waiting when the travelers reached the United States.[27] Supporting these efforts in the United States were organizations aimed at specific groups. Among them were the Irish Catholic Colonization Society, the Swedish Agricultural Company, and the Hebrew Union Agricultural Society, which directed immigrants away from metropolitan centers to rural areas.

Many of these immigrant groups traveled and settled as colonies of extended families and neighbors. Sometimes whole villages packed up and traveled as a unit. People not only moved themselves, they transported their customs and traditions. Immigrants did not need to fear isolation from what was once familiar, promised one German-language publication, for they would find "many neighborhoods just as German as the one he left in the old country."[28] Group travel provided immigrants with social contact, aid, and a sense of continuity. Some pooled their financial resources to the benefit of all. Said a member of a Prussian colony: "We put all our savings in a common treasury, part of which we invested in buying things we thought necessary to start a settlement. Our intention was to buy a tract of land to be held in common, and later to locate our individual claims."[29] Many colonists followed this formula, building and replicating villages and homes similar to those left behind. In these environments, youngsters were more insulated from other immigrant groups and U.S.-born settlers, and they were more likely to retain language, values, and customs of their national and religious heritage.

Outside these homogeneous communities, the West was an international mix. At times this generated prejudices and racism, as it did in urban environments. Often, the reaction was one of curiosity and acceptance. Remembering the people in his rural community, a boy settler said: "On one side [was] a German who could scarce speak English married to a Bohemian who could speak little English and no German: on another side a family of Swedes fresh from the old country ... nearby a family from Iowa; another family from Illinois." They were old and young, educated and illiterate. Despite their differences, they were all "engaged in the same enterprise."[30] Settlement, farming, and survival bound together this disparate group of people. It was little wonder that when youngsters wrote or spoke of their families and communities, the two were regarded as connected. Children understood their relationship to family and relatives, but they also considered themselves as members of a community that comprised people with a shared goal. Children watched and remembered how people joined together to help one another, build schools and churches, and celebrate special occasions. It was little wonder that years later, these children could recall in detail the names and personalities of neighbors.

Children went to school (when they were available), found time to play, and generally felt that there was a community of adults looking out for them. They also worked at varied and numerous jobs. Many of these, such as herding cattle or working in gardens, freed adults to do heavier, more skilled work. Many jobs assigned to children and adolescents were performed without adult supervision. Children worked alone, with siblings, or with neighbor children. It might seem that urban children working at jobs away from their families had nothing in common with rural youngsters. In fact, there were similarities. Work could be labor intensive; much of it was tedious. And, while some jobs were done with parents, a great deal were not. This meant that parents "were in no position to oversee closely how their girls and boys passed their days, to guide with much precision their steps into adulthood."[31]

Affecting children, too, was the fluid nature of settlement and adaptation. Perhaps nowhere else was the sense of a stable community challenged more than in western settlement. Many "settlers" would simply not stay put. Hardships brought on by economic downturns in the regional or national economy, local-ized droughts, poor crops, and personal losses forced any number of families to move on to a promise of something better. And, for some, just the hint of greener pastures elsewhere was enough to make them pack up and move. Youngsters were aware of the ebb and flow. Of would-be settlers in his area, one boy noted that some moved on "without a backward look or even a good-bye to their neighbors."[32] Those who stayed adopted a certain attitude about western settlement. It was a test of character. Children internalized the message and expressed pride in themselves and those around them who had the "vim and back-bone," the "courage," to remain. Children learned that among the things the western community valued was hard work and a stick-to-it attitude. Exhibiting those attributes provided children with a feeling of belonging.[33]

COMMUNITY AND PUBLIC POLICIES

While youngsters were influenced by their immediate communities, these were, in turn, affected by outside forces. Social commentators worried that

FIGURE 2.3: The children of western settlers, like those shown here working in a potato field, did many chores without adult interaction or supervision. Kansas State Historical Society, Topeka, Kansas.

"the factory system [had a] ... tendency to destroy family life and ties ... and ultimately the home."[34] When the home was threatened, so was community and, ultimately, national stability. Protecting and preserving the family and its children was of utmost importance. Local and state governments, urged on by reformers, more clearly defined the role of government in private life and enterprise. By the end of the century, commentators and reformers were discussing what constituted "good" and "bad" child labor. The most apparent examples of the bad were children literally chained to the machines where they worked or long hours spent in the mines. In agriculture, the worst conditions were among U.S. migrant workers and in the English "gang system," which became notorious for its exploitation of children. Despite these examples, both European and U.S. culture considered agricultural work good labor, and attempts to enact labor legislation was weakened by arguments that family farms could not survive without the labor of children working with their parents. The result in the United States was no farm legislation during the nineteenth century and only a weak attempt in Britain to prohibit employment of children under the age of eight in the gang system.[35]

Labor laws focused on controlling the employment of youngsters in the most apparently dangerous and debilitating occupations associated with industrialization and mining. Some laws banned outright the employment of children and adolescents, and a cornerstone of child labor legislation was imposing age limits. Parents and employers might conspire to circumvent the laws, but they found it more difficult when compulsory school laws became more stringent and enforceable. Legislation allowed reformers, government entities, and public policy to insinuate themselves into community life as never before. School and labor laws took decisions about work and schooling out of parents' hands. Other laws that dealt with child abuse and parental obligations brought welfare workers and the police into the family home. When parents and the immediate community failed to provide children with a childhood that corresponded to middle-class expectations, welfare agencies felt it their "sacred obligation to intercede."[36]

By the end of the century, what happened in children's lives was increasingly governed by factors outside the family and community. This is not to say that these were less important than they had once been. Nor can it be said that youngsters across the broad spectrum of social and economic lines and classes came to experience exactly similar childhoods. Yet, in many ways, it was the case that the standardization of rules that called for control of child labor and education for all placed youngsters on a more even field. So did the social propensity of segregating children by age. This occurred in graded classrooms, Sunday schools, youth clubs, sports groups, and in workplaces where age limits on employment were enforced. Children's limited contact with youngsters outside their age range reinforced the idea that childhood consisted of stages. Children were segregated into miniature communities of their peers.

CONCLUSION

What constituted a community was influenced by social attitudes about childhood. The physical community in which youngsters lived, played, and worked was determined by economics and the rapidly changing industrial patterns of the century. Industrialization both consolidated and eradicated communities. Migration and immigration often forced the families within a community to struggle for solidarity and continuity. And, in the story of western settlement, children's sense of permanency was tempered by a fluid mobility. Communities might differ considerably in physical makeup and what they could offer materially to a child, but the essence of belonging to a place remained a strong element of childhood.

Group participation in forming set values and common goals included attitudes about the nature of children and their place within the family and community. Biological kinship and neighbors, as well as relationships connected to church and work, directly influenced children. Not every influence was positive, as reformers and commentators were quick to note when they spoke of lax community standards that allowed youngsters to patronize disreputable establishments such as taverns and gaming houses. Unsavory aspects of urban neighborhoods bore the brunt of criticism, but rural communities were not immune. There is abundant evidence, for instance, that children living in the American West were exposed to gambling, alcohol, and tobacco use by adults who considered these harmless vices. Writing of these conditions, one western historian has noted that, despite children learning "some alarming habits," there is no indication that western life produced a generation of indolent adults.[37] In fact, the very opposite was the case, not least because there were many influences on youngsters from within their communities in both rural and urban surroundings. Alongside the negatives were the positive aspects of family nurturing, playmates, and adults who felt a responsibility to set good examples as child protectors, religious advisors, and teachers. Children, in turn, defined themselves within the context of a community bond of shared experiences and values. For better or for worse, children were shaped by their sense of community and the people who surrounded them.

CHAPTER THREE

Economy

CAROLYN TUTTLE

The transformation of the economy accompanying nineteenth-century Western industrialization permanently altered the way families lived and worked. There was a degree of interdependence between the survival of a family and the success of the economy. In the nineteenth century, family survival depended on the occupation and earnings of each family member. The Industrial Revolution, which began first in Great Britain, created more opportunities for family members to earn income outside the home in the formal market. This increased the family's dependence on money wages from factory work in the formal economy and reduced its dependence on jobs in domestic workshops and on the land in the informal economy. The growth of the industrial sector increased employment and income, eventually improving the standard of living for hard-working families.

Industrialization also changed the dynamics among family members and their roles within the family. As families moved into urban areas to take up employment in the manufacturing sector, the family economy changed permanently. Family members who were used to working together in the home now found themselves employed by strangers in such workplaces as paper mills, textile mills, and coal mines. In some of the early mills, women and children performed essential tasks, and fathers' skills were of little value. The family experienced considerable upheaval as women and children were able to make significant contributions to the family purse, and men were still unable to support their families on their own. The employment of children in industry was substantial and stimulated considerable debate.

Eventually, though, the successes of industrialization made it possible for mothers to return home and focus their efforts on housekeeping and child rearing and for children to concentrate on school. The father's position in the family as breadwinner was reestablished and solidified. These changes within families and childhood experiences spread from Great Britain to Belgium and France, and then to the United States and Canada. However, families living in the rest of eastern and southern Europe, in countries that still had primarily agricultural economies, continued working and living together under the same roof.

THE EMERGENCE OF SOCIOECONOMIC CLASSES: THE MIDDLE AND UPPER CLASSES

The survival and perpetuation of society in the West depended on a family's ability to provide for itself and transmit any assets it had accumulated from one generation to another. The degree of success a family had in self-preservation depended upon the value of the economic resources owned by the family in the form of land, labor, raw materials, and capital. These resources were either used by the family to produce what they needed or sold in the market for money to pay for the goods and services essential for their survival. A family's social class was determined by the value of their resources to producers and the degree to which they relied on their physical labor for survival. In the nineteenth century, families fell into a number of social classes whose boundaries are difficult to delineate: a wealthy upper class, a very diverse middle class, and an emergent working class.

Families among the titled nobility or landed gentry in Europe (or the wealthy in the United States) were particularly successful at accumulating wealth and passing it on to future generations during the nineteenth century. They worried less about daily survival and more about preserving ancestral property and accumulating new assets for future generations. Their survival depended on the establishment and protection of property rights and the value of the land they owned. Their success did not depend on their hard work but instead on the productivity of those who worked for them. The wealthy enjoyed the comforts of life and hired domestic servants to care for their children, clean their homes, and cook their meals. They watched their wealth increase as the harvests from their land yielded valuable crops. Their ability to feed, clothe, and house their family was secured by the efforts of previous generations and therefore largely insulated from the business cycles of the local economy.

The middle class, who had first appeared in Europe in the late Middle Ages, grew dramatically with industrialization. Innovations and inventions during the Industrial Revolution created new investment opportunities to increase wealth. Returns to physical capital increased greatly during this period as innovations led to many new factories equipped with power-driven machinery. This increase in wealth resulted in better access to education, more job opportunities in manufacturing, and greater market power for the middle class. The new middle class that emerged was not homogeneous and included shopkeepers, machinists, factory owners, and investors. Among these, entrepreneurs and industrialists needed capital to adopt new machinery, mechanize production using steam power, apply specialization to the production process, and expand the scale of production. Their survival and success depended upon the return on their investments, which were determined by the foresight and technical skills of inventors and manufacturers. When the projects were successful, investors' wealth grew from profits and capital gains. This was one of the advantages of proprietorships and partnerships: owners kept all of the profits for themselves because they were the ones who had taken the risks. When the projects were unsuccessful, however, investors could potentially lose everything—the money they had invested as well as any personal property of value. This unlimited liability was one of the disadvantages of proprietorships and partnerships. By the end of the nineteenth century, the middle class as a whole was better off, although considerable income disparities existed. Successful entrepreneurs, investors, capitalists, and business owners became more exclusive as they filled the ranks of the wealthy middle class, separating themselves from the managers, clerks, and teachers in the lower middle class. The middle class was not as comfortable as the wealthy but was more secure than the working class. Their ability to provide for their family was vulnerable to the business cycle but was insulated from the daily preoccupations with survival.

Although those in the growing European middle class were deeply divided by their social identities, occupations, politics, and religion, they were unified by their economic philosophy. They were strong proponents of classical economics and Darwinism. Most of the middle class believed in the pure laissez-faire market economy of Adam Smith, where individuals, by pursuing their own self-interest, would lead to the success of society as a whole. In their pursuit of prosperity, moreover, individuals should not be restricted by any sort of government intervention. Some members diverged from this free market approach, proposing more government involvement to help the less fortunate, but their voices and policies were largely ignored. In a free market, demand and supply would determine the value of resources and the goods and services they created. This open market economy would stimulate individuals to do their best because of their inherent competitive nature. As each person followed his or her own interests and did his or her best, society would benefit tremendously. According to their understanding of Darwin's theory, each generation was more successful than the last because only the strongest survived. When individuals failed and were unable to provide for themselves, no one else was to blame and nothing was to be done.

THE EMERGENCE OF A WORKING CLASS

Industrialization not only transformed the economy, but it changed society as well. As the agricultural sector of the economy declined and the industrial sector grew, more and more families found themselves dependent on others for their livelihood. Some families began to work outside the home in medium-sized factories or small workshops, which developed and persisted alongside larger factories.[1] Working on one stage of the production process, they were dependent on subcontractors to purchase their intermediate goods. The change in the role and function of the household in society was a dramatic departure from the past. Households that had been self-sufficient, where production was for their own consumption, became reliant on commercially produced goods that had to be purchased in the market. Family survival depended less on the land and more on securing employment in factories and mines. Those who had been self-sufficient became dependent on money to buy the necessities they had once produced themselves. Money, which was necessary for everyday transactions, became the unit of account and was used as a store of value. Earning money, whether it was a local currency or a national currency, became necessary for survival. With this shift to a money economy, a working class emerged beside the existing middle class.

This working class first emerged in Britain at the turn of the century (1790–1830) as the laborers behind the Industrial Revolution, growing in numbers as the rest of Europe and the United States industrialized. It was the changing productive relations and working conditions of the Industrial Revolution that created a class of people whose livelihood was entirely dependent on the owners of workshops, mills, factories, and mines. All across Europe, families were busy in small workshops (the metal trades in Birmingham, silk weaving in Lyon, woolen crafts in Florence, and lace making in Catalonia), large textile factories (cotton in Lancashire, Barcelona, Ghent, and the Rhine) and mines (coal in Yorkshire, Mid Lothian, Pembrokeshire, the Loire, and Westphalia). The technological innovations of specialization, division of labor, and mechanization, while making the tasks performed by the worker easier, made the job itself harder. Workers' survival depended on the contract they signed with the manufacturer and the relative power they had with other workers to make sure it was honored. Their success depended on their ability to cope with the monotony and alienation of performing simple tasks quickly and correctly hour after hour, day after day. Due to this demanding industrial regimen, working-class families experienced a loss of leisure and amenities, because their wages barely paid for household essentials. Their ability to support their family was vulnerable to business cycles and during downturns was dominated by the daily preoccupations of survival. Many working-class families rented apartments or small houses because they had recently moved to urban areas in search of employment. There was nothing but a job at the mill or mine to inherit, because workers were unskilled and were paid so little that they could not accumulate savings. The only legacy a family might leave was a reputation of being a hard worker.

Feeling threatened by this new social class, members of richer classes created ideologies that blamed many of the problems of the working class on the morals and ethics of the working class themselves. Members of the working class were allegedly careless, indolent, idle, and disaffected and therefore unable to provide for themselves. They were considered to be "shiftless and thriftless" because of their excessive consumption of alcohol, perceived laziness, and inability to save money. People who were already successful thought the working classes could move up the social ladder if they just worked harder. But they remained relatively poor because they spent everything they earned and did not save. Wanting instant gratification, they would buy and consume large quantities of food and alcohol. However, it is now clear from the documented increase in the participation of women and children in the labor market, and from the intensification of industrial work that accompanied industrialization, that there is little justification for this view.[2]

Families among the poor or peasant class struggled to survive, rarely accumulated any wealth, and were considered fortunate if they had a few material possessions to pass on to future generations. The perpetuation of the family's name was consequently determined by the success of the family enterprise and the prevailing peasant custom of partible or impartible inheritance. In families where there were no tangible possessions to pass on to future generations, children were viewed as assets. Families "invested" in strong, healthy children, because they contributed more to the family than they consumed. Poor families were large, because children contributed to either family production or family income and were a form of insurance for parents in old age. The survival of these families was inextricably tied to the ebbs and flows of the local economy. It was literally feast or famine for families whose livelihood depended upon the land or a trade. Their success depended on the productivity of each family member. Suzanne Voilquin wrote in her autobiography in 1865 of her family's dire predicament brought on by her father's illness (he had a small hat-making shop in Paris). She recorded a conversation with her mother,

> When I'd gathered what I could, I would bring it home, boil it with a bit of salt, and serve it to him several times a day in enormous quantities. It was on this same diet, insubstantial as it was, that your father had to return to work. All of our resources had been exhausted. Everything we could carry had been taken off to the pawnshop. Only your father's labor could save us.[3]

Poor families had no wealth or savings to fall back on, making their ability to provide for their family entirely dependent on the fruits of their labor. In addition, there was no government safety net to provide for family members when natural disasters ruined crops or when illness, injury, or death reduced family production. When the economy expanded, every member of the family contributed to the family enterprise, whether it was household maintenance, farming, or a trade. Families were able to keep themselves warm with clothing and coal and satisfy their appetites with vegetables and possibly meat. When there was an economic decline, securing the inputs for producing or buying food, clothing, and coal was much more difficult. These periods of famine pushed families below consumption levels necessary for survival. Sickness and death stood at their doorstep, often taking the youngest or weakest members of the family. Poor families worried far less about future generations, because they were completely preoccupied with surviving the present.

THE CHANGING FAMILY ECONOMY
AND WORKPLACE

The dynamics among family members, who worked and who did not, and how much each contributed to the family's survival, depended on the type of industry in which the family was employed. During the nineteenth century, the organization of production evolved from household production to the sweating system and finally to the factory system. Families who worked in agriculture on farms used household production. Families working in cottages on various trades first relied on household production but, by the end of the century, were trapped in the sweating system. Families who worked in manufacturing in mills and mines used the factory system. The creation of a new factory system, however, did not completely replace traditional methods. Custom and pride prevented many of the struggling family farms and enterprises from switching to more efficient methods of production. As a result, throughout the nineteenth century, it was not unusual to observe all three systems existing side by side in a village.

Household production was the predominant form of organization in the countryside. The agricultural sector still employed the majority of the population in Europe and the United States. It dominated in both the pre-industrial and industrial phase of the economy. Initial gains in output and productivity of this sector in Great Britain have been revised downward.[4] By the mid-nineteenth century, agriculture experienced only modest increases in output, and these were mainly due to increases in the productivity of land and not that of capital or labor. All sizes of farms dotted the landscape—small farms that produced enough to sustain a family, medium-sized farms that produced enough to sell in the local market, and commercial agriculture that produced primarily for the national market. On small family farms, the entire household contributed to daily production for their own consumption. Medium-sized farms operated in a similar fashion except that they often hired additional laborers to plant and harvest the crops and either paid them in kind or by piece rates. On larger commercial farms, workers were recruited, hired, and paid by supervisors for specific tasks. The British overseers or the American padrones often recruited entire families and brought them to the farms by wagon. Farming had been mechanized in these commercial farms such that crop production increased dramatically. On the larger farms in the United States, agricultural labor and food processing were beginning to be reorganized under industrial models.[5] Much of this rural life has been romanticized, depicting the peasantry of Europe as people living a tranquil life spent in the wholesome outdoors, where work and leisure were intertwined as the family enjoyed its independence. Similarly in the United States, the legacy of the yeoman and his family as a self-sufficient productive unit has dominated the discussion of rural life in America. The reality was much harsher for the family and its members.

The household production model required every member of the family to work, starting children on little tasks when they were able to walk. This interdependence of each family member in both production and consumption has been called the "family economy," described by Tilly and Scott as "the interdependence of work and residence, of household labor needs, subsistence requirements, and family relationships."[6] Fathers planted seeds and harvested the crop while children pulled weeds, sifted out the rocks, fetched the water, and watched over the animals. Mothers worked with the children when they were not cooking, cleaning, and caring for infants. This division of labor was described by Tullos for the Carolinas in the United States as follows,

> Most women's work on Piedmont farmsteads consisted of tending children, preparing and preserving food, washing and cleaning, perhaps helping to plant, hoe, and harvest field crops, tending gardens, providing medical care, and making clothes, coverlets, and quilts. The oldest and the youngest family members, male and female, were set to such tasks as spinning thread, making baskets, gathering herbs, milking cows, and feeding chickens.[7]

The days began at sunrise and ended at sunset. The work, although intermittent, was mentally and physically exhausting. The reward for standing on their feet all day, outside in the rain or hot sun, was enough food and water to stop the hunger pains. The final output of the farm was the result of a collective effort of the entire family. The family naturally went through periods of poverty and prosperity. The survival of the family depended on seasonal conditions as well as the number and ages of the children. Because children worked in home production, their ability to contribute led to what has been called the "family life cycle." When children were young and unable to work, families struggled to survive, because there were more mouths to feed on a smaller output. As children became old enough to work, families prospered, because they were able to produce more. Once children were older and left home, the family fell back into poverty without the contribution of the children.

The organizational structure of production in the cottage industry resembled the family farm initially. Families who did not own land but instead had a trade worked out of their homes. The cottage industry existed in rural areas and small towns as well as large urban centers. Mothers and children gathered around the kitchen table late into the night, making buckles and hairpins in Birmingham, sewing lace and embroidery in Catalonia, and assembling artificial flowers for hats and purses in New York. Every member of the family did what he or she could to contribute to the total output of the family enterprise, whether it was spinning yarn, making baskets, weaving, or straw plaiting. Children began to assist their families in cottage production at slightly younger ages than they had in farming. The days were long and arduous, but the whole family worked together. Sheltered from the weather, families worked twelve-hour days, although the hours were neither regular throughout the week nor consistent from day to day. Because families worked together and for each other, they took breaks when they wanted and enjoyed leisure on Sundays. Fathers who were artisans and tradesmen took on the tasks that required strength and skill, while youths assisted them by performing auxiliary tasks. Mothers and children performed simple, repetitive tasks and did chores around the house.

As the population in England and Wales increased steadily after 1650, the demand for food and necessities grew.[8] The small independent family enterprise could not work fast enough to keep up with the increasing consumer demand. A new system arose where families sold their output to a subcontractor who coordinated the production of inputs and sold the final product to retailers. Workers were separated from the final product and no longer worked for themselves. The production process was broken down into several stages, and the subcontractor would transport the intermediate goods between workshops until the final product was complete. The stores (retailers) then bought the products they wanted to sell from the subcontractor. The subcontracting system, also referred to as the putting-out system, industrial homework, or workshops, was extensive in most of northern and West Europe as well as the United States. Contemporaries commented on the hustle and bustle in the urban areas. It seemed as though inside every home and workshop, every hand was busy making shoes, straw hats, baskets, shirts, sweaters, and blankets.

This new system, however, was infamous for mistreating workers and creating the first sweatshops. Subcontractors earned their living from the margin between the amount they received for a contract and the amount they paid the workers. This margin was said to be "sweated" from the workers, because they received minimal wages for excessive hours working in unsanitary conditions. Photos taken by Lewis Hine provide images of women and children sewing garments in New York City, crowded into a small room that was poorly lit and not well ventilated. The stench and humidity hung in the air as the sweat rolled down their brow and onto the cloth. Several economic historians argue that the working conditions in these sweatshops were the worst of the century.[9] Ivy Pinchbeck, for example, asserted that "crowded into the tiny room of insanitary cottages, stimulated by competition to work at fearful pressure and under the threat of punishment, children in the domestic industries must have often fared worse than those in the factories."[10] Thus, there is a consensus that the putting-out system placed intolerable physical demands and inhumane emotional pressures on the men, women, and children who worked there.

The concept of the family economy took on new meaning when fathers, mothers, and children no longer worked together in the home. The family was still an economic unit where all members contributed to family income, but production and consumption were no longer connected and performed in the home. During the next stage, the family economy that produced the family wage ventured into the formal market for employment. The onset of industrialization increased the family's dependence on the health of the formal economy. As Britain and then Europe and the United States industrialized, two realities emerged. On the one hand, the countryside remained largely agrarian, with fields stretching as far as the eye could see. Small farms dotted the landscape, and the livelihood of most families depended upon their harvest or husbandry. On the other hand, cities grew up around the large textile factories, with cramped housing in the form of apartments and row houses. They were easy to identify from a distance by the tall smokestacks protruding from the red brick factories—in Lancashire and Yorkshire in Great Britain, Ghent in Belgium, Normandy and Alsace in France, and New Hampshire and Rhode Island in the United States. The farmer and the factory worker knowingly coexisted, but their lives were very different.

The industrial regimen was very different from the rhythms of rural life. The factory clock replaced the sun in determining the beginning and end of the workday. Rules and regulations replaced family preferences and customs. And an impersonal and formal attitude among coworkers replaced family ties. This dramatic shift in the nature of work made it difficult to recruit workers, because the work in the factory or mine was so different from what had been customary for centuries.[11] Men who had worked for themselves on the farm or in the cottage industry were reluctant to give up their trade and control over their own time to work in a factory where their skill had no value and their time and effort were controlled by the factory clock. Women and children, however, who were accustomed to subordination, became ideal factory workers. The family wage took on a whole new meaning. As the Hammonds put it, "the idea of the family wage as the economic unit, though not of course explicitly formulated, governed men's thinking about the industrial system, and thus factories seemed to offer special advantages to the poor by providing employment for their children."[12]

The employment of children increased considerably as the West industrialized. In Great Britain, children were predominantly found in the textile and mining industries but were also employed in the potteries, glassworks, and lace industries. In 1833, nearly half of the workforce in the northern cotton, wool, flax, and silk factories were children under the age of sixteen.[13] In 1842, the year of the Mining Act, children under the age of eighteen comprised between twenty-one and forty percent of the labor forces in the coal mines of England, Scotland, and Wales.[14] A similar pattern emerged as other European countries industrialized. After 1800, Ghent became the "Manchester of the Continent," and the textile industry was the largest employer of children. The linen, hemp, and lace industries hired forty percent of its workers younger than the age of sixteen, while twenty-seven percent of the cotton textiles workforce was younger than sixteen years of age. As in Britain, the percentage of children working in Belgian coal mines was considerable, with 22 percent of its employees under sixteen in 1846. In 1822, a census of factory hands from Alsace revealed that roughly one-third of its workers were under the age of sixteen. In France, an industrial survey in 1845 revealed that the larger workshops employed 143,665 children under sixteen, nearly 12 percent of the total workforce.[15] In the United States, the employment of children followed the development of the textile industry, which began in the Northeast and, by the end of the century, was established in the South. In 1820, children aged fifteen and younger comprised roughly one-quarter of the manufacturing labor force of the industrializing Northeast.[16] Toward the end of the century, in 1870, children younger than sixteen comprised 14 percent of the workforces of the New England cotton textile mills and 23 percent of the mills in the South.[17] The pattern was similar from country to country as industrialization unfolded, with children concentrated above all in the textile and mining industries. Child labor thus played a major role in the economic growth that Great Britain, Europe, and the United States experienced during the industrial phase.

Writers, travelers, and inspectors chronicled the lives of these child laborers in factories and mines. Some observers admired the new industry and were impressed with the abilities of the children. Andrew Ure, a proponent of the factory system, wrote of them, "They seemed to be always cheerful and alert, taking pleasure in the light play of their muscles, enjoying the mobility natural to their age. The scene of industry, so far from exciting sad emotions in my mind, was always exhilarating."[18] The journals of travelers such as David Davies and historians like Peter Gaskell often highlighted the beauty of the British textile industry where women and children were busily making fine cloth.[19] Charles Dickens, a staunch critic of British industrialization, toured the Lowell mills in Massachusetts in 1842. He discovered that the "New England Lowell girls" worked in clean, well-lit, and ventilated factories and lived in nicely furnished boardinghouses. Other observers loathed the large factories and were shocked with the burdens placed on children. In Great Britain during the 1840s and 1850s, several social novels focused on describing the suffering of factory children. The works of Benjamin Disraeli, Elizabeth Gaskell, and Frances Trollope described the misery and cruelty children experienced working in large factories. The writings of Karl Marx, Frederick Engels, and, more recently, the historian E. J. Hobsbawn painted a picture of the "dark Satanic mills," where young children worked in dimly lit, stuffy, overcrowded factories for twelve hours a day. One of the mining inspectors, J. R. Leifchild, described what he saw as he descended into a coal pit in Monkwearmouth, England,

> But what have we got here? A little mite of a boy, sitting behind this door, crouched up in a corner. Looking anything but like a free, joyous boy of playful propensities! What can he be doing here? This is the little "trapper boy," the youngest piece of humanity employed in the mines.[20]

Several of the familiar images associated with child labor in the mines have been captured in sketches and photographs. Underground in British coal mines, child "trappers" opened and closed the tunnel doors while "hurriers" pushed and pulled the wagons full of coal to the shaft. Inspectors of the mines sketched what they saw underground and included them with their reports. In the United States, the photograph of the "breaker boy," whose face and hands were blackened from the coal and who is crouched over a conveyor belt removing the rocks and slate as the coal rushed by, is infamous.

FIGURE 3.1: *Child trapper working underground.* British Parliamentary Papers.

FIGURE 3.2: *Lewis Hine,* Noon Hour in the Coal Breaker, *January 1911*. Photography Collection, Miriam and Ira D. Wallach Division of Arts, Prints and Photographs. New York Public Library, Astor, Lenox and Tilden Foundations.

THE CHILD LABOR DEBATE

Contemporaries began to worry as the number of the children working grew and as images of the child laborer became more familiar to families of every social class. Out of concern for the future of children and the country, an emotionally charged debate around the issue of child labor developed. Alfred (Samuel Kydd), Arnold Toynbee, Karl Marx, and Sidney and Beatrice Webb, later referred to as Pessimists, were shocked at the plight of children who worked in the British factories and mines. Pessimists believed it was their moral duty to expose and denounce the deplorable conditions under which the children were employed. They believed the exploitation of child labor was a new phenomenon that arose from industrialization. A similar debate arose in almost every country that industrialized after Great Britain. In France in 1819, it was the economist Jean Simonde de Sismondi and the conservative Vicomte de Bonald who first argued there were profound differences between the employment of children in factories and in agriculture.[21] And the passionate statements of

Robert Hunter and Edgar Gardner Murphy on the evils of child labor in the United States were becoming more and more convincing.[22] Recent research by historians and economists such as Sarah Horrell and Jane Humphries, Michael Lavalette, and Carolyn Tuttle has revealed that, although the exploitation was not new, it was extreme.[23] They found evidence of girls in factories who were "forced into unnatural activity by blows from the heavy hands and feet of the merciless over-looker" and boys underground in mines where the "ways (were) so low that only very little boys can work in them, which they do naked, and often in mud and water, dragging sledge-tubs by the girdle and chain."[24] As the use of child labor in industry accompanied industrialization, critics demanding reforms gathered evidence and proposed legislation.

Critics of this view, from contemporaries such as Andrew Ure and from the historians J. H. Clapham, R. M. Hartwell, Clark Nardinelli, and Neil Smelser claimed the Pessimists had exaggerated the problem. In particular, they alleged that critics had focused on a few factories where the Sadler Committee's Report had documented abuses in 1831 for the British Parliament. They believed quite the contrary, that the conditions and wages in the factories and mines were better than the conditions on the farms and in the home workshops. The Optimists, as they were later called, argued that the vast majority of working children were treated well and actually enjoyed their work. Factory children were not exploited but instead gained valuable skills, good work habits, and independence.

Suffice it to say that the nature of the work and the working conditions faced by children in these new factories were dramatically different from anything they had previously experienced, whether on the farm, in their homes, or in a cottage workshop. Although working conditions did vary from factory to factory, the nature of the work did not. Considerable research on the evidence that was collected by the Factory Inspectors in Britain for the House of Commons has revealed the conditions of work were inhumane at best. The 1848 Enquiry on Labour in France uncovered children working thirteen-hour days with two hours off for meals.[25] In the 1890s, future members of the National Child Labor Committee in the United States found children working all night in damp and dusty cotton mills.[26] The temperature in British factories ranged between seventy-one and eighty-seven degrees because most of the factories built had only a few small windows that allowed the air to circulate.[27] In almost all factories with the new machines powered by the steam engine, the smell of oil and metal filled the air as the clamoring noise deafened the ear. The children had to work faster and continuously to keep up with the new mechanized production processes. Their hand movements had to be precise and calculated.

Their legs had to be strong and flexible to permit them to stand over machines for ten hours and longer. The children showed tremendous self-discipline since they were not allowed to stop when they got tired nor eat when they got hungry. Children of poor and working-class families spent most of their childhood slaving over machines instead of playing or going to school.

WOMEN'S CHANGING ROLE IN THE ECONOMY

Industrialization increased the opportunities for women to work outside the home. The labor force participation of women increased significantly in the first half of the century. The most common occupational categories for women's paid employment were domestic service, factory work, and the clothing trades (in workshops or outwork). Many working-class women labored beside children in the textile factories and mines. Factory owners in these industries preferred women's labor because it was docile, cheap, and hard working.[28] Two of the three most familiar and appealing images of Victorian women during this period focus on their work. The first is the factory girl who was a symbol of the new industrial economy. She worked almost all day outside the home in a Lancashire cotton mill. This girl was exposed to both physical and moral dangers and lacked domestic training. The factory girl acquired a reputation of an immoral, indecent, impulsive woman who was not capable of keeping a good home. The second image was of the domestic servant who lived "below the stairs" and served the leisured middle class doing hard domestic work. This woman was more respectable, because her occupation gave her the opportunity to cook, clean, and care for the children. The final image was that of the "angel in the house" who had been described in a poem in 1854 written by Coventry Patmore. These women were pure, asexual, submissive yet morally superior, and concerned with the spiritual and not the practical.[29]

Economic considerations often shaped the choice of a partner, the time of marriage, and perhaps childbearing. For the working class, marriage meant an improvement in material comfort, because two incomes were better than one. In communities dependent on an industry, women's earning power was sought after, and there was a good deal of intermarriage in weaving and mining communities. Working outside the home, however, made the dual responsibilities of women much more difficult. Single women may have been liberated by social and economic independence associated with factory work, but married women were not. Married women and mothers experienced a greater burden now that the two spheres—work and family—were no longer under the same roof. Once they had finished working ten hours in the factory, women returned home to cook dinner, clean the house, and care for the children. As working-class families became more successful, women were more likely to retreat into a purely domestic household. Middle-class women had the luxury of confining themselves to the private life of home and children. Rising income also placed the new focus on the home as a consuming household rather than a producing household. Men and women now operated in entirely different spheres, with men in the workplace (the public sphere) and women in the house (the private sphere). Women were to work only out of necessity. Withdrawal of the wife and daughters from the labor market was seen as a defining characteristic of a successful early-nineteenth-century family. The change from the family economy to the man breadwinner–woman homemaker household evolved from a middle-class ideology to a working-class practice by 1850.

A RISE IN THE STANDARD OF LIVING AND THE CONSUMER REVOLUTION

We would expect that, as industrialization swept over Europe and the United States, the standard of living of the owners of capital and the workers should increase. The gains, however, were unevenly distributed and gradual. Those who gained worked in the formal labor market—the factory workers and miners—and those who lost worked in the informal labor markets—domestic workers, outworkers, spinners, handloom weavers, and farm laborers.

The evidence on wages, income, and consumption spending supports gains in material living standards by the working class, but the path was not smooth or continuous. The large gains of sixty percent to ninety percent in living standards for blue-collar workers in Great Britain after 1810 calculated by Lindert and Williamson[30] have been reduced considerably to modest gains of ten percent after 1840 by Brown.[31] Horrell and Humphries estimated the average annual earnings of British families from 1787 to 1865. By midcentury, families working in factories or mines earned the most, forty-nine pounds and forty-three pounds, respectively, while families working in agriculture (twenty-two pounds), and outwork (seventeen pounds) earned considerably less.[32] Similarly, research based on statistics of consumption of tea, sugar, and tobacco confirm that British living standards had improved by midcentury. The tradeoff between the poor quality of life in urban locations (with high rent, poor water quality, and the distance to the mill) and the higher adult earnings was significant in the industrial textile and mining towns. "If there were economic gains, they did not lead to physical improvements in the lives of English men and women."[33]

Industrialization was followed by an expansion of consumer demand and the growth of a consumer revolution. New consumption patterns emerged after 1850 in Europe as consumer demand grew in the cities, towns, and eventually rural communities. Families began to purchase more than the bare necessities as new standards of domesticity and comfort in the home arose. The desire to purchase commodities associated with hygiene, nutrition, and the health and education of children created a demand for housing, plumbing, furniture, and cooking stoves and utensils. There was also a flourishing trade in books, games, and toys for children on both sides of the Atlantic.

These changes in consumer demand originated in the wealthy and middle classes and, by the end of the century, were felt by the working class and even the poor. Families in the wealthiest classes in Europe—the nobility, the landed gentry, and the aristocracy—had enjoyed purchases of fine wines, teas, and tobacco for centuries, while the families in the lowest classes—the poor, the peasants, the farmers, and tradesmen—produced most of the goods they needed for survival and rarely purchased products in the marketplace. Families purchased domestically produced goods such as coal and cotton textiles in addition to imported consumer goods such as tobacco, sugar, and tea. The change in household behavior caused by industrialization and the dependence on wages and money was accompanied by an intensification of work and the suppression of leisure. The industrious working class was accused of self-exploitation, because they "are forced to labor now because they are slaves to their own wants."[34]

FAMILY PRESERVATION

By the end of the nineteenth century, more and more families were surviving, and many were actually better off than their parents and grandparents. To ensure the perpetuation of the family name, families used a range of strategies to preserve family possessions and wealth. Most inheritance systems in countries that protected property rights tried to strike a balance between security and equity. For example, in England and Germany, the system of yielding heirs required the heir to compensate the other siblings for their exclusion from the family farm. It was important to families to both preserve ancestral property and provide the foundation for future generations. Children were by far the most important form of insurance to preserve the current family and perpetuate the family name. Family property was either handed down to one child (the oldest son, the next-to-oldest son, or the last born) or divided among all of the children (partible inheritance). Fathers normally gave daughters and sons comparable shares of the inheritance, although girls usually inherited personal property while boys usually inherited real property. In the absence of a will, the rules of primogeniture were invoked, giving the oldest son the rights to all real property. The custom of primogeniture was applied more strictly in England than elsewhere in Europe.

Inheritance laws and property rights applied only to men as the head of the household. The property rights of women were dependent upon their marital status. In England, once women married, their property rights were governed by common law. This required that the property women took into the marriage, or acquired subsequently, be legally absorbed by their husbands. A married woman could not make a will or dispose of any property without her husband's consent. Once married, the only legal avenue through which women could reclaim property was widowhood. Women who never married maintained control over all of their property, including their inheritance. The women's movement eventually gained supporters and pushed through the Married Women's Property Law in 1882, which gave divorced women possession of their own earnings and some private property and small sums of money.

CONCLUSION

As the century came to a close, the family had successfully made the transition from a producer household to a consumer household. This new family model moved swiftly from the middle class to the working class and eventually to the poor, from West Europe to North America and then to South and East Europe. Increasing numbers of women and children were no longer working outside the home. Where they could afford to do so, mothers returned home and focused all of their efforts on caring for their children and maintaining a clean household. Children returned home and were no longer viewed as providers but instead as "treasures" that required considerable time and money to protect. Fathers remained outside the home, working in the formal economy and earning higher wages that allowed the family to eat better and live more comfortably than ever before.

CHAPTER FOUR

Geography and the Environment

NING DE CONINCK-SMITH

The twentieth century has been named the Century of the Child, indicating that childhood received a new importance socially as well as politically. Some have even spoken in terms of the "islanding" of childhood, indicating that children have ended up living a life isolated from society.[1] The focus on the twentieth century, however, has made us overlook the importance of the nineteenth century as a period when the construction of a new, modern, urbanized childhood took place. Nowhere is this more visible than when the history of childhood and the family is approached from a cultural geographical perspective, focusing on children's territories and the material and spatial changes of childhood. At the beginning of the nineteenth century, few people had ideas about what schools should look like. By the end, the Prussian three- or four-story version, with its cellular classes, big windows, and specially designed furniture, had become the norm, spreading from Central Europe to Scandinavia and onward from Europe to North America. This is one of many examples of the way ideas on how to confront the challenges related to industrialization and urbanization have traveled. Other examples would be the family parlor and the well-equipped nursery, both new phenomena in the middle-class home, and the Playground Movement.

This chapter will discuss these ideas and their impact on public and domestic spaces for children. Are we witnessing the first steps of what the

German sociologist Jürgen Zinnecker has called *Die Verhäuslichung* [the domestication] of childhood, meaning that children were beginning to spend their lives indoors—or at least as close to home as possible? Or does it make better sense to conclude that life changed for all children, but not at the same speed? There were still great differences between children of working-class families, those of middle-class families, children of immigrant families, slave children, boys, girls, and children living in various regions and nations.[2] This chapter is written with these questions in mind, but also with a curiosity about the similarities and differences in the solutions chosen by various generations of parents, educators, and child savers when confronted with the influences of urbanization and industrialization on the lives of children.

APPROACHES TO THE MATERIAL CULTURE
OF THE FAMILY AND ITS CHILDREN

There is no such thing as a general reference work on the historical geography of children and their private and domestic environment during the nineteenth century. However, a number of historians have investigated the material culture of childhood and the family in the past. Scholars might turn to the seminal text by Philippe Ariès, *Centuries of Childhood* (1962), to be convinced of the role of spaces and objects in the formation of modern childhood. According to Ariès, schools, clothes, and toys supported the sense that the world of a child ought to be different from that of an adult. Another important text is *Die Kindheit: Kleidung und Wohnen, Arbeit und Spiel: Eine Kulturgeschichte* (1979) by the German ethnographer Ingeborg Weber-Kellermann. Even though Weber-Kellermann also included children of the poor, it is the middle class child who—as in Ariès's study—is central to her description of the materiality of children. In 1991, she also published a book on the history of the nursery, *Die Kinderstube*. A U.S. perspective can be found in the frequently quoted 1992 book by Karin Calvert, *Children in the House*. This study focuses on the material culture of early American childhood between 1600 and 1900, with a special emphasis on children's clothes, furniture, and toys. Once childhood in the West had become a valued part of human life from the late eighteenth century, middle-class parents began to create a separate world for their children far away from the harsher realities of adult life. Children had not only a special right to happiness, but also a duty, as the British historian Hugh Cunningham once phrased it with reference to a character in Robert Tressell's *The Ragged Trousered Philanthropists*. With this came the nursery and new white clothes, stressing the innocence of children. The change in the understanding of children, from little adults to beings in their own right, also influenced the design and the use of toys. Before the middle of the nineteenth century, toys were scarce and exceptional, frequently made with adults as much as with children in mind. Afterward, they were designed with the purpose of educating as well as entertaining children, especially boys. Girls had to be content with sewing, playing the piano, or reading. According to the U.S. cultural historian Gary Cross, toys were markedly sex stereotyped, with miniatures of adults' tools and work settings. The lives of middle-class children are generally depicted as isolated from the world of their parents. We read more about the days spent in the nursery with siblings and nurses than with parents in the garden or in the family parlor. Exceptions to this rule include Linda Pollock's study of parent-child relations from 1500 to 1900 and the history of wealthy middle-class Canadian families by Annemarie Adams and Peter Gossage, which notes the attention paid to the needs of children in the design of the family home.[3]

The material culture of working-class children in the United States and Britain has been explored in some detail by David Nasaw and Anna Davin, respectively. In these studies, clothes and toys take up limited space, given the fact that poverty prevented working-class children from owning much of them. In contrast, children's spaces became of higher importance—especially the street, which, for many children living in overcrowded tenement houses, functioned as a twenty-four-hour playground. David Nasaw's study *Children of the City: At Work and at Play* (1985) is a history of boys in particular who roamed the streets of the new cities on the East Coast of the United States in search of work, fun, and food. In *Growing Up Poor: Home, School and Street in London 1870–1914* (1996), Anna Davin's focus is on girls caught between being children and little mothers. While their mothers were absent, it fell to them to care for homes and babies. Despite differences in geographical and gendered perspectives, both books draw a picture of working-class childhood of the nineteenth century as very different from the world of middle-class children of the same era. There were no magic moments between childhood and adult life, as David Nasaw has phrased it, and, even though girls were kept closer to the home than boys, the middle-class ideal of a domesticated childhood spent learning and playing was still far away. The same conclusions were reached by a team of German scholars, based on a comparative study of children's lives in the German town of Wiesbaden and the Dutch town of Leiden.[4] Their study showed that, because the urban space was of higher importance than the domestic space, the topographies of the two towns influenced the way children played. In Wiesbaden, the hilly streets were used for sled runs in winter, whereas the Dutch children used the numerous canals for swimming in summer and ice skating in winter.

The creation and understanding of children's objects and spaces, according to Michel Foucault's seminal work *Discipline and Punish: The Birth of the Prison* (1979), was described using a language of discipline and power. Schools, like prisons, were seen as tools of governance, serving to create docile bodies suited to the economics, politics, and warfare of modern societies. Instead of excessive use of force, discipline could be obtained, according to Foucault, through careful observation and the molding of bodies into the correct form based on this observation.[5] A particular form of institution was required, which Foucault argues was exemplified by the panopticon—a design that was developed for nineteenth-century prisons but that was also clearly visible in the way schools were constructed and furnished. The influence of Foucault's work on the study of the spaces and material culture of children can be seen in a series of studies of educational buildings in various national contexts.[6] All studies point to the importance of medical hygiene, order, and discipline in the design of schools. The many similarities between school design in Europe and the United States have led scholars to discuss the role of world exhibitions, international scientific conferences, and study tours for the exchange of ideas and plans.[7]

It is the changes rather than the continuities in the lives of children that have dominated the existing research into the history of children's spaces and material culture in the nineteenth century. The focus has been on children living in the cities rather than on those living in the countryside, where they were preoccupied with herding cattle, helping on the farm, and going to school during the winter.[8] Whereas the earliest studies depicted children in the role of victims, more recent ones have depicted children in the role of agents, wrestling with the challenges and opportunities of social change. Memoirs and children's literature form a substantial part of the source material. The end result seems to be that the middle-class ideal of the domesticated childhood was a normative point of reference for all children—and more of a reality to some than to others. How, then, did these ideas materialize in the creation of a new, primarily urban landscape for a good childhood?

A NEW URBAN LANDSCAPE
FOR THE GOOD CHILDHOOD

Cities grew enormously during the nineteenth century. New York, London, Paris—and even smaller cities like Copenhagen—more than doubled their number of inhabitants during the second half of the century. People came from the countryside to find work in the new factories or service industries, or they came as immigrants from countries overseas. Most of the new inhabitants were young people, and with them came even younger members of their family. Between a third and half of the population in these new urban centers were children younger than the age of fifteen. The number of destitute street children peaked in U.S. cities during the second half of the century. Because apartments in the tenements were small and families large, the street and vacant lots ended up being used as playgrounds.[9] The many street children were also a consequence of a rising unemployment among children, especially boys. While the girls had their hands full helping out at home and minding younger siblings, few opportunities existed for younger boys. There were no animals to herd in the city; no farm work to participate in; and, with the enforcement of obligatory schooling during the latter decades of the nineteenth century, child labor changed from full time to part time. Finding part-time work either before or after school was not always easy. Selling newspapers was one option, delivering milk early in the mornings another. The "newsies" (newspaper boys) of New York and the milk boys of Copenhagen formed an independent child labor culture. They had their own songs and pranks, recruitment system, membership of unions, and instigation of strikes to protect their rights and income. The newsies and the milk delivery boys were kings of the schoolyard, with their grown-up manners and money to spend on candy and inviting girls to the penny theaters, nickelodeons, and cinemas. By the outbreak of the First World War, these occupations had been taken over by adults. Distribution systems had changed, as newspapers were sold from kiosks and milk was sold from stores. But attitudes to child labor had also changed. The positive sentiment that child labor could prevent children from hanging on street corners and help them to support their families was replaced by an understanding of child labor as harmful for children's mental and physical health. After this, there was no doubt that the primary work of children would be conducted in the classroom. As such, it was not the factory laws that curbed child labor but the enforcement of elementary schooling in combination with improved living conditions and a new understanding of the ideal childhood, even among children of the poor.[10]

NEW EDUCATIONAL SPACES: SCHOOLS, KINDERGARTENS, AND PLAYGROUNDS

In the early 1870s, Philip Robson, the first architect of the London School Board, visited schools throughout the United States, Switzerland, Germany, Austria, France, Belgium, and the Netherlands. Robson was neither the first nor the last educational architect to travel, but his handbook, *School Architecture,* was published at a time when compulsory schooling was becoming a phenomenon in most children's lives, especially for children living in the cities. Social unrest and growing class tensions made the ruling classes look toward elementary education as a remedy to preserve social hierarchies and order. One important precondition for this was the existence of school buildings and state engagement.[11] Urban immigration made it necessary throughout the industrial world to build new schools, and, as a result, the design of school buildings became a professional occupation for doctors, engineers, and architects. Ideas were exchanged at large international hygienic conferences and at the World Exhibitions. At the World Exhibition in Vienna in 1873, for example, a model rural school was constructed on the premises, and drawings of school buildings and furniture were on display.[12]

The earliest schools had been housed in a mixture of buildings, some of which had been built for this purpose and others not. The elementary educational system of the second half of the nineteenth century would be based on purpose-built schools. Whereas the first part of the century had witnessed a variation of teaching methods, from the Lancastrian mutual teaching method to simultaneous teaching in galleries and classes, the Prussian classroom teaching method became the norm from the 1860s onward. Schools were seen as "beacons of civilization" and as social hygienic institutions, which should contribute to the improvement of children's health. The size and design of furniture, the ventilation, the lightning of the rooms, the outdoor playground facilities, and the wash basins and latrines were of the utmost importance. Growing state engagement made room for standardization, and many schools across national borders looked very much alike. "An agreed grammar of schools" was created. The variations were greatest when it came to the exterior styles. Bricks were the preferred building material, but schools in Sweden, Norway, and the American prairie could also be built of wood. Historical references were frequently used in the design to underline the importance of schools. It could be the Italian Renaissance, the Nordic Middle Ages on the continent, and the Gothic revival or the so-called Queen Anne style in the Anglo-Saxon world. The new types of school buildings were functional. From the outside, the big windows, entrance gates, and surrounding walls left no doubt as to their purpose as symbols of modernization and urban pride.[13] In Copenhagen, schools were equipped with entrance doors so heavy and handles placed so high that children had difficulty opening them. But the message was not to be missed: The gate to enlightenment was difficult to open. It is frequently claimed that the class teaching method as well as modern school architecture spread from Prussia to continental Europe and to the Anglo-Saxon world, replacing older forms of teaching like the Bell-Lancaster monitorial system or simultaneous instruction, where children were divided into smaller groups, placed on a raised gallery.[14] This may be true, but the Prussian inventions only caught on because similar experiments could be found in other continental European countries and in Britain.

The first purpose-built schools in England and Ireland were constructed by the Sunday school movement around 1800. The school on School Street in Dublin, dating from 1798, was a three-story building. Children entered directly from the street, and it had two big schoolrooms, one for boys and one for girls, on the first floor and several smaller classes on the top floor. The ground floor housed staff rooms and a soup kitchen. The interior layout suggests that both monitorial and classroom teaching were in use. Experiments within the infant school movement were also important, especially the use of object teaching as a reaction to the mechanistic Lancastrian teaching method. At the infant schools, children spent their time singing or dancing, played in the outdoor playground, or were grouped together on benches in an elevated gallery. The intention was that children's character and moral behavior would be built up through play and cooperation.[15] In France, the inspiration came from the Jesuit schools of the seventeenth century. These schools had small classrooms, with windows placed so high that the boys could not be distracted. Both principles were to be found in the schools of the late nineteenth century.[16]

The class teaching method did not imply that students were of the same age group, as we understand it today. North American prairie schools as well as Danish rural public schools were ungraded, with younger and older pupils in the same class or alternating during the week. In Denmark, which had tried to institute a system of compulsory schooling in the eighteenth and early nineteenth centuries, there was a long tradition of state-authorized normal plan rural schools. Until the late nineteenth century, normal plan schools had one room for all students. The interior design changed over the years from the teacher sitting in the middle with the students around him to the teacher placed on a raised podium at the head of the class with the students on benches in front of him. The model of the new urban schools, constructed in accordance with the insight of the school hygiene movement, was gradually transferred to the rural schools. Light had to come from the left, children's clothes had to be placed in a separate wardrobe, and schools had to be equipped with latrines. But it was not until after the Second World War that the age-graded class teaching method materialized in rural areas.[17]

One challenge for the education authorities was the design of new school buildings; another was their location. In urban centers, where land was scarce and costly, schools were located on former rubbish dumps, on grounds with odd shapes, or on the outskirts of the city. In France, the school and the town hall were frequently built together. In other countries, over the years, different schools were built next to each other, forming a "Latin quarter," as in the Swedish town of Norrköping, where a high school (a *gymnasium*) was flanked by a girls' school and an elementary school. With the growing importance of education, schools were given a central location in town planning. In the city of Hälsingborg, Sweden, the new high school was built in 1896 overlooking the city from a hill; in other Swedish cities, the school formed one side of a central square. The location was thought to be important both for the health of the students and for the shaping of their taste for beauty. In several cases, a location close to nature or by the sea was preferred.[18] In France from 1850, there was a ban on locating schools next to bars, inns, markets, slaughterhouses, and cemeteries, because they could all risk harming the moral and physical constitution of children. The location of schools in former chapels was quite common, which had the unfortunate side effect of children stumbling over human remains when they used the cemetery as a playground.[19] Frequently, rural children had a long way to go to school. They went to school on skis or snowshoes in winter, and they walked or ran during summer. In Denmark, the 1814 educational act stipulated that children should not have more than a quarter of a Danish mile (about four and a half miles or seven and a half kilometers) to school. In many regions, the teacher came to see the children, teaching in a barn or at a local farmer's house. When school buildings were erected, teachers divided their time between different schools.

The schools set new standards for children's spatial and bodily behavior. Handbooks in school design prescribed children's posture for when they were working at their desks. An upright position was expected, legs were not to be crossed, and hands had to be kept above the desk. Ideally, desks should be open at the front so that the teacher could see and control what happened below the table. But lack of space made these demands impossible to implement in many cases. Children were rearranged once a month according to their marks. In the London board schools, the top of the class were seated closest to the fireplace. In Copenhagen schools, the brightest children were placed at the desks closest to the teacher, and the students who did not do so well were located at the back of the class. For serious offences, detention was used, but it was gradually replaced by physical punishment, because staying late after school clashed with children's working hours and parents fiercely protested the use of detention. In the city of Frederiksberg, near Copenhagen, students who played truant were sent to a children's prison with a window facing the schoolyard as a warning

FIGURE 4.1: *Anton Dorph (1831–1914),* Young Girls Who Play in the Dunes on Their Way Home from School, *1863.* © Statens Museum for Kunst, Denmark.

to other students. As in England, Copenhagen and the Swedish town of Malmö had specific truant schools.[20]

School space was also gendered. In some cases, boys and girls went to separate schools. In others, they were separated at the entrance, with the schoolyard being divided by a high wall, and boys and girls having separate gyms. Their curricula also diverged at certain points: Boys took classes in woodworking, and girls studied home economics. Children experienced schools differently. Girls found it a place where they could leave their child minding and other obligations outside the door, sometimes in the literal sense. In London, the school board decided in the 1870s to equip new schools with baby rooms.[21] Boys were more inclined to challenge the hard discipline and the patience of the teacher. Late into the nineteenth century, child labor was more important to many families than schooling. Girls had to stay at home when mothers did the laundry, and both boys and girls skipped school during the harvest. As a consequence, school hours had to follow the rhythm of working life.

Spaces for younger children also changed. Infant schools, *salles d'asiles,* and kindergartens were known from the 1830s, but most young children were cared for at home by mothers, neighbors, or older siblings. For this age group, the playground movement that originated in London in the 1860s was of greater importance than the school. Play areas were included in new parks, and some centrally located churchyards were open for play.[22] By the late 1880s, playgrounds could be found in all major cities, from Berlin to Boston. In the summer of 1885, the Massachusetts Emergency and Hygiene Association placed a pile of sand in the yard of a chapel in an immigrant neighborhood of Boston. The pile became so popular with the children that the society opened three more the following summer. At the 1893 Chicago World Exhibition, model kindergartens and playgrounds were exhibited. The sand pile was one of the idea visitors took back home, and the idea spread quickly on the European continent. By 1900, sand piles or sandboxes had become fundamental to playground design. The idea behind the sand pile—the stimulation of cooperative play—went hand in with the other playground equipment such as the seesaw and the merry-go-round.[23]

The playground movement was a specific urban phenomenon connected to the child saving and settlement movements. It was driven by a few entrepreneurs, such as the Danish teacher Hans Dragehjelm, who was decorated by the king as the inventor of the sandbox. The sandbox was originally meant to be a tool to prevent boys from playing in the streets, by introducing them to the "wonders of the sand," as Dragehjelm framed it, since things made out of sand could be made over and over again. This idea never worked. Sand could never compete with the street when it came to action—and instead it was young children who found a play space here. Sand piles were soon supplemented by small ponds, where children could sail boats or play with water. Again, the hope was to make playing in public fountains and swimming in the harbor less attractive. Even though playgrounds were popular, children continued to play in the streets. It was closer to home, and, for older children, it was also where they worked minding younger siblings, collecting coal and odd bits and pieces, selling newspapers, or running errands.

NEW EDUCATIONAL SPACES: ORPHANAGES AND REFORMATORIES

In the 1840s, there were about 30,000 destitute children in London. At the turn of the century, 100,000 children were cared for in orphanages across the United States.[24] Destitute children were an integral part of the industrialization and urbanization processes that swept across Europe and North America during the nineteenth century—and their number grew explosively. Children and parents lost track of each other during the immigration process, parents died or split up, living conditions were tight, and some children ended up living on the street. Casual forms of child labor became a way of living for many of these children; petty theft and prostitution were other alternatives, as described so vividly in the novels of Charles Dickens.

At the same time as these big social changes, new ideas about how to treat destitute children arose. Homeless, poor, destitute, and delinquent children were no longer to be kept in poor houses or in prisons together with adults. In contrast to adults, there was still hope for children, who should receive education and be isolated from the influence of vicious adults. Children could be saved from society, and for society, and be brought up in the right Christian spirit. From the late eighteenth century, religious congregations organized Sunday schools, collected money, and rented or built facilities to care for these children. The child saving movement began by looking after orphaned children, who were either placed in foster care or taken to an orphanage. During the 1830s and 1840s, the child saving movement joined forces with the prison reform movement in the creation of reformatories designed to care for criminal children. From the 1870s, child saving gradually became a state responsibility, especially when it came to the education of juvenile delinquents.[25]

To house the large numbers of children, specialized buildings were necessary. Orphanages tended to be small and owned by private, religious organizations with a single woman in charge. They could be housed in city houses or on estates donated by wealthy benefactors. The new interest in hygiene and the importance given to fresh air and sunshine led to the addition of balconies, where small children could nap in their cots during the day. The interior design was kept similar to that of a middle-class home, with a living and dining room and frequently a garden for the children to play in. But, in contrast to middle-class children, who eventually had their own bedrooms, children in orphanages slept in large dormitories with a nurse sleeping among them. Memoirs provide the impression that life at an orphanage could be a relief to some children who had been living on the street or in poor family conditions; to others, it was a world of coldness, hard labor—children scrubbed floors, washed, and worked in the garden—and harsh physical punishment.

Institutions for delinquent children tended to be very large. A group of four or five reform schools inspired the building of similar schools in European countries. Information on these institutions was obtained through the international conferences of criminologists and philanthropists or by visits to them. In the summer of 1865, the Norwegian theologian Ole Irgens visited Das rauhe Haus [The house of Mr. Ruge, a former owner] in Hamburg and its director,

Dr. Wichern. Das rauhe Haus was opened in 1833 as a home for about three hundred destitute boys and girls. From its earliest days, it positioned itself as different from other orphanages. Das rauhe Haus wanted to replace the child's lost family. It was a so-called moral institution, where children were educated, not punished. The direct inspiration came from the Swiss educational philosopher Johan Heinrich Pestallozzi and his work with orphaned children at the school at Yverdon in the first decades of the nineteenth century.[26]

In a famous phrase, Pestallozzi declared: "There can be no doubt that within the living room of every household are united the basic elements of all true human education in its whole range."[27] At Das rauhe Haus, children lived in small family groups consisting of children of varying ages and placed in individual houses on the premises. Pestalozzi stressed the importance of combining education with work and the need to create a balance between head, hands, and heart. At Das rauhe Haus, children had plenty of opportunity to work and play in the large garden. The day the Norwegian visitor came by, strict order reigned everywhere, children were found happy and satisfied, and the director explained his educational principles in great detail. Children should receive love and care, but they should also be punished, as they would be punished in a family.[28] Punishment was administered differently in the many new reform schools. At another model school, the New York State Reformatory in Elmira, from 1877, the director Frederick Wines underlined the importance of causing the criminal youth pain. He argued, "some illnesses cannot be treated with out the knife of the surgeon." The treatment consisted of the director punishing the inmates with a leather strap soaked in water so that it stuck to the body.[29]

A third, much-visited type of model institution was the French *colonie agricole*. Around seventy institutions were created between 1840 and 1885, the first of which also became the most well known, the *colonie* of Mettray, founded by the philanthropist Demetz in 1839. The purpose was to educate and civilize delinquent boys through hard agricultural labor far away from the temptations of the city. The system was famous in its own time and later achieved greater notoriety through the work of Michel Foucault, who included the colonies in his study on *Discipline and Punish*. The highly supervised and disciplined life, with no possibilities of hiding or escaping, made Foucault see the colonies as a model "in which are concentrated all the coercive technologies of behavior." In it were to be found "cloister, prison, school and regiment."[30] This statement has been questioned by the French historian Ivan Jablonka, who argues that the colonies were—like Das rauhe Haus—created as an alternative to prison. Their failure as future agricultural colleges had both discursive and social explanations. The discourses that framed the initiative were contradictory, advocating both education and punishment. Children were seen as both innocent victims and as vicious, mean, and dangerous. Even though the colonies received money from the state, they were expected to cover the expenses of the children's food, lodging, and education. This pushed the directors toward exploiting the boys for their labor and leaving them little time for education. According to Jablonka, the failure of the system tells us that there was more than a superficial likeness to the adult prison system. It is a story about children falling victim to grand ideas and experiments—and also a story about how the creation of children's territories cannot be separated from the question of gender and class.[31]

NEW DOMESTIC SPACES: THE HOME, THE NURSERY, THE PARK, AND THE STREET

It was not only the public spaces of childhood that changed with the building of schools and reformatories. Private life and domestic spaces also changed for the children of both rich and poor. Grim housing conditions forced children to play in the streets. With their younger siblings, girls played with dolls on the stoops, while boys played with hoops or marbles in the middle of the street. Growing traffic, police officers, and gas lamps gradually restricted this unlimited use of urban space. When asking why the police were always in the way, New Yorker Mike Gold spoke for many poor children from Stockholm to Los Angeles. They had their ball games broken up by police officers, were caught picking coal at the harbor front, and were beaten for splashing under fire hydrants and clinging to carts. According to Harpo Marx, the cops were sworn enemies in New York at the turn of the twentieth century. The same goes for Copenhagen, where it was not unusual for police officers to be harassed and stripped of their helmets and uniforms by working-class boys, who found the officers inhumane, unjust, and violent. "We hated the officers with the whole of our young hearts," as the author Christian Christensen later remembered.[32]

From the Swedish provincial town of Gothenburg to New York, gangs of boys were an integral part of child life in the nineteenth century. Territory was everything to the children, as the historian David Nasaw states. For children living in overpopulated apartments in tenement buildings, it was the only place they could call their own.[33] Gangs were rooted in a neighborhood with the purpose of defending it. Boys were recruited when playing in the streets or through older siblings. Armed with fists, sticks, and slingshots, the boys attacked and harassed each other. Jewish boys who were caught by a group of Irish boys in New York were certain to be "cockalized." This meant that the boy was thrown to the ground and had his pants pulled down, while the enemy kids spat and urinated on his circumcised penis and shouted "Christ killer." With parents preoccupied with making a living and thus out of the way, gang life became a way of growing up to many poor children. Besides fighting with each other, gangs also challenged the social order when members stole fruit or candy, cheated their way into penny theaters, put firecrackers in letterboxes, threw stones and snowballs at horses and pedestrians, and drank alcohol and smoked.[34]

FIGURE 4.2: *Marie Bashkirtseff (1858–1884)*, Un Meeting, *1884.* Oil on canvas, 76 × 70 inches (193 × 177 centimeters). © RMN (Musée d'Orsay)/Jean Schormans.

Before the 1870s, poor children's toys were primarily homemade, frequently by the children themselves. Most boys knew how to handle a knife. They could carve boats or weapons out of odd pieces of wood, make a bow and arrow, or a craft a flute from a willow tree. Younger children made cows and pigs out of sticks and cones. Old rags could be turned into dolls or balls if a pig bladder was put inside. In many games, the body was the main "toy," as in girls' singing games, boys' ball games, and the game of hide-and-seek, which was played by boys and girls together.[35]

Both in the city and in the countryside, boys could roam much farther than girls. A survey conducted in the winter of 1883–1884 of boys and girls from a rural parish on the island of Fynen in Denmark revealed that the children of farmers were heavier and taller than the children of smallholders and that the daughters of smallholders were in the worst physical condition of all. The explanation was simple: They always had to help out around the house and rarely spent time outdoors. Even boys, who at a tender age had been sent away from home to work, had more time to play outdoors, when herding cattle or geese, for example.[36] Playing in the streets and roaming the countryside had their price, however. Children were often victims of traffic accidents and of drowning while swimming in streams or marsh pits. A mixture of ignorance, curiosity, and poverty also led them to accept offers from men. In New York City, in the middle of the nineteenth century, an estimated five percent to ten percent of young women in their teens and early twenties engaged in prostitution. Concern about child prostitution led the state of New York to raise the age of consent from ten to eighteen in 1895. Ten years earlier, newspaper stories about children, especially girls, recruited into prostitution had led the English Parliament to raise the age of consent from thirteen to sixteen.[37]

Children of the middle classes were, as a rule, banned from playing in the streets with poor children. They went for walks in the park or followed the street play from the windows of their nursery. A new spatial construction related to the development of the nuclear middle-class family and the sentimentalized understanding of the "good childhood." Nurseries had existed in wealthy families before the nineteenth century, but normally only as room where children slept. Children otherwise played and lived in the same rooms as adults. With the development of the nuclear middle-class family, children were placed center stage. Paradoxically, this also meant that children were stowed away in a special wing of the manor, on a top floor, or behind the kitchen.[38] Together in the same room with the nanny, they slept in beds made especially for children and had little tables and chairs their size where they did their homework. Just before bedtime, they were brought into the salons to say goodnight to their parents.

Memoirs contain descriptions of family life and of how children spent time together with their parents, either in the mother's room during the afternoon or in the family parlor, playing music, putting together a jigsaw puzzle, reading, or playing quiet board games. The mass production of the high chair from the 1830s onward signaled a wish for parents and children to be together at meal times. In the Victorian household, the family dinner table became the place where children's upbringing and manners were in focus. One of the earliest versions of the high chair had an angel with a bent knee as its back, pushing the child to sit in an upright position.

During the second half of the nineteenth century, doctors entered the nursery. Beds replaced cots since rocking could harm children's health, the temperature had to be kept low at night, and children needed to spend time outdoors. The new garden and park culture made this possible without mixing with children of the street. From the 1860s, prams became the fashion. Nannies and mothers pushed the child in front of them and did not face the child (in contrast to what became the norm since the 1920s). There was no notion

FIGURE 4.3: *Fritz Uhde (1848–1911)*, Die Kinderstube, *1889*. Oil on Canvas, 43.6 × 54.5 inches (110.7 × 138.5 centimeters). © bpk/Hamburger Kunsthalle/Elke Walford.

that young children needed intellectual stimulation. Quite the opposite was the case: young children were thought to be like vegetables, needing quiet and healthy surroundings to grow and flourish.[39]

Middle-class parents kept a close eye on their children, boys as well as girls. Children went on trips to the park with their nanny, and this was not always an enjoyable experience. A German woman born in 1904 was later in life full of resentment toward the park, where, as a child, she and her sister were forced to walk every day together with a very strict nanny. All their clothes were white, even their shoes. "When other children ran off to have fun, we were not allowed. Once back home, the shoes were just as white as when we left."[40] Very wealthy children, like the daughters of the Vanderbilt family in the United States, had a playhouse made for them. They cooked meals with their nanny and invited family and friends over to visit.[41] Boys seem to have paid a high price for protection under the watchful eyes of their parents, and the memoir literature contains many descriptions of lonely middle-class boyhoods. Boys often became quite dependent on their parents, especially their mothers. They read books and played with toy soldiers, or they became good at inventing things when playing by themselves. Like many other children, the German critic Walter Benjamin liked to hide under the dinner table, which his imagination transformed into a Greek temple. At other times, he hid behind a curtain, pretending to be a ghost.[42]

Once these middle-class children started school, the walk to and from class gave them an opportunity to explore the city. Children like Walter Benjamin experienced the city in all its sensual details. Rushing through town, they noted everything from the women in the market hall to the fire engine drawn by four horses, which left a shower of sparks behind it. In New York, children marveled in front of the windows of the big department stores, and when penny theaters, nickelodeons, and candy stores mushroomed in the cities, children were among the first and most faithful customers. The movie industry was well aware of this. In Vienna, even infants could be admitted at a reduced price. In Copenhagen, dogs were allowed in theaters so that children did not have to leave their pets outside.[43]

CONCLUSION: DIFFERENT TERRITORIES— DIFFERENT FAMILY LIVES AND CHILDHOODS

This chapter has told the story of the changing territories of families and their children during the nineteenth century. It begins at a time when child rearing and education were private matters for the family and ends when education was considered one of the pillars of the modern nation state. At the outset, children's lives were closely integrated with those of adults; later, children were separated from the rest of society. The changes did not occur overnight, and their impact varied according to children's gender and the social and cultural backgrounds of their families. In the working-class city of Leiden, for example, children had less time for play than their wealthier counterparts in the German town of Wiesbaden. In Wiesbaden, children tended to play indoors with their toys, whereas the Leiden children played outdoors with their friends.[44] The chapter has dealt primarily with children living in cities, because changes came first and were most visible there. Even though there were many differences between the lives of families in the nineteenth-century Western world, there were also important similarities. The growing focus on children's upbringing and education brought a decline in child labor and more time available for play and study. This resulted in the creation of a new urban landscape for children. Spaces unregulated by adults were no longer deemed suitable for children. The alternative was a highly regulated public landscape for urban children. Schools, kindergartens, and playgrounds were situated at the center, with orphanages and reformatories at the periphery.[45] Children's private spaces within the family home also changed, especially for middle-class children when they had their own nurseries. Poor children, meanwhile, still slept together with their parents at the end of the century.

The nineteenth century must be considered a century of experiments. Immigration, urbanization, and industrialization produced new social challenges—and new solutions. This chapter has stressed the similarities in the way these challenges and solutions were handled and pointed to the importance of the international conferences and world exhibitions. Ideas traveled back and forth between Europe and North America. Mass schooling was one answer; playgrounds to keep children off the streets a second; the creation of reformatories a third. All of these solutions were anchored in a conflicting discourse, where a balance between protection and punishment, the child as victim or villain, was not easily reached. These dilemmas were evident in the solutions. In the end, there was no doubt that the new spatial constructions were meant to be instruments of social order, regulating children's bodies and social relations. The changes have been termed the "islanding" or the domestication of childhood, and the two processes went hand in hand. Children were gradually separated from the world of adults, and the home was seen as the ideal space for children. For children without homes, reformatories were created as a replacement, and for children with potentially failing homes, school was the best alternative. Even in the homes of the middle class, children were both isolated and domesticated in their nursery or in the family parlor.

CHAPTER FIVE

Education

BENGT SANDIN

This chapter will discuss the way schooling in the West emerged as one of the main influences on the definition of childhood and on the lives of children and their families. The educational systems were in the process of dramatic change and development during the nineteenth century, but only slowly did educational institutions become important in the everyday lives of children. Children's lives were primarily influenced by other formal and informal systems of socialization in the family and in the local community. For children working as apprentices, factory hands, or farm laborers, childhood was not defined by educational institutions. However, toward the end of the century, schooling would become a dominant aspect of children's lives. It would come to define the parameters of childhood, the role of work, and the nature of family life and parenting.

The history of education and schooling is also an expression of the important social and political changes that occurred during the nineteenth century. The educational systems reflected the expansion of citizenship and nation building at this period. Populations and nations were defined at the same time as decisions were made on those who were to be included and excluded from the schools. The educational systems expressed equality and nationhood but also inequalities, exclusion and marginalization based on gender, ethnic, and religious distinctions. These were not only aspects of the same process, but also an expression of a struggle over the identity of children and the normative meanings of childhood. They defined, for example, where children were supposed to grow up: in the home, the school, or the workplace.

The irony of schooling is that it ties ideals of freedom to the demands of social administration and compulsion. It also expresses norms around acceptable social spaces for children. This, in turn, makes it possible to discern the underlying controversies over the role of children and the character of childhood as they were expressed through the organization of educational systems.[1]

Ambitious campaigns to promote educational systems invariably had to confront the reality of a multitude of children and families for whom schooling was a foreign project. However, in time, the families learned to accommodate to the requirements of the school and even to use it for purposes other than those the elites and governments had intended. Childhood is at the core of such processes as a compromise between different interests, but the processes have different meanings depending on whether they are approached from the top-down perspective of the elites or from below.

EDUCATION AND THE NATURE OF CHILDHOOD: A PROJECT FROM ABOVE

The education reform movement in Europe gained momentum from the political elites during the late eighteenth century rather than originating from the masses. Educational institutions were met with suspicion and resistance among broad layers of the population in West Europe, and were not a response to popular demand—although there were some exceptions. The significance of the movement rests in the long-range consequences of the reforms. Education merged with the principle of a national identity and nation building. The imposition of compulsory schooling marked a turning point in the way in which educational politics were envisioned, for example, in Denmark (1814), Greece (1834), Spain (1838), Sweden (1842), Portugal (1844), Norway, (1848), Austria (1864), Switzerland (1874), Italy (1877), the United Kingdom (1880), and France (1882).[2]

Three paths to the construction of educational systems can be distinguished. The earliest was based on an organizational initiative by the state, as in the Scandinavian countries and Prussia. The second, in Greece, Italy, Portugal, and Spain, involved the construction of an educational system that was more a matter of rhetoric than reality on the ground. The introduction and success of the schooling in the first case was closely associated with the organization and legitimacy of the national church. In southern Europe, by contrast, no national church could support the educational efforts by the state, but at least the nation state could be displayed symbolically through the educational system. Third, in France, the Netherlands, Switzerland, Britain, and the United States, schooling expanded ahead of state involvement, though with certain differences in the content and organization of education stemming from competition between religious groups and various secular organizations. In the United States, education was organized through local and state government. In France, Britain, and the Netherlands, different religious associations organized schooling, balancing state initiatives.[3]

The establishment of educational institutions was by no means uncontroversial, because it involved taking a stand on central political issues concerning governance, nation building, and citizenship. The different positions regarding whether the education of the masses should be encouraged also reflected contrasting stances on the nature of childhood and the political role of schools. Those who objected to the creation of educational institutions feared that instruction would lead the poor to feel able to change their social station and would indeed endanger the stability of society. For others, schooling as an aspect of childhood implied political change and development, but it could also guarantee stability. Hostility toward popular education was entrenched in some national elites, while others saw it as a way to further their own political positions. Such conflicts were evident in the Nordic countries and in the German states, as well as in Britain and France. In Britain in particular, many saw it as a threat to the social order, while elites in the newly created United States understood education to be a vehicle for building civic identity and national independence.[4]

At the same time, a widened but carefully screened education was seen as a source of social and political stability in Europe. The terms for this can reflect the beliefs that individual ambition benefited the state and the overall good of the society and that obedience to the law required knowledge of divine and secular laws. Knowledge did not run contrary to social stability, as the Prussian model exemplified and for which it was appreciated.[5]

Children in this manner embodied the association between citizenship and childhood. Citizenship was conceptually linked to national identity, and schooling played a central role in the processes of symbolizing and building national identities as well as forming the criteria for citizenship and the legitimacy of the state. The school reform movements have to be understood as the harbinger of a new way of governing, transforming subjects into citizens while simultaneously creating new links between individuals and the state or the nation.[6]

SCHOOLING AND THE DEFINITION OF CHILDHOOD

Compulsion to go to school and the right to education became in this process indistinct and conceptually blurred, but they also had other important cultural consequences. The creation of schools was instrumental in creating national boundaries. It defined national identity through the curricula that were adopted and the language used for teaching. Regional identities and linguistic minorities were subsumed by means of the school system under a standardized pronunciation and spelling as well as under a series of national symbols. The importance of this for childhood is that a unified national identity, imposed from the center, meant that all children were to speak a similar tongue and appreciate the same monuments of national glory.[7]

Schooling was established as an important aspect of the culture of nations. Common people were at the core of the nation, and at the same time they were the uncivilized "other," sometimes with a regional identity, in need of education. This influenced legislation as well as the concepts used. In the Scandinavian countries and Germans states, the common schools were called *Folkskola* or *Volkschule,* expressing the identification of education, citizenship, and nation. Schooling also demonstrated the need to include the "ignorant" broad layers of the population in national projects. However, colonized territories and ethnic minorities in the defined territories, who might form a numerical majority, were excluded from incorporation in the nation building project. The language and cultural symbols thus interacted with ethnic and racial definitions.[8]

Educational provision also included girls in the comprehensive educational systems, as the future mothers in the nation. It was felt that social maladies, immorality, and political danger would be avoided through the inclusion of all children. The distinction between schools and orphanages was not always very clear. The expansion of educational provision ran parallel to the expansion of other types of institutions for children and the regulation of children's use of urban space.[9]

The emphasis during the Romantic period on the formative and malleable character of children led the discussion to focus on the quality, disposition, and moral character of the environment in which children grew up. Working-class mothers, for example, were deemed incompetent to care for children, underscoring the need for educational institutions for younger children. This sentiment was an important feature of debates in many European countries during the seventeenth century, and, by the early eighteenth century, it was clear to many reformers that schools were particularly important, because they could provide a substitute for a family upbringing. Children of the masses needed to spend time in school during their formative years—particularly children of the poor, because this group, it was felt, continually displayed an inability to provide a proper home environment. Such educational ambitions also included relatively young children, under the age of six.[10]

Childhood also became associated with schooling among the lower classes in a positive way. Although this was not the case universally, what was on offer from various educational institutions was closely related to the harsh realities of life in the poorer neighborhoods. The schools in urban Sweden during the early nineteenth century, for example, showed that they could attract students when they offered material support, especially food and clothing. Schools in Stockholm and other cities systematically offered meals to their pupils. This had the effect of extending social control over the leisure time and family life of children from the lower classes, using such material rewards as a means of education and discipline. It was also a way of organizing the activities of children in the urban environment. The middle classes expected their investment in the education of the poor to result in fewer children begging in the parks and at the doorstep of bourgeois homes.[11]

However, the encouragement of education among the masses also reinforced the desire to separate children from different social classes, to avoid any form of "contamination." In Stockholm, a royal commission made it clear, during the second half of the nineteenth century, that the schooling of the lower classes should be separate from that of other children, because the former was primarily associated with poor relief and was therefore a matter of policing. Such mass education was also to include children of both sexes or else immorality would pervade the social system. Thus, childhood and education were not only associated with boys but also included those who would hold the primary responsibility for the upbringing of the next generation. The morality of the lower classes was at the center of educational reform in Sweden, as it was in other European countries.[12]

The evolving systems of schools made a clear distinction between primary and secondary education. The French lyceum, the German and Scandinavian gymnasium, and the U.S. high school were created to supply a more advanced curriculum and, in some cases, a more applied training in the interest of the middle and professional classes. There was no direct link leading from the primary to the secondary level. In this way education systems were created and designed to form separate avenues of socialization. In Britain, for example, the late and reluctant engagement of the state in the creation of an educational system resulted in a much differentiated system of schools and a lower level of enrollments. The parallel avenues reflected different worlds for children according to their class, gender, and ethnic background. In the United States, by contrast, the emphasis was more on inclusion into a common school for all citizens, which evolved into the creation of the U.S. high school. This, at least, was the vision; the reality was separate educational avenues based on the social geography of the urban and rural landscape and division by ethnicity.[13]

The British case shows how class interests and a lack of central initiatives until relatively late marked the creation of a socially differentiated school system. Yet even in more state-oriented systems, educational philosophies and initiatives influenced by class interests were influential in the setting up of schools. The Danish and Scandinavian folk high schools represented an educational idea closely associated with the social and class interests of commercially oriented farmers. Moreover, the creation of a national system of inspection reinforced both the responsibility to live up to the standards of a national system and made visible the deviations from the expectations of such norms.

BENGT SANDIN

| 1. What shall become of this child? | 2. School/ street | 3. Continued studies/ drunkenness | 4. Successful work/ vice and misery | 5. Honored old age/ despised beggary |

FIGURE 5.1: *The understanding of schools as the only place where children could grow up and mature to a respectable adulthood was dramatically expressed in the illustrations in a school textbook from late-nineteenth-century Sweden.* Neither upbringing in the family, work, nor life in the street was given any credit in contribution to such progress. The irony is that the great majority of children to whom this textbook was addressed had very short school careers. The imagery of the normal childhood was closely associated with the educational system in the Western experience.

The inspections were an expression of a conflict between central and local authorities and ambitions to enforce national standards and central legislation. School inspection made policies in the local communities as well as parenting and the living conditions of children objects of national debates, renewed interests, and disciplinary action.[14]

Educational provision that was created in Europe during the first half of the eighteenth century made clear the need to distinguish between education for citizens, depending on their role in society, their class, and their gender. At the same time, education became symbolic of national sentiments and a new system of governance. The learning child became a powerful image of a positive child-hood in accordance with social stability, while ignorance was associated with rebelliousness and conflict. A still more important aspect of change was the notion of schooling as a necessary substitute for socialization in the lower-class family. Proletarian family life was not seen as compatible with a good child-hood. Childhood was consequently constructed as an ideal, with a number of variations of the schooled childhood. But for most children, the schools that predated the compulsory education of the latter part of the century had little relevance. The impact of education on the life course of children was limited. Schools did not form the reality of childhood even if the concept of childhood was perceived as consonant with education.

CHILDHOOD AND EDUCATION:
A PERSPECTIVE FROM BELOW

The educational efforts of the secular and religious authorities during the late eighteenth and early nineteenth centuries stretched into many parts of the countryside. Children could have some kind of formal education in a village school or with an itinerant teacher. Children would typically start to participate in the family's economic activities at an early age, and any such educational experience was limited by the much more important task of earn-ing their keep. The lives of most children were dominated by traditional forms of socialization in the family, religious institutions, and the workplaces rather than by the schools.[15]

Certainly children were allowed a period of growing up close to home during which they played in the company of other young people. Village life also included playful interaction between the generations. Attitudes toward the phases of growth were well established but were also subject to change because of the development of the economy. The demographic transition and population growth of the late eighteenth and early nineteenth centuries increased the pressure to support more surviving children. In any household, the number of young workers would reflect how many of their own children a family could put to work. The labor of children was well suited to many simple and time-consuming tasks on the farm. As a result of proletarianization in the countryside, the socialization of the young changed during the early nineteenth century. Families could not always provide their children with work and so were forced to send them off to other households. The development of manufacturing industries allowed some families to give work to their children in their homes or to send them to workshops in other villages. The age when children left home to take up employment with other families was influenced by the poverty of the family and its access to work. Many children were sent off at very young ages. The accessibility of work as apprentices was limited, and the character of craft work in some areas changed, reinforcing the proletarian nature of work for young people in the early manufacturing industries. Such was the case, for example, in the textile and tobacco industries, and also in the sawmills.[16]

The socialization of children at work proceeded according to their maturity, strength, and gender—a school of learning by doing. This learning often took place in strange households, and it could be a brutal and abusive experience, because children placed with other families might be exploited harshly. However, being brought up in the bosom of one's own family was no guarantee of better treatment, as poverty and destitution all too often blighted the lives of children. In many cases, the introduction to work involved caring for and herding animals. This allowed for moments of play, but it was also a lonely and dangerous occupation; wild animals and rough weather were a constant hazard.[17]

At an older age, other tasks on the farms became possible. Some of these involved training in specific skills such as carpentry and working with livestock, which could lead to future employment as an adult. For children living with a family of some means and property, such socialization reflected parental ambitions and care. For children sent away to work far from home, the situation must have been different, merely preparing for a life of hard, semiskilled labor. In either case, the introduction to what might be expected later in life as a grown-up followed a traditional path. It was most formalized in the craft sector, with a system of acquiring positions as a journeyman following long-established traditions in craft associations.

Formal schooling might be of use in this context. Reading skills helped commercially or politically oriented farmers and villagers who migrated seasonally to urban centers to work on building sites or to market their wares. For others, the contribution of the schools was limited to the skills needed to show deference at the Sunday sermon. Schools might also be appreciated in the case of small children, given that they freed adults from the need to supervise their offspring. For the families of landless laborers, however, the obligation to send their children to school not only added to the costs of child support but also deprived them of potential earnings. There is no doubt that formal education added to the burden of bringing up children.[18]

Reports from school inspectors showed a distinct reluctance among the rural population to accept the demands of the educational system. Poverty and periodic shortages of labor during periods of agricultural expansion made demand for the work of children among the landless proletariat and family farmers clash with the ambition to send them to school. Even the most ambitious school reformers had to adapt to such realities and allow a certain amount of flexibility in terms of the absence of children during periods of high demand of child labor. The structure of summer, spring, and fall breaks in different countries still reflect this historic ancestry. School enrollment and attendance patterns also reflected the character of the labor market and its demands for boys or girls and for older or younger children. Typically, a higher degree of presence in school would be expected from younger children and during the less labor-intensive periods. The regulations allowed for some degree of negotiation.[19]

A basic undertone in attitudes to the lower classes was a critique of their child-rearing practices. A connection was made between child rearing and the popular culture from which the upper classes distanced themselves. The resistance to participation in education was for them a sign of a lack of civilization, culture, and civil responsibility. Such a critique included a questioning of the behavior of young people, and notably journeymen and apprentices, in the transition period between first communion and the establishment of an independent household. Street children were a further source of concern. Secondary education for the masses was not seriously considered at this period, but youths who were independent from household control comprised a social category that was a source of worry. The influence of an early educational experience was believed to form the moral base for such a period of transition to adulthood. Examples of this can be found in both the countryside and in the urban environment. Among the more prosperous citizens, children's existence was no doubt more strictly controlled by the demands and expectations of the adult world.[20]

The transitions between life phases had ramifications for the way in which education was defined. The process of growing up was shaped by the age at

FIGURE 5.2: *The freedom of errand boys to test the privileges of adult life outside the normalizing influence of schools worried urban middle classes all over the Western world.* This photograph is undated but probably dates from the early twentieth century. Stockholm Stadsmuseum Fa 13658.

which children were expected to start an apprenticeship or a work contract and when the church expected them to take communion for the first time. In Sweden, reading instruction in the household had followed such a pattern since the seventeenth century, but it proved difficult to sustain during the early nineteenth century as a result of proletarianization and population growth. The household control system was based on a smaller and more stable population. Reading instruction of the rural poor could no longer be managed within the framework of the household when the population expanded and the number of surviving children grew dramatically. Initiatives were taken to formalize educational provision in order to make sure that children could read at the age of first communion. The collapse of such attempts as these to preserve the traditional system of control and integration underpinned the fear of the consequences of proletarianization and supported the arguments for a state-controlled, compulsory educational system.[21]

Education and schooling should not be equated: reading skills might be appreciated but not necessarily acquired in schools, and schools as well as education could be organized in many ways. Teachers in the countryside were sometimes required to teach in the home so that children would not have to walk to distant schools. Home instruction could correspond to the Lutheran system, allowing for parental supervision over both children and teachers. In other areas, it allowed for control of these agents in a system under construction. The role of the teacher needed to be negotiated over a long period.[22]

The attitude of families and children to education consequently varied according to cultural attitudes and material conditions. Educational institutions served a multitude of purposes both before and after the intervention of the state or other central agencies. Before such regulations were implemented, toward the middle or end of the nineteenth century, schools were founded by different interests, such as reform societies, aristocrats, city burghers, philanthropists, and clergy. In Britain, this system maintained the division of the educational system along the lines of class and gender—and continued to do so after regulation during the late nineteenth century.[23] Such schools had different effects depending on the circumstances of the children involved, because they were founded and financed with different purposes in mind: to instill religious values, to keep children from begging or loitering on the streets, to create a work ethic, to teach trade skills, or to create a national identity. Schools were also directed toward meeting the needs of middle-class interests—for example, for the education of girls from this background. Schools like these were partially replaced over the course of the nineteenth century by the system of compulsory elementary schooling but also remained a as a parallel system of education throughout the period.[24]

GOVERNANCE, THE STANDARDIZATION
OF SCHOOLING, AND CHILDHOOD

Laws about schooling had a different focus relating to the expectation that local communities would take responsibility for financing schools, buildings, and wages for teachers as well as for implementing a central curriculum. There was also an assumption that children would spend a number of years in the educational system. These laws, designed to improve education, allowed for a degree of negotiation with both the school authorities and parents. Compulsion might force the local community to build schools, as in the Swedish case, but only a number of years later did it actually aim at the presence of children in schools.

The introduction of compulsory schooling was a multistep process, with a series of educational acts that reflected the negotiation between local and central authorities, between local school boards and families, and between children and parents. Children might drop out early from school once they had learned to read, mastered other parts of the curriculum, or knew their catechism. The reverse might also be the case. Children leaving school with poor knowledge of the catechism and inadequate reading skills created demands for a more prolonged schooling. The age span when children attended school could be rather wide, and it could vary depending on a number of factors, including proximity to schools, poverty, the local labor market, and an appreciation of the value of literacy. The organization of the schools evolved slowly during the century to bring the now-familiar equation of age with school grade and class.[25]

Education was consequently as varied an experience as that of childhood. But the principles of education became clearer and more standardized during the nineteenth century. Clearly, the establishment of schools on a mass scale introduced a novel way of governing the population and simultaneously produced new notions of childhood. The techniques of ruling and the philosophy behind them changed, resorting less to physical violence and overt displays of power, and more to the shaping of minds through subtle techniques of pedagogy. Institutions of mass education demonstrated the application of such pedagogical thinking and the structuring of schools as an expression of such governance, with their reduced emphasis on corporal punishment and the regimentation of the monitorial schools. The challenge of teaching two hundred to three hundred pupils in one room made heavy demands on control and surveillance techniques in order to interrupt possible alliances between children. At all times during the rise and decline of this monitorial system, the question of visibility, the construction of a field of vision for the master and overall control, remained a central educational issue.[26]

The education system made children visible and, following Michel Foucault, made childhood an embodiment of the practice of standardization. Monitorial schooling represented a crucial movement in this standardization of educational practices and institutions. The system was developed in Britain, but it corresponded to educational models in other countries. It was labeled after its British initiators, Bell and Lancaster, and became an important model for the way schooling was conceptualized. This model was based on a strict routine in the classroom, carried out by numerous children in the role of monitors assisting the teachers. In this pedagogical system, a hierarchical structure guaranteed the continuous activity of a well-ordered mass of pupils. Its attraction for the authorities was the possibility of teaching large groups of pupils at low cost, modeled on the organization of a system of mass production.[27]

The monitorial schools were an important part of the attempt to establish and motivate schools throughout the first part of the century. The system appeared in schools directed toward the laboring poor, and also in middle-class schools and such institutions as military academies. Its principles were probably expressed and applied in different ways depending on the social and political context. Different versions of this handling of large groups of children through maintaining visibility can be demonstrated in German and Spanish schools. In the German states, a general concern about the position of the teacher led to questioning the role of the monitors. The presence of the adult's gaze became important not only in the moments of direct teaching but also in the administration of punishments. In Spain, attitudes to the monitorial system were quite different. After an opening phase in which the original was closely copied, Spanish anxieties about the stability of authority led to criticisms of the practice of rotating monitors. Spanish pedagogues accepted the active role of children in the supervision of the pupils, but they insisted on the importance of the monitors.[28]

The monitorial school contained a clear arrangement for children in a hierarchal order of learning and also visualized regimentation in the same way that society was structured. The idea of teaching many students as if they were only one student entailed a transition from a tutoring pedagogy (the teacher talks and works face-to-face with each student) to a simultaneous method (the teacher talks directly to a group of students organized in a class) was a path-breaking innovation. This "grammar of education" revolved around students grouped in graded classes with a relatively homogeneous composition; teachers who were trained either as generalists (in primary schools) or as specialists (in secondary schools) working as individuals; structured spaces for teaching and classroom-based pedagogy; a rigid schedule that established social control over time; knowledge formed into standardized disciplines (which had the effect of defining how teaching was to be organized). Such an organizational framework would function as the only way of conceiving schools and, by doing so, exclude all other alternatives. It became the only system that was either possible or imaginable, what David Tyack described as "the one best system."[29]

DIFFERENT EDUCATIONAL AVENUES
AND CHILDHOOD AS A NORM

The educational system had to confront the problems of legitimacy and acceptance by broad layers of the population whose living conditions did not immediately conform to the requirements of the school institutions. School attendance patterns and truancy during the latter part of the nineteenth century continued to demonstrate the tradeoff between schooling and work, reflecting differences in the demand for children of different ages and gender in the labor market. It also reflected seasonal conditions and, in the countryside, the agricultural cycle. The patterns of attendance indicate that parents would send children to school if it did not conflict with family activities. Debates over education and reports from school inspectors indicate that school reformers were aware that parents were reluctant to send children to school when they could find employment. In urban centers, children who participated in neither education nor employment created a further problem. Debates took place over street children and the moral consequences of poverty and a lack of schooling.[30]

The child labor debates focused on different issues, including the danger to both the health and morals of working children. These were expressed differently, depending on the kind of child labor that was involved. Reports on the deplorable health conditions created concerns about the future of the labor supply. Naturally, school inspectors in the countryside worried about the disruption of schoolwork when children helped out on the farm or worked long hours as hired hands. For many rural children, this remained a reality throughout the century, but the family setting, the small scale, and the dispersed population made it seem less of a problem. In urban and heavily industrial settings, low levels of school attendance provoked anxiety over the working-class family, the socialization of children, and even political unrest. Consequently, child labor laws in different countries were designed to improve the morals and schooling of the children of the poor, as well as to counter their physical deterioration. Such measures were evidently open to negotiation, because exceptions were made for industrial work in some sectors and for the agricultural sector.[31]

During the latter part of the nineteenth century, with some variation, governments concentrated on improving school attendance. They tightened their legislation and developed an administrative and legal framework aimed at increasing the number of working-class children in schools. The ages for starting and leaving school came under scrutiny. A school entry age of around six or seven was deemed appropriate, indicating a clearer differentiation between a preschool age and a school age. Similarly, thirteen or fourteen was considered an ideal age for leaving school. This ran parallel to greater precision in the definitions of the national norms for the curriculum and the level of knowledge expected at different ages.[32]

For the educators of the time, this process was sometimes motivated by the developmental needs of children, sometimes by ambitions to control the urban environment. They sought to bring children's schooling in line with protective legislation against child labor, the age of confirmation, or regulations in the penal code. Their arguments were based on a combination of educational, political, and practical considerations. Such debate focused on urban centers but had consequences for the organization of rural education as well. Rural schooling became increasingly valued after the establishment of a national framework by large school bureaucracies and departments of education. These processes also indicate the relationship between the visibility of children on the streets of the towns and in factories on the one hand and an urge among political elites to regulate the life of children of the lower classes on the other.[33]

Enrollment improved toward the end of the nineteenth century but still displayed large regional variations. Girls, as future mothers, were central to educational efforts for the lower classes, but the education of girls remained a private matter in other social classes. Such an attitude reflected a negative evaluation of the moral character of the working-class family and a lack of commitment on the part of the state to the education of women. The school systems kept primary and secondary education separate. Education that aimed at preparing children for higher education was to be arranged in the homes of the wealthier classes as private instruction or in private educational facilities.

FIGURE 5.3: *On the way to or from school, opportunities to play were ample.* School children playing with boats in the streams of the melting snow in Stockholm around the turn of the century. Stockholm Stadsmuseum E 30739.

At this level, the schools again reflected gender divisions. In this way, education reinforced children's economic and social backgrounds.

Very little public (government) support was at first given to the education of upper- and middle-class girls, leaving them in the hands of domestic and private teaching before the middle of the century. In most countries, the teaching of girls was not accepted as a responsibility of the state. During the second half of the century, however, an increased interest arose that was closely associated with both the feminist movement and the changing cultural values of the middle-class family. Most important here was the problem of family reproduction. Middle-class women were forced to seek employment outside the home, as schoolteachers or post office clerks, for example. The expansion of the primary education system created a market for educated women from the middle classes. This resulted in a gradual feminization of the teaching profession in elementary schools and an interest in sending children of all classes to cheap state schools.[34]

The differences between children and between the different types of childhood were obvious in the way they were reflected in the structure of education. Social geography made certain that children from different backgrounds were channeled into different schools. At the secondary level, the educational system that was created was distinctly gendered and marked by class in France, Britain, and the German states. In Scandinavia, a parallel school system was developed, while in the United States, the public high school was formally designed to include children from different layers of society—though in reality it also reflected varying strategies marked by class and the cultural backgrounds of immigrant groups.

Immigrant families in the United States who had toiled as farm hands and factory workers looked at schooling with suspicion, as working-class parents tended to do elsewhere, but aggravated by their status as newcomers with a foreign cultural background. The usefulness of skills acquired in schools was questioned, as were the attitudes to life and the future that children might pick up in schools. Schools also imparted routines and values that were grounded in conceptions of time associated with factory routines, foreign to the rhythm of the agricultural background of the parents. However, an education that could lead to a profession or degree, and thus serve the family interest, was potentially of interest to the new citizens—even if it was in conflict with the background of the parental generation. To immigrant groups like the Irish, Polish, and Italians, schooling beyond the minimum was no longer alien by the turn of the century. However, the consequences for the identity of their young adolescents remained a concern. The detachment of the cognitive, emotional, and social growth of the youth from the families was difficult to accept among immigrant families. A separate cultural space for young people, distanced from the loyalty to and demands from family, threatened the core values immigrant parents had taught their children. Education also produced cultural distance from family, new patterns of peer culture, and unfamiliar notions of development nourished by the extended schooling. This tended to underpin the creation of a youth culture in the following century, the very foundation of which the U.S. high schools came to symbolize more than any other educational system because of its ambition to reach out to children of all social classes. An important legacy for the future, though, was the establishment of the idea, and in some locations the reality, that national educational institutions as a whole should include children from different social backgrounds, governments having a responsibility to provide similar opportunities for all children.[35]

The appropriateness of a comprehensive school for all classes of society influenced the discussion in countries with parallel school systems as well in the United States. The apparent democratization of education, with more middle-class children in public education, made the problem of transferring from one school system to another, between public and private and educational facilities, problematic for those children who aspired for a longer education, because the curricula and educational norms differed. Demands for public elementary schools not designed solely for working-class children were formulated by a middle class for whom it had become more difficult and more expensive to send their children to private education. The cost of the investment in children and the demographic transition, with the fall in birth rate and the emergence of smaller families, might have influenced rising educational investment. Childhood had a definite price for these parents. Schools institutionalized different childhoods that reflected class and gender divisions as well as the division between urban and rural environments. During the latter half of the nineteenth century, an enormous expansion of school building took place in urban centers that reflected the expansion of elementary education.[36]

The development of school administration and a greater number of children in education led to conflicts over the meaning of childhood. The consequences of a broader recruitment of children also created problems. In southern Sweden, a school inspector commented during the early 1880s on such issues in a report after visiting schools and orphanages in other European countries. He wanted to share his observations and illuminate the problems of the comprehensive schools:

A public school cannot select its pupils. It has to accept them as they are when they are sent to it, and to keep them no matter how they shape up.

The school has no more right to turn away the intellectually disadvantaged than the depraved. On the contrary, it is the duty of the school itself to seek out and gather up all those children, regardless of which category they belong to, who do not come to school of their own accord. Anyone who has had anything to do with the public school knows how harmful this circumstance is for the success of the school's work, how the ungifted children impede the progress of the gifted, how the depraved children have a detrimental effect on those who are as yet unspoiled.[37]

It was necessary to separate out the physically and intellectually handicapped. Delinquents and children living under moral and material depravation had to be weeded out from the public schools and placed in other institutions. The effect of legislation on deviance was that classes should be smaller, and education for national citizenship should be introduced. The ability to follow the teaching in ordinary schools also became a criterion of normality: a way of defining difference but also a way of defining citizenship. The deviation from this new normality of education was easily detected and could be described and measured. Children of the poor became visible, not only from the pulpit and as an item in the registers, but in overt contrast to all other children. In this project, the teachers, physicians, and philanthropists began to try transforming the children of the poor into children of the nation, subjects of the new nation.[38]

The moral coherence and identity of the nation put a special emphasis on the meaning of childhood. Children were not only a matter for the family but also for the survival of the nation, both morally and genetically. This came out differently in various national contexts, depending on the character of the demands for national cohesion, social responsibility, and the democratization of education. Children in the schools and in summer camps began to be described and measured in different ways with the aid of the newly emerging medical and psychological sciences. The Child Study Movement became an international intellectual movement. The educational system provided a channel for many of these initiatives. This movement led to the development of programs to feed hungry school children and others to improve hygiene, such as school baths on Saturday afternoons while clothing was treated for vermin. Afternoon leisure activities and holiday camps for the poor were initiated to keep children off the streets during the long summer vacations. Classes were introduced and curricula developed in the urban schools to fill out the spare time of otherwise idle children. Social programs were developed around the educational system or in proximity to it. The playground movement took initiatives in the cities for the benefit of the children of the urban poor. The Child Study Movement thrived on the large numbers of children assembled in the educational system. This led to the creation of legislation that normalized the child in accordance with the needs of the educational system through a wide variety of instruments, ranging from organized play and summer schools to action directed at those defined as delinquents.[39]

The new demands on children to participate in education also involved demands on families. Mothers were expected to be able to send clean, healthy children to school, at the right time. It was important to create a childhood—a longer childhood. The men were expected to provide for the whole family, nonworking wife and children alike. The ideal of motherhood, which was so strongly emphasized in national sentiment at the turn of the century, complemented such a childhood: a nonuseful child, a school child, dependent on a breadwinning father and a caring mother. The emotional dimension to family life—the caring element—was also consistent with this kind of change. A childhood of universal validity had been established based on the demands of educational systems and with consequences for the definition of men's and women's parenting; a childhood that did not always match up with reality but that could at least be measured against it.[40]

FIGURE 5.4: *August Malmström (1829–1901),* The Tell Tale. Oil on canvas, 26 × 39 inches (66 × 100 centimeters). Stockholm Stadsmuseum, NM 1440. Girls and boys on the way to or from school in the Swedish countryside during the early nineteenth century. This is perhaps an example of what we would now call bullying outside school, captured by the artist.

CONCLUSION

At the beginning of the nineteenth century, schools had little impact on the daily life of most children and their families. However, a transformation of the understanding of childhood as it was expressed in educational and philosophical writings at this period did influence the way childhood was conceptualized. It was only toward the end of the century that formal education had a major impact on the character of children's lives in urban and in many rural areas and came to influence thinking about childhood at all levels of society. By their classification of the pupils, the experts of the soul, mind, and body of children made their presence felt in their nineteenth-century versions. Clergy and teachers as well as doctors, hygienists, and philanthropists participated in the production of notions of the normal or deviant child and defined citizenship according to class, gender, and racial categorizations. Educational systems made children and childhood visible for study and discussion. Their classification of children created a legacy for the twentieth century. It also took on a meaning for the children themselves, since they were the objects of categorization and discipline. Furthermore, it forced children and their families to choose whether to comply with the demands of the emerging regulatory system. Children interacted and formed the everyday life and policies of educational institutions by reacting on school regulations and educational demand, necessitating compromises and alterations.

The long-term significance of the creation of educational institutions also reflected a dependency on children's own agency. The frontier between the spheres of education and welfare became more difficult to delineate as educational institutions gave birth to, or propped up, systems of welfare support and disciplinary institutions, in the form of child welfare boards and juvenile courts. A history of childhood and education needs to take into account the fact that schooling was forced on children and their families—and was in turn influenced by them.

CHAPTER SIX

Life Cycle

CARL IPSEN

This chapter explores the life cycle in the West in the nineteenth century. It focuses inevitably on the demographic transition—the dramatic, unprecedented, and irreversible declines in Western mortality and fertility—that began in that period. Mortality decline had, of course, been a universal desideratum, and fertility decline seems to be its inevitable accompaniment. Europe led the way in this regard, and, in the twentieth century, most of the rest of the world also experienced this dual shift away from traditionally higher levels of births and deaths, so much so that there exists a broadly and implicitly accepted "developmental paradigm," according to which the Western family represents the final stage in a process through which families and societies around the world are evolving. According to this view, the diverse types of family still observed today are simply less modern rungs on a developmental ladder atop which sits the Western nuclear family. Put in these terms, that paradigm seems easily discarded, but, as its major critic, Arland Thornton, writes, the tendency to "read history sideways" is widespread and entails an insidious and entrenched critique of not only non-Western families but a whole series of social institutions: "That is, with development, these societies too would eventually be characterized by political liberty, many non-family institutions, an individualistic orientation, nuclear families, later marriages, many people never marrying, marriages that were love matches and higher status for women."[1]

The risk of reading history sideways is particularly acute when exploring the history of the Western family in the nineteenth century. It was precisely then that the two universal changes that distinguish modern families first became widespread: longer life and fewer children. It is important then to emphasize that European mortality decline occurred in a unique and nonreproducible context, one largely unaffected by the medical advances that eliminated or at least attenuated so many killer diseases in the twentieth century. Similarly, fertility decline in Europe was achieved in family regimes that differed from those found in other parts of the world. Nor, for example, did the state play a significant role in achieving low fertility in Europe, as it would in other parts of the world. As an antidote to reading history sideways, we begin with a non-Western anecdote that should provide a test case for similarity and difference. This story of a Chinese family invites reflection on a contemporary but very different demographic and social context.

GUOJUN AND HIS HEIRS

Guojun was born in 1852 in Zhejiang, China, fourth son to Bingbiao and his wife; the other three had died in childhood. When Guojun was six, Bingbiao, then in his thirties, also died. Guojun and his mother soon left Zhejiang and went to Xi'an, where she too fell victim to an early death. Cared for by a childless uncle and aunt, death struck Guojun's family twice more, and, as a teenager, he found himself on his own, heir to both father and uncle and responsible for continuing both family lines. Like his father, Guojun entered the class of scholar-officials. At some point, perhaps while still a child, he was betrothed to Miss Qiu, the daughter of a subprefect in Zhejiang and one year his senior. By the time he was twenty, Guojun had returned to Zhejiang, married Miss Qiu, and fathered a daughter. Their family subsequently grew to five daughters and two sons over a sixteen-year period; we have no information on survivorship.

Guojun eventually rose to the position of magistrate. He traveled frequently on government business, and the family moved several times. At the age of about forty, he fell in love with a young girl who had been sold by her parents into domestic service. Following tradition, Guojun's wife, Qiu, bought the girl's freedom and presented her to Guojun as a concubine. Qiu died in 1905 at the age of fifty-six. Guojun survived until 1912, aged sixty, just after the fall of the Qing dynasty and declaration of the Chinese Republic.

By that time, Guojun's youngest son, Liankui, was twenty-four years old and had earned a law degree. He would become a prominent Shanghai lawyer in the republican period. A couple of years later, Liankui formed a liaison with Cao Yuehung, a courtesan. Eventually he took her into his home along with her mother and Cao's daughter by another man. Cao subsequently bore Liankui six children, one of whom died in infancy. In 1914, Liankui also took a formal wife, Xu Peihua, aged twenty-one, though she lived in a separate house while Liankui continued to reside with Cao. To ease Xu's loneliness, Liankui gave her Cao's first son to care for. The boy died at the age of four, after which Liankui, at Xu's insistence, went to live with her until she became pregnant. That project was successful, and she bore a son, but that child also died, as did Xu herself in 1932 at the age of thirty-nine. Cao too died at about that time. Other women in the family brought up her children, and Liankui, in his forties, apparently lived the bachelor's life.

Liankui's cousin, Tongli, also kept both a formal wife and a concubine. Attending an opera in which Tongli, the concubine, and Tongli's daughter, Zhaohua, all performed, Liankui became enchanted with Zhaohua, whom he had previously met when she was a young girl. Liankui contrived to see more of Zhaohua, courted her, and, in 1933, the middle-aged man married the seventeen-year-old girl over her father's objection. Zhaohua bore Liankui two children in Shanghai and two more after they moved to Hong Kong in 1938 under the threat of Japanese invasion. After a period back in Shanghai (under Japanese occupation), the family went once more to Hong Kong. Liankui grew old and irascible and, jealous of his young wife, he divorced her. That event did not alter their family life much, because Liankui was little involved with the children. He died in 1959 at the age of seventy.[2]

This non-Western example affords insight into several important and general characteristics of historical families and life cycles in a global context, including high levels of infant and general mortality, geographic mobility, and moderate levels of fertility. Bingbiao's four children, for example, only one of whom survived to adulthood, probably suffered above average mortality, while Liankui's children—eight or nine survivors out of eleven births—were fortunate, likely more so than most. The average fertility of the family's various wives and concubines meanwhile was close to the estimated Chinese average of about five births per woman, which is also the level for old regime Europe. Nor was it too unusual in the 1850s or before for a child like Guojun, in China or elsewhere, to lose both parents while still a boy.

More striking to the historian of the West, instead, are the differences this anecdote exposes when compared to traditional European patterns: childhood betrothal, young ages at marriage, the sale of servants, the maintenance of concubines and multiple households, the problem of continuing family lines, and divorce. None of these were characteristic of Western patterns throughout the same period, though examples of middle-aged men marrying teenaged girls can occasionally be found.[3]

Keeping these differences in mind and realizing that the Western model is just one of many, there is considerable intrinsic interest in exploring mortality and fertility decline in nineteenth-century Europe and the ways in which those declines influenced families and children. The pages that follow will explore those declines against the backdrop of the Western human life cycle in that century, from birth to, in some cases, marriage and childbearing to, in all cases, death. Following the perhaps inevitable emphases in relevant scholarship, much of what follows applies especially to northwestern Europe, and divergence from those models tends to increase as one travels south and east. It is also the case that, insofar as one can generalize about the European life cycle, those generalizations apply in varying degrees to the "neo-Europes" in North America and the antipodes as well.

BIRTH AND INFANCY

Life in Europe prior to World War I (and indeed World War II) began at home for the vast majority of the population, just as it had for centuries before. Women—in particular a "good mother" with experience in traditional birthing methods or a midwife—normally attended births. Both the training and regulation of midwives made notable advances over the course of the nineteenth century. And that time span also saw the first steps toward the medicalization of childbirth, steps that would, in the latter half of the twentieth century, move the locus of childbirth from the home to the hospital. For the mother in traditional societies, childbearing was one of the most dangerous moments of her life, and maternal mortality in the nineteenth century likely fell somewhere between five and ten deaths per thousand births (meaning that a woman who experienced an average five births might run a one in twenty risk of dying at one of them). Given that Europe (and the neo-Europes) was predominantly Christian, baptism usually followed closely after birth. That sacrament involved some form of ablution and sacred words spoken by a priest or minister. Most Christian sects practiced infant baptism, though a minority of Protestants believed that the child must knowingly partake of the sacrament and so waited until older ages while others eliminated the sacrament entirely. Among Catholics and others who considered baptism essential to salvation, it might even be administered by lay people such as midwives in emergency situations or even to infants after they had already died. Baptism might include naming, and the adult sponsors or godparents of the baptism assumed responsibility for the

child's spiritual upbringing. Jews also had naming ceremonies for infants over-
seen by a religious authority; the Jewish version notably included circumcision
for boys.[4]

The nineteenth century witnessed the broad adoption of civil registration
and regulation of demographic events. Births had traditionally been recorded
in parish registers. To take England as an example, civil registration began in
1836, though the process only became reasonably thorough in 1874 (meaning
poor data in between for the unfortunate historical demographer). By 1910,
one could report that: "Registration is very efficiently carried out in practi-
cally every European country, with the exceptions of Turkey and Russia. In the
United States laws requiring registration vary in different states."[5]

The most striking aspect of the human life cycle at the beginning of the
nineteenth century is that, in many cases, it was exceedingly brief. Statistical
series and historical reconstructions reveal that infant mortality in the demographic old regime, say around 1750, hovered near 250 per 1,000. In other
words, one child in four died before reaching his or her first birthday. Most
of that mortality was concentrated in the first hours, days, and weeks of life
owing to birth defects, infections, and other complications related to birth;
neonatal mortality (in the first month of life) accounted for fully 150 to 180 of
the 250-per-1,000 figure cited above. Children who died after the first month
usually did so for different reasons. Gastrointestinal infections were frequent
causes in warm climates and in the summer, while respiratory ailments struck
more often in wintry, cold places. Infectious diseases, of course, continued to
take their toll. And, while breast-feeding might provide protection, practices
varied: most women in Bavaria, for example, did not breast-feed their children,
while in other parts of Germany (and elsewhere), average periods might extend
to nearly a year. The moment of weaning, whether early or late, was, in any
case, a dangerous one. In addition, some small and unknowable proportion of
infant deaths—one estimate for eighteenth-century England suggests about two
percent—were infanticides; and that proportion may have peaked in the fertility "crisis" years of the mid-nineteenth century. Nor were children out of the
woods after their first birthday; another 250 of those 1,000 born would perish
before the age of fifteen. European parents then, on average, could count on
about half of their children reaching adulthood, which means that their four or
five children on average would translate to a replacement level of two to two
and a half potential parents for the next generation.[6]

The scenario sketched above implies that infants and children lived with
their parents, though that was not always the case. Child abandonment, for
example, was widely practiced in Catholic Europe, and foundling mortality

could easily be double the overall infant rate. One study of abandonment in late-eighteenth-century Paris found that, out of 1,000 foundlings left at the foundling hospital, about 350 died before reaching the rural wet nurses to whom they were traditionally entrusted—ideally within days of birth—and another 540 failed to see their fourth birthday. In other words, only about ten percent ultimately survived the trauma of abandonment.[7] Where abandonment was practiced, the mid-nineteenth century witnessed a European foundling crisis brought on by a combination of population growth and the social disruption caused by modernization and economic change. In several major cities (Paris, St. Petersburg, and Milan, for example), studies have revealed abandonment rates ranging from 20 percent to 50 percent of all births at that time, though doubtless these figures were inflated by foundlings brought into the cities from the surrounding regions.[8]

Abandonment was not the only thing that separated children from their parents. Death could do that, too. Under the old demographic regime, approximately 14 percent of English children lost one parent by the age of fifteen, and another 2 percent lost both.[9] Some of these children, like Guojun in China, would be cared for by other family members. Others, especially lower down the social ladder, and including children orphaned of one parent, might end up in orphanages or other institutions.

How large was the population of institutionalized orphans and foundlings, and indeed of institutionalized children generally? The figures on parental death cited above are certainly significant, though the frequency of motherless and fatherless children must have strengthened the social and family networks that could absorb them. To take one example, Italian orphans in public care circa 1900 numbered about thirty-six thousand. In a population of about ten million children aged zero to fifteen, that comes to less than half of 1 percent. That figure may have been higher in earlier decades, though it seems unlikely that institutionalized orphans in Italy (and so perhaps elsewhere) ever amounted to more than about 1 percent of children. Abandonments at that date instead numbered about thirty thousand per year, down from a midcentury peak of about forty thousand, or about 3 percent to 4 percent of births (significantly less than the metropolitan rates cited above). That figure may also be close to the pretransition situation in France and other countries with institutionalized abandonment. Meanwhile, the Italian state supported about 130,000 foundlings of all ages, some in foundling homes but most farmed out with nurses. If we add another five thousand or so children confined in jails and reformatories, it would seem that, around the turn of the century, the state maintained in all about 2 percent of Italy's children. The annual abandonment percentage is close to the eighteenth-century infanticide estimate cited earlier, both indices of fertility surplus in the past. The corollary is that, even in traditional societies characterized by at times desperate poverty, over 95 percent of children were taken care of by families. Nor were any of the populations listed above static in the period. With declining mortality, the orphan population likely declined slowly over the course of the century. Meanwhile, the midcentury foundling crisis passed, thanks to better standards of living and fertility control, and, in the twentieth century, abandonment declined to low levels. Though of a different nature, the expansion of policing and the incarceration of unruly children led to something of an explosion of juvenile incarceration in the late nineteenth and early twentieth centuries.[10]

DEATH

The most dramatic demographic change in nineteenth-century Europe was, as stated above, mortality decline. At the beginning of the century, national crude death rates ranged generally between 25 per thousand and 35 per thousand per annum. The overall rate declined slowly in the first three quarters of the century and then rapidly in the last one, so that, by the early twentieth century, the best rates were below fifteen and the worst were in the upper twenties. The greatest improvements in survivorship, however, were those of infants and children, and, although available data are limited and variation is the order of the day, the largest declines in mortality seem to have been enjoyed by older children. For example, the risk of dying for French children aged five to fifteen seems to have declined by about 80 percent between the mid-eighteenth century and World War I. Although gains for the first five years of life were less—about two-thirds—the starting levels were higher, and so these gains had a still greater impact on overall survivorship. Undoubtedly it is for this latter reason that historical infant mortality (deaths in the first year of life divided by total births) has been so intensively studied. Old regime regional rates varied considerably, from below 100 per thousand to over 300 per thousand, presumably as a function of the health of the mother, breast-feeding practices, hygiene, and other environmental factors. Figures 6.1 and 6.2 show that some European mortality rates had already begun to decline in the eighteenth century and most followed by the late nineteenth. As noted below, mortality in the United States was on the higher end of this range. An important factor in infant mortality was breast-feeding, and practices seem to have varied considerably. In the best cases, infants were nursed for a year, or even through a second summer, and so enjoyed the full health benefits of colostrum and breast milk. Custom and economic necessity, though, often translated into shorter periods of nursing and higher levels of mortality. There were even instances in the nineteenth century of increasing infant mortality over time linked to an increase in women's out-of-home employment (for example, in textile factories), because that sort of work could separate mothers from their nursing children and so reduce breast-feeding. In France, in particular, there was also much concern about the farming out of infants to paid wet nurses by their parents and the negative impact that practice may have had on infant mortality. Inevitably, some of these children experienced interruptions in feeding; nurses might misrepresent their ability to lactate in order to get a paid charge (wet nurses were paid more than dry nurses); and, until late in the century, little effort was made to control the quality of care farmed-out infants received. Among some groups—for example, silk workers and shopkeepers in mid-nineteenth-century Lyon—rates of mercenary wet-nursing might be as high as 75 percent. The introduction of so-called artificial feeding of infants, usually with cow's milk, generally produced negative results, often disastrous ones prior to the development of pasteurization around the turn of the century.[11]

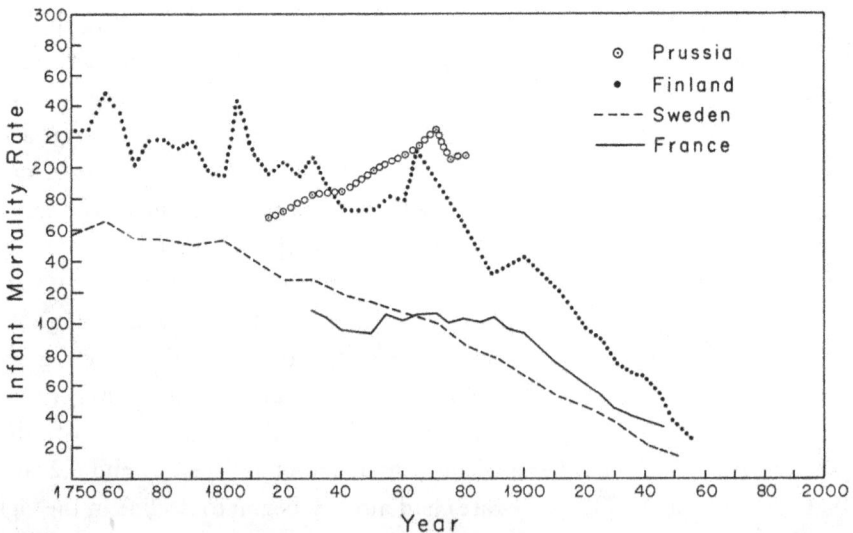

FIGURE 6.1: *Infant Mortality Rates for Four Countries with Extended Series.* From Francine van de Walle, "Infant Mortality and the European Demographic Transition," in *The Decline of Fertility in Europe,* eds. Ansley J. Coale and Susan Cotts Watkins, 213–214. Princeton, NJ: Princeton University Press, 1986.

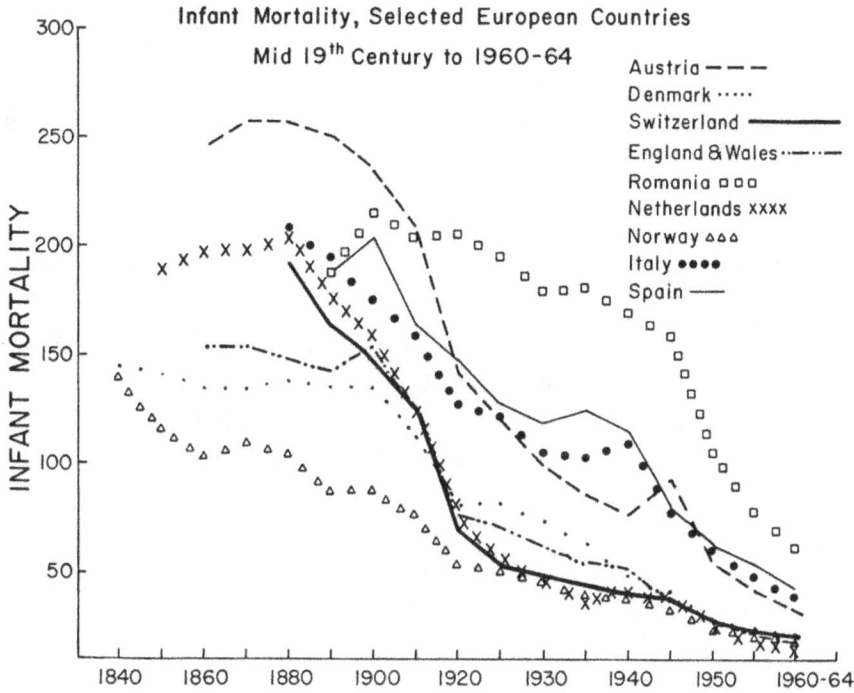

FIGURE 6.2: *Infant Mortality Rates: Selected European Countries.* From Francine van de Walle, "Infant Mortality and the European Demographic Transition," in *The Decline of Fertility in Europe,* eds. Ansley J. Coale and Susan Cotts Watkins, 213–214. Princeton, NJ: Princeton University Press, 1986.

Why did mortality decline? One theory looks to improved diet. Subsistence crises declined in the nineteenth century (with some notable setbacks like the potato famines of the 1840s in Ireland and elsewhere) while agricultural production increased. But population was increasing, too, and there are indices that suggest dietary stagnation or decline in various parts of Europe until about 1850, by which time mortality decline was already underway. Nor were any of the significant pre-World War I advances in medicine (except the smallpox vaccine) achieved before mortality from the diseases they attacked was much reduced. Public hygiene improved in the nineteenth century—draining of marshes, improvement of water supply, and sewage—but, as with better diets, these developments became significant in the latter half of the century when their links to combating diseases such as cholera, tuberculosis, and malaria became apparent. One intriguing hypothesis suggests instead that better personal hygiene may have played an important role in initiating mortality decline. In England, at any rate, the consumption of soap and washable cotton clothing—then becoming widely available thanks to industrial production—was on the rise in the early part of the century.[12] Better personal hygiene, then, followed by improvements in public hygiene and diet may have been the formula for improved survivorship of infants, children, and adults.

CHILDHOOD

After weaning, children normally stayed in the parental home, where the mother might combine child care with other domestic work. That work likely included agricultural tasks or care of livestock, because most of the European population still lived in rural settings. The nineteenth century, however, saw increasing numbers of men and women living in cities and engaging in wage labor outside the home. From preindustrial levels of 60 percent to 80 percent, the European population dependent on agriculture in some areas dropped by mid-century to levels as low as 25 percent (England) while remaining high in others (Italy, Spain). By World War I, that level had dropped to generally low levels: 9 percent in the United Kingdom, 37 percent in Germany, though still 54 percent in Italy.[13] Both urbanization and work outside the home complicated caregiving, and it is no accident that the first half of the nineteenth century saw the development of *crèche* or day care movements in various parts of Europe.[14]

By the age of six or seven, children might start to work. In rural settings, this was nothing new. Children had always helped around the farm as they grew up to become fully productive adult laborers by about age fifteen. But the nineteenth century saw a new development. Industrialization led to the creation of factories and the expansion of mining to retrieve the minerals needed to run those factories (coal, sulfur, and others). Children found employment in both factories and mines and so created some of the most typical, and mournful, images of the Industrial Revolution. Outraged public opinion led to the introduction of laws that sought to establish minimum ages and maximum workdays for industrial and mining work; though many historians agree that, by the time these laws became effective, other social and economic forces were drawing children out of the factories and mines.[15]

Industry was not the only force that removed children from their parents' domestic sphere. An older tradition saw children leave home altogether through the placing of children in other people's homes as "life cycle servants." Starting usually between the ages of nine and twelve, large numbers of boys and girls went to work for a number of years as servants in homes and on farms (and a smaller percentage as apprentices), until they were able to set up their own household. Various studies have estimated that, for some regions, as many as 25 percent to 75 percent of all children spent some period in service. In addition to providing gainful employment to youth, the generalized system of "transferred children" supplied the pool of labor demanded by an agricultural economy. This practice characterized in particular northwestern Europe and North America; in other parts of Europe, serfdom or extended families achieved a similar end. The experience of living away from home at young ages also served to initiate boys and girls, for better or worse, into the outside world.[16] The life cycle service phenomenon declined in the nineteenth century. It would seem that, toward the end of the nineteenth century, as economies industrialized and standards of living improved, ever larger numbers of older children continued to live with their parents, both while attending school and undertaking wage-earning employment that was compatible with living at home. At the same time, both of those activities (school and wage work) might also entail moving away from home, especially if that move was from country to city.[17]

Hugh Cunningham has written that "there is ... little doubt that the introduction of compulsory schooling, normally in the late nineteenth century, did more than any other factor in these five centuries [since 1500] to transform the experience and the meanings attached to childhood by removing children ... from the labour market."[18] Combined with a growing recognition on the part of parents that schooling was desirable, compulsory state schooling was the force that ultimately drove children out of both the industrial and service employments described above. In some parts of Europe (Germany, Scotland, Sweden), high rates of literacy had been achieved prior to the nineteenth century under a regimen of, primarily, church schools. Compulsory state schooling instead, like the factory, traces its origins to the eighteenth century but only found full development in the nineteenth century. It was in the last decades of that century that universal schooling (elementary school, in any case) became not only required in much of Europe but to some degree achieved. The institution of state schools responded to the need for a better-educated workforce while also encouraging a sense of national identity, patriotism, obedience, and the reinforcement of specific class and gender roles. By World War I, most Europeans went to school for at least two or three years and learned to read and write.[19]

MARRIAGE

Most Europeans in the nineteenth century married, whether at the end of a period as a servant or else once established in a wage-earning job, ever more frequently preceded by a few years in elementary school, or, of course, after a host of other possibilities. Marriage in the West, like infant mortality, has been the focus of intense study, and many of the misconceptions about the timing of marriage, marital fertility, and the sorts of households marriage precipitated in past times have by now been overturned. What we have learned most of all is probably the danger of generalization. Still, the outlines of a distinctive European demographic system, consisting of relatively late marriage and a high percentage of the population remaining unmarried, seems to have characterized northwestern Europe (and its extensions) for much of the modern age. Average ages at marriage ranged from about twenty-eight to twenty-nine for men and twenty-six to twenty-seven for women, while the celibacy rate ran 10 percent to 20 percent. Given that nuptiality traditionally regulated fertility, this system was the "great contraceptive weapon of modern Europe." Nor did it function in the same fashion throughout all of Europe. Ages at marriage were lower in Spain and England (under twenty-five) and help to explain the dramatic population growth experienced by the latter. They were still lower in Eastern Europe (twenty-three to twenty-five for men, twenty to twenty-one for women), where celibacy rates were also low (1 percent to 6 percent). A lower age at marriage and high nuptiality also characterized the British and French "pioneer" populations in North America.

Most marriages led to the creation of nuclear households (that is, a married couple and their children), though this arrangement was more prevalent in the northwest and Britain and in the United States (perhaps 80 percent of families). Moving into southern and eastern Europe, other family forms became more important; these included stem families organized around a privileged child, often the firstborn male, who inherited the property and continued the family line (while other siblings might continue to cohabit, often unmarried) and extended families comprising more than two generations or extended laterally to include aunts and uncles or other relatives. Any of these might be complemented by the presence of servants. Marriage generally lasted until the death of one partner, and, while divorce began to be possible late in the nineteenth century, only a small percentage of marriages ended that way. Traditionally high mortality, however, meant that widowhood and remarriage were common, so that in the demographic old regime, at least one marriage in four was a remarriage. As mortality improved, that rate declined (and so presumably the pressure for legal divorce increased).[20]

The nineteenth century witnessed several fundamental changes in European marriage (though they began earlier and continued after). On the one hand, marriages based on love and affection became increasingly more prevalent compared to marriages based on family and economic considerations. As something of a legal corollary, the traditional proprietary right of husbands to their wives gave way gradually to relative equality before the law. The institution of marriage also became secularized as state legislation came to replace religious authority in its regulation. Whereas weddings had traditionally been performed by a religious authority (and, whether Christian or Jewish, might involve the exchange or bestowal of rings, vows, other rituals, and a feast), the Napoleonic code, much imitated on the continent, only recognized civil marriage as legitimate, while the English introduced a hybrid system—imitated in the United States—over the course of the century that recognized both church marriages and those celebrated by a public registrar. The introduction of civil marriage laws of one form or another generally spans the century or so between the 1780s and the 1880s. The Catholic Church sought to maintain its authority in this regard, which could create odd situations like that in postunification Italy, where a significant segment of the population celebrated their weddings only in church and so were considered unmarried (and their children illegitimate). Whether church or civil, marriages usually required some combination of posting of banns, consent of parents for minors, and witnesses. Starting in 1896, some of the United States forbade marriage for certain categories of people, including epileptics, those afflicted with venereal disease or confined to public asylums, and the insane and the feeble minded; the fear was that they would pass on their afflictions to their offspring.[21]

PARENTHOOD

In the past, as now, most births took place within marriage. Premarital pregnancies, however, were common. A study of German villages finds that over 10 percent of first births were conceived before marriage in the eighteenth century and over 20 percent in the early to mid-nineteenth century; the rates in England were probably even higher. Nor were so-called illegitimate births rare. In the German villages, they grew from 2 percent to 5 percent of total births in the eighteenth century to over 10 percent in the early to mid-nineteenth century; and similar rates have been estimated for England. Economic and social change associated with industrialization and urbanization likely lay behind these trends, because increased opportunity and mobility meant that pregnancy outside of marriage might precipitate migration and the breaking of marriage vows rather than lead, as traditionally, to a wedding. Doubtless this development contributed to the midcentury foundling crisis referred to above (and perhaps also to an increase in infanticide).[22]

What is most notable about fertility in the nineteenth century is its decline *within* marriage. This phenomenon has, again, been so well studied as to defy generalization. Traditionally, a woman's reproductive life began with marriage (or a little before) and continued to about age forty, the rhythm of births determined primarily by breast-feeding practices and the presence of the husband (who might be a migrating worker) but undoubtedly also by recourse to abstinence and abortion as fertility levels were always well below the biological maximum. Beginning in the eighteenth century, specific groups of cultural elites (aristocrats, commercial classes, some Jewish communities, and others) began to practice stricter and measurable birth control within marriage, presumably coitus interruptus, abstinence, and abortion. The result was fewer children and possibly the cessation of childbearing at an earlier age. In the nineteenth century, instead, birth control became a mass phenomenon. Recourse to abortion by traditional methods increased as well, and, while scholars disagree about its prevalence, contemporary observations and retrospective studies argue for a level between 10 percent and two-thirds of all conceptions in the period during which the birth rate was declining.

The diffusion of fertility limitation is as intriguing as it is complex. A massive provincial-level study reveals that French marital fertility had experienced a 10 percent decline by 1827, the start of an irreversible process. The most precocious provinces began their decline before the revolution of 1789. Starting from a much higher level, fertility also declined in the United States beginning about 1800 (in colonial New England, completed family size was six to eight children). The rest of Europe followed, but only much later. Sixty percent of European provinces experienced the 10 percent decline between 1890 and 1920, almost a century after the French, and some did not experience it until the 1940s. Generally speaking, fertility decline was earlier and more rapid in cities and among higher social classes, but the exceptions to this generalization are many and perplexing: rural France embarked on its decline before urban/industrial England; rural Hungary and urban Germany did so at about the same time. There are indications that birth control practices spread from France to other parts of Europe, following generally cultural-linguistic pathways, but the mechanisms involved remain unknown.

Why did the French and Americans limit fertility in marriage, and why did others follow suit? At a societal level, traditional levels of fertility were incompatible with declining mortality, because they would have led to unsustainable population growth. In fact, the population of Europe more than doubled in the nineteenth century despite both the drop in births and the migration of tens of millions of Europeans to the New World and the antipodes. (By comparison, the northeastern United States combined both positive natural growth and in-migration to grow tenfold over the course of that century, while the overall U.S. population increased from five million to over seventy-five million.) At a family level, increased confidence about infant survival may have encouraged couples to aim for fewer births. The crowding of urban life also may have discouraged having large families, and the gradual shift of children from work to school undoubtedly increased the economic burden of child rearing and so argued for smaller families. There is much debate about these questions, and evidence can be marshaled for and against all of these suggestions.

What is not debated is that fertility eventually declined everywhere and irreversibly. European crude birth rates were almost everywhere above 30 per thousand in 1850; by 1910, they were almost everywhere below that figure. The total fertility rate is a synthetic measure that estimates the average number of children born to a woman who lives to the end of her reproductive life. By 1860 to 1870, total fertility rates in the United States had declined to match the traditional European level, still at about five (outside of France). By 1900 to 1910, the level was about three and a half on both sides of the Atlantic (and it would continue to decline in the twentieth century, falling to two and below in many areas).[23]

MIGRATION

As suggested, migration was an important life cycle event that might occur at any point in the progression from birth (conception, in fact) to childhood to marriage, adulthood, and old age. Europeans had always migrated, often multiple times in a single lifetime: for marriage; to work on farms, as apprentices, or as domestic servants in the population-hungry cities (where death rates normally exceeded birth rates); for seasonal work; and generally in search of economic opportunity. With the development of manufacturing, new factory towns sprouted up and attracted masses of workers. The circulation of population intensified in the nineteenth century as that population grew and economies continued to industrialize, incorporating eventually that great engine of mobility, the railroad. Individual movements might be temporary and frequent, a characteristic, as noted above, that injected disruption into fertility and nuptiality patterns. Migration overseas grew throughout the century as well, especially after the development of the steamship in the 1860s. Many migrants were working-age men, and many returned home after shorter or longer periods. In one extreme example, Italians migrated back and forth to Argentina for seasonal agricultural work. But many also stayed, and migrants also included women and children (possibly joining an already migrated husband or father) as well as whole families.

It may help to briefly put these European migrations into a quantitative context. At the beginning of the period, the population of Europe was a bit under two hundred million, and several hundred thousand people (mostly workers) migrated each year. Most of this migration took place within Europe, though the European population of the Americas at that point was approaching ten million (deriving in part from migration and in part from natural increase). Between 1800 and 1914, the population of Europe grew from about 188 million to about 458 million, a historically unprecedented growth rate of nearly one percent per year. Over that same period, the percentage of population engaged in agriculture declined from about three-quarters to about one-third, which means that the total number of agricultural workers did not change much, but that number, thanks to increased productivity (and also the importation of foodstuffs), was able to feed a much larger population in 1914 as compared to 1800. Much of the nineteenth-century population growth, then, was necessarily dominated by the children of agricultural laborers who did not follow in their parents' footsteps but engaged instead in new economic activities that often necessitated migration. As a result, migration within Europe increased (notably but not only to the cities) as did migration overseas. With regard to the latter, between 1860 and 1914, an estimated fifty-two million Europeans migrated, mostly to North and South America. And while a significant percentage of those millions eventually returned, the scale of this migration siphoned off some of the dramatic growth of the European population referred to above. We can imagine that migration of some sort became the norm for most Europeans in the Age of Empire, and, for a significant percentage, that meant migration to the New World.[24]

To extend this brief discussion of migration as a phase of the life cycle to the New World would introduce considerable complications and highlights the initial caution about focusing on the Western family as a model. For migration to the Americas came not only from Europe but from Asia and Africa as well, and American internal migration included not only the advance of the neo-European frontier but also the displacement of indigenous populations from the arctic north to the cone of South America. Those migrations undoubtedly tell a very different story of life cycle changes in the Age of Empire.

DEATH AGAIN

The life cycle necessarily ended with death, and, as already noted, death came progressively later over the course of the nineteenth century. To use one more

measure, life expectancy at birth—approximately equal to the average age
of death—increased everywhere over the course of the century, from thirty-
seven to fifty-four in Sweden, from thirty-seven to forty-eight in England,
from thirty-four to forty-seven in France, and from twenty-eight to thirty-five
in Spain.[25] These numbers, however, require some interpretation to convey a
better sense of lived experience. Because low life expectancy generally reflects
high rates of infant mortality, a rate like twenty-eight in Spain in 1800 does
not mean that most or even many people died at age twenty-eight. For those
Spaniards, life expectancy in fact increased if they survived the first years of
life. Death may have taken away half of all children by the age of five, but
those who survived to that age were likely to live to almost fifty, or more than
twenty years beyond "life expectancy at birth." The long-lived Swedes of 1900
lost about one hundred per thousand of their children, and surviving five-
year-olds were likely to live to about sixty-four, still fully ten years more than
life expectancy.[26] Those numbers are significant. To die at fifty in the Spain of
1800 meant to die in the prime of productive life and likely leave behind pre-
teenage children. To die at sixty-four in 1900 Sweden, by which date women
might well cease childbearing before the age of forty, meant to expire at an
age that, in the twentieth century, came to be generally accepted as an age of
retirement and not before one's children were grown and economically independent. The mortality experience of the United States differed significantly
from that of the rest of Europe, because life expectancy there seems to have
declined during the first half of the nineteenth century, reaching about thirty-
seven in 1850. Thereafter it improved and crossed the threshold of fifty before
1900, probably about where it had been a century before. African Americans,
the majority of whom passed from enslavement to freedom over the course of
the century, experienced a life expectancy about ten years below that of the
white majority.[27]

   Like birth and marriage, death too became an event widely recorded in
civil registries over the course of the nineteenth century. Traditionally, both
Christians and Jews buried their dead following rituals that might include
confession of sins, extreme unction, sitting with the corpse, a religious service
of some sort, and perhaps a feast (Jews insist on prompt burial following
death). Burial of the dead seems to have been a mostly European (and neo-
European) practice, as most of the rest of the world cremated their dead.
Partially in response to overcrowding in cemeteries and health concerns,
the nineteenth century saw the (re)introduction of cremation in the West.
Early advocates and technology seem to have come from Italy around 1860.
The practice spread so that, by 1907, there were, for example, twenty-eight

crematoria in Italy, thirteen in the United Kingdom, and thirty-three in the United States.[28]

CONCLUSION

This chapter has explored the Western life cycle as it evolved in a period of unprecedented declines in mortality and fertility. Over the course of the nineteenth century, infants and children in particular died less frequently as life expectancy extended. The restriction of childbearing within marriage was partially disrupted by the forces of modernization and produced something of a crisis of illegitimate births to which child abandonment and infanticide were unhappy responses. Fertility came to be better controlled—it was never uncontrolled—and reached low levels, precociously in France and most everywhere by the end of the period. Childhood patterns of labor and life cycle service began to give way to universal schooling and longer periods spent at home. Better adult mortality meant less disruption of marriage at young ages and probably contributed to the introduction and expansion of divorce. All these experiences could be contrasted and compared with those from other parts of the world to get at what is unique about Western patterns. They do, in any case, provide the background to subsequent changes in the West, including very low levels of fertility, high levels of divorce, single-person households, and alternative family forms. But those are all topics for the next volume.

CHAPTER SEVEN

The State

RACHEL G. FUCHS

Modernization, industrialization, and urbanization during the nineteenth century, accompanied by the increasing visibility of impoverished children, prompted state involvement in the lives of families. Public officials redefined the social questions in ways that led them to take responsibility that previously had been the duty of religious charities or private philanthropies. The idea that a modern state protects its children from danger, and protects society from the dangerous children, became prevalent, with reformers distinguishing between deserving and delinquent children. Deserving children were destitute or marginalized through no fault of their own when they became orphans or were abandoned. Delinquent children were miscreants, but often because of poverty. To a limited extent, state officials tried to direct family lives prior to the last third of the century, usually in the form of legislation and judicial action. Activity to save the children, however, increased during the last third of the nineteenth century and the beginning of the twentieth century, with synchronicity across West Europe and the United States.

State involvement in families usually focused on the indigent and children without families. Reformers and policymakers generally did not want to interfere with the conjugal middle- or upper-class family. This chapter, therefore, concentrates on state provisions for the poor, such as welfare, child-saving movements, legislation pertaining to the protection of children, and the perceived criminality of youth. Children, including those within as well as those outside a family, often lived in a climate of calamities and survived by fashioning a culture of expediencies. They sought useful methods to manage situations, adapting their behavior as they went along, usually within the larger cultural parameters of ethics, morality, economics, and the law.[1]

Politicians and reformers regarded children and poor families as malleable material for the creation of a healthy citizenry and in turn a healthy state. Therefore, state actions were linked to nineteenth-century state formation. Public policymakers suggested that local and national governments invest in children as building blocks of a modern state. Ideas of what comprised a modern state, along with widespread fears of national or racial degeneration and the increased visibility of poverty in the face of economic depression, industrialization, and migration, furthered state efforts to save the children for the good of the nation—and for the good of the children. In most instances, municipal authorities, including jurists, functioning as representatives of the state, took the lead in designing and implementing policies for children and families, paving the way for national legislation and programs.

Until recently, histories of state policies toward families have tended to posit a public–private dichotomy, placing the secular state in opposition to private philanthropies and charities, usually religious. They have argued that state welfare took over from failed philanthropies and charities, for nation-building purposes, starting in the last decades of the nineteenth century. Although on one level, that transformation from private charity to public welfare occurred as the welfare state developed, on another, more practical and fundamental level, the dichotomy between public and private is specious. State governments would partially fund private initiatives, and religious or secular private volunteers staffed and implemented government programs and institutions—despite the efforts of many national governments to suppress religious organizations in the process of creating a modern national, often republican, state. State policies toward families and children tended to occur as part of state building after wars.

WAR AS AN IMPETUS TO STATE ACTIONS

The customary deprivation and dislocation in people's lives during war left many children parentless, or at least fatherless, and often homeless. This spurred state action to try to provide for the widows and orphans of those who had died in war. In France, the devastating loss to Germany in 1870 spurred the new republican government to take measures to save the children. French politicians, overcome with fear of depopulation and stating that the nation loses "a battalion a year" to infant mortality, began programs to save infant lives, such as providing aid to mothers to encourage them to breast-feed their infants and regulating the wet-nursing industry that fed hundreds of thousands of infants. Nevertheless, it was not until 1923, after the astounding number of deaths during the First World War, that French law permitted the adoption of orphans and abandoned children. In England, the Boer War (1899–1902) preceded many of the social welfare reforms for children, because British politicians attributed their loss in that war in part to the physical deterioration of the youth.

Across the Atlantic Ocean, the American Civil War "greatly intensified public concern over children's welfare and convinced reformers that state action was necessary to protect the young."[2] The Civil War affected all children, North and South, who suffered material and emotional deprivation. As one young child declared, "Santa Claus forgot to come to the Shenandoah Valley."[3] The Civil War especially transformed slave children's lives; their workloads became even more overwhelming. Numerous slave children escaped to the North, and, after the war, some went to school for the first time. In 1865, Congress created the Freedmen's Bureau to alleviate poverty in the South, help settle displaced persons, support parents looking for their children, and assist in the transition from slavery to independence. However, it provided no funding. Some states, such as Illinois and New York, responded more quickly than others did to families' wartime and postwar needs, with the creation of orphanages and pensions for widows and children. On a national level, in 1873, Congress created funds for the widows and children of men who had died in the war.[4]

STATE REGULATION OF FAMILIES THROUGH LEGISLATION AND JUDICIAL DECISIONS

Throughout West Europe and the United States, the dominant ideologies that formed the bases of law codes and culture regarded conjugal families as the bedrock of the state. Consequently, laws and legislation protected men's individualism and family property. Paternal authority in the home was sacrosanct, thereby limiting state action in families with fathers. However, by means of legislation and judicial activism, the concept of *parens patriae* (the state's legal authority over children's welfare) legitimated state intrusion into the once inviolable domain of the father. The state, with its "tutelary complex" of judges, social workers, teachers, and other representatives, sought to take over some aspects of paternal authority, but predominantly in families without fathers.[5] During the last quarter of the century, the principle of doing what was in the best interests of the child prevailed.

All states enacted laws requiring the registration of births. Often these laws replaced religious custom and canon law that had required baptism within specified time periods to save infants' souls. For example, in England, the Birth and Death Registration Act of 1874 required a parent or other official to report a birth within forty-two days and a death within eight days. Failure to report finding an abandoned child within a week was punishable by a fine. Loopholes still allowed parents to conceal a birth and perhaps commit infanticide.

States enacted marriage laws that determined the legal age of independence and the legitimation of children. Marriage laws were also a means whereby the state could control the family, its most important institution for raising future citizens. In France, marriage laws reduced the age of consent in order to free love relationships from parental restraint and encourage legitimate births. Because the conjugal family was a foundation of the state, many governments tried to limit out-of-wedlock births, and one way to do this was through lowering the age of marriage. Too often, under these circumstances, however, the father disappeared. In the United States, the age of majority varied by the state, and, during the later decades of the century, social purity movements campaigned to raise the age of marriage to promote sexual restraint. Another means to avoid illegitimacy and prevent condemnation of extranuptial children and their mothers was to accept common law marriages.

By midcentury, many states not only recognized common law marriages, but they also declared the offspring of annulled marriages as legitimate, as well as those of parents who subsequently married. French law enabled the legitimation of children upon the marriage of their parents, if the parents took the necessary legal action. Some laws in the United States and Europe also gave inheritance rights to illegitimate children whose parents legally acknowledged them. In part to support the white male patriarchy, U.S. states prohibited slave marriages and interracial marriages in the post-Civil War era.[6]

Custody disputes, settled by public magistrates, arose in the case of parental death or, on rare occasions, in the case of separation or divorce. Divorce was extremely difficult, if not impossible, in most countries during the nineteenth century. In many child custody cases, as early as the 1830s, judges advanced the doctrine of "the best interests of the child," which they frequently invoked along with *parens patriae* at the expense of patriarchal rights and privileges, in awarding custody to the mother, if her conduct had been beyond reproach.[7] Despite the paternalistic English law declaring that fathers had custody over all legitimate children, the Custody of Infants Act of 1839 in that country gave mothers of "unblemished character" access to their children in the event of separation or divorce. Judges customarily granted mothers custody of daughters and all children under the age of seven, but any hint of adultery would result in custody going to the father. The English 1873 Custody of Infants Act extended access to children to mothers in the event of separation or divorce, and, by the Guardianship of Infants Act in 1886, women could be made the sole guardian of their children if their husband died. In France, judges in civil courts also acted in the best interests of the children and followed similar procedures; in contested custody, they granted custody to the mother unless she committed adultery.[8]

Courts could separate actual physical custody of the child from legal guardianship. Fathers usually retained guardianship of their children, at least until after midcentury. In the last quarter of the century, however, custody and guardianship could go to the mothers as often as to the fathers—especially if children were younger than seven or were girls. Judges held discretionary power—in the best interests of the child. By 1900, only nine of the United States (and the District of Columbia) granted mothers and fathers equal statutory rights to guardianship, although magistrates in all states based their decisions on their own judgment about children's welfare and parental fitness in awarding custody and guardianship to the mother or the father.[9]

Custody of illegitimate children was rarely disputed. It went to mothers since they were outside the legitimate patriarchal household. Out-of-wedlock children, including those born of adultery, had long been excluded from any membership in a legal family in order to protect the conjugal family.[10] In U.S. and English law, the illegitimate child could inherit from no one, not even the mother. French law, on the other hand, made out-of-wedlock children the responsibility of the mother.

The two major state concerns about extranuptial children—public cost and the children's welfare—existed in tension. Paternity suits could alleviate that tension by reducing public cost for extranuptial children and also increase the children's welfare. In France, until the law changed in 1912, the civil code forbad paternity suits. The code stipulated that a father bore responsibility for a natural child only if he had legally recognized that child. In the United States, legislators wanted to fix paternity upon a man so a mother could obtain child support and thus save the state money in poor relief. German law permitted paternity suits, but jurists limited a mother's claims to the cost of delivery and some limited child support. The German Civil Code of 1896 stipulated that an unrecognized illegitimate child and his or her father were unrelated and made the illegitimate child a member of the maternal kinship group. However, it required the father to pay child support. Paternity searches legalized in Portugal (1867) and Spain (1889) had limitations and exceptions comparable to those of Germany and the 1912 law in France; they were possible in cases of rape, if the couple had lived together in a union resembling marriage, and if there had been written avowal from the father. In England, after 1834, a mother had the right to bring a putative father to justice if he refused to marry her or help raise the child. She had to bring proof of his paternity, and it was up to the man to demonstrate that she had had relations with someone else during the time of conception. If the mother succeeded in her case, the man was compelled to help support the child until the child's teen years, depending on the situation. A child without support was charged to the parish. English laws of 1872 and 1873 fixed the sums the fathers had to pay.[11]

By the end of the first decade of the twentieth century, most states in Western Europe and across the Atlantic were inclined to permit paternity suits to save the state money and protect the welfare of illegitimate children. Furthermore, the dominant middle-class culture more frequently viewed illegitimate children as objects of compassion and less as bearing the vices of their mothers, paving the way for legal adoption.

Attention to the protection of the sacrosanct conjugal family, to the property rights of blood relatives, and to the sense of the inviolability of inheritance rights for legitimate children delayed legal child adoption in all countries, although in some countries, childless adults could adopt other adults for the sake of property transmission. As the homeless, neglected, and abandoned children became more visible, sometimes after wars, and with the emergence of custody laws, some legislatures considered the creation of legal child adoption as a means to provide for children in need. Children could join new families, often called "fictive families" to distinguish them from blood relations, but those children could not inherit from the adopting family. In the United States, an 1851 Massachusetts statute, which became the model for other states' laws, legalized adoption of children to new families who could nurture and educate a child. Legal adoption severed the child's ties with the biological family in favor of the creation of new ties with the adopting parents. The key point was the best interests of the child. By the beginning of the twentieth century, most of the U.S. states had legalized adoption.[12] Most other countries did so as well, with similar terms as in many of the United States. When full legal adoption was recognized as a new family construction, and not merely as a means to save the children, the adoptee was integrated into the adopting family.

ABANDONED CHILDREN

Without the possibility of legal adoption, birth mothers who were unwilling or unable to care for their newborns legally abandoned them. Policies regarding child abandonment served both public and private purposes. For the state, providing for infant abandonment fulfilled the public interest in preventing abortion and infanticide as well as in raising a working and fighting force. To a large extent, the dominant religion of the state influenced the characteristics of child abandonment. Protestant countries, such as England and some German states, strongly discouraged child abandonment. In predominantly Catholic countries such as France, Portugal, and Spain, and in cities such as Brussels and those on the Italian peninsula, foundling hospitals became the most important form of state involvement with children's lives until the twentieth century. In France, Russia, and the Hapsburg monarchy, the national governments set policy establishing foundling hospitals, but local agencies oversaw the administration of the institutions. In Portugal and on the Italian peninsula, local communities, cities, and other administrative units dealt with abandoned children until the turn of the century. Throughout continental Europe, in Russia, and in some cities of the United States, the Catholic Church worked with secular agencies in staffing the foundling homes.

In France, Italy, Spain, and Portugal most foundling asylums had a turning cradle—a wooden, cylindrical, concave box constructed in a windowlike aperture in the wall of the foundling home. One half of the cradle was exposed to the street. The cradle swiveled, enabling a desperate person, usually the mother, to deposit a baby in the half facing the street and then turn it so the baby went inside, leaving an empty cradle to receive the next infant. The person depositing the baby would then ring a bell, alerting the attendant inside (usually a nun) that a new baby had been left. In 1811, Napoleon mandated foundling hospitals equipped with a turning cradle in every major city of France, thereby secularizing and nationalizing a system that had been operating for centuries under the auspices of the Catholic Church. Orthodox Russia followed the Catholic model in creating open admissions to metropolitan foundling homes.

In the 1830s and 1840s, the increase in out-of-wedlock births and periods of severe economic depression contributed to a vast increase in the numbers of abandoned infants. To save money, some foundling hospitals sought to make child abandonment more difficult and curtail the freedom of admissions. This led to a decline in the abandonment of legitimate infants in many countries but only moderately altered the numbers of abandoned children. Foundling asylums in all countries sent the infants out to wet nurses in the countryside. Few survived infancy.[13]

Most of the women who abandoned their babies were not married; this is especially true in France and Russia because of the higher rates of illegitimacy.

Illegitimacy alone, however, is insufficient as an explanation for infant abandonment. Extreme poverty and lack of alternatives to abandonment were the most likely reasons. Some families tried to use foundling asylums as part of their culture of expediencies, a type of temporary welfare system during a climate of calamities, even though the child's chances for survival were slim. The notes attached to the abandoned babies giving the reasons for abandonment are similar: "I am unable to nurse and care for my baby." Or "I have had to put down this little child out of the direst poverty. It is a healthy baby but it is as thin as a ghost, and I can no longer feed it." Another mother wrote, "It breaks my heart, but I cannot cope any longer; I have used up all I have, and I can no longer feed my baby. Please take pity on my child, because it will otherwise die of starvation."[14] It was unlikely that the babies lived.

In areas where parents abandoned legitimate children, more girls than boys were left at foundling homes; in areas where most abandoned children were extranuptial, baby girls and boys were abandoned in equal numbers, indicating that a single mother, either out of dire economic need or for honor, could not keep her baby, regardless of sex. The plight of abandoned babies eventually penetrated the popular imagination, leading to reforms in all countries at the end of the century, restricting the flow of abandoned infants, and coinciding with the growth of public welfare.

Social welfare programs designed to keep mothers and babies together started in the early 1870s. International competition over population size, along with a desire to protect children, was so intense that child protection took similar forms and materialized at roughly the same time everywhere. Although most reformers believed that children were better off with their mothers than in foundling asylums, with wet nurses, or in poorhouses, they also agreed that the family alone was no longer sufficient for socializing children. Politicians and reformers became increasingly willing to intervene directly in the family in order to protect children. State authorities urged women to have children for the good of the nation, and some politicians understood the state's responsibility to support the children. The high rates of foundling mortality and new notions of maternal responsibility led to programs designed to curtail infant abandonment and to keep the babies with their mothers, even unwed mothers. Because abandoned children died at more than twice the rate of nonabandoned children, the new fears of depopulation spurred welfare polices to keep families together.

Authorities made it increasingly difficult, and less acceptable, for mothers to abandon their infants. In France and Italy, most turning cradles had closed by the 1870s, with a decrease in the number of abandoned babies. In St. Petersburg and Moscow, reforms restricting foundling-asylum admissions and requiring the mother's identification and child's birth certificate went into effect in 1869. In 1891, the Russian reforms abolished open admissions. These restrictions on admissions had the short-term effect of reducing the number of babies left at the homes; the long-term rates of abandonment fluctuated. Restrictions on abandonment were often accompanied by other sources of child support for mothers, such as aid for maternal breast-feeding, free milk dispensaries, and municipal day care centers that were sparsely located in several cities.

In antebellum New York, no public foundling asylums existed, and no private charities admitted abandoned children. Only the almshouses took in foundlings, as the law mandated, but almshouse officials sent those infants out as soon as possible to poor women who acted as wet nurses or foster parents. After the Civil War, city officials opened a foundling asylum, called the Infant's Home, and delegated the administration to private individuals. In a pattern similar to Europe, private religious charities staffed municipal foundling asylums, and the state sometimes chartered and granted funds to foundling asylums run by religious charities.

The Infant Hospital on Randall's Island in New York City, which opened in 1869, housed about six hundred homeless and destitute children. The majority of them died, as almost all abandoned children did, wherever they were. Children in this hospital were not all abandoned infants as in the European foundling hospitals. It housed true foundlings and single mothers with newborns who sought refuge there. Most babies came from the streets, doorsteps, and the police. Public horror over the "slaughter of the innocents" led authorities to seek a more humane treatment of the foundlings. Operating in the children's best interest and to save children's lives and institutional costs, from 1871 to 1891, the Randall Island Infant Hospital "placed foundlings with lactating women," many of whom doctors supervised; older children were placed in apprenticeship, as factory workers, as farm laborers, or as indentured servants. The numbers of institutionalized children increased after passage of the Children's Law of 1875, although, by the turn of the century, most Progressive Era (1890–1920) social workers believed that home placement was preferable to institutionalization of children. The Randall's Island Infant Hospital closed in 1905.[15]

POOR RELIEF AND MUNICIPAL
WELFARE PROGRAMS, 1780 TO 1880

State involvement in child-saving programs was complex. Charity and welfare during the first two-thirds of the nineteenth century separated the deserving poor from the undeserving, who were typically able-bodied men. Orphans, abandoned children, and married women with several young children whose husbands had died, become disabled, or had abandoned them were the most deserving of poor relief.

Between 1780 and 1815, municipal governments began assuming some responsibility for poor children in the absence of family, community, or religious charities. By 1815, most cities had institutions for the confinement of the destitute: hospitals, asylums for orphans, foundling homes, prisons for the vagrants, and "reformatories" for prostitutes. The Prussian law code of 1794 stipulated that each community had the responsibility to take care of all residents who had the "right of domicile" *(Heimatrecht)*. In 1842 and 1855, some German states, including Prussia, passed laws abolishing *Heimatrecht* and substituted a more easily obtainable proof of local residence. After 1870, these regulations extended to all of Germany. Similarly, in other countries, local charities, poor relief bureaus, and hospitals required local residency.

Poorhouses or almshouses dominated poor relief. They increased in number and size during the nineteenth century, fueled by disease, urban poverty, economic downturns, and immigration. As municipal public institutions, they collaborated and cooperated with private volunteers and religious societies. They were filthy, overcrowded, ill-kept, large institutions that functioned as prisonlike asylums to house destitute family members of all ages. These institutions combined moralization, punishment, and work and were highly criticized. In Prussia, some workhouses were orphanages. Italy had a long history of the institutionalization of endangered girls who lacked economic or emotional support and were in danger of falling into prostitution. The changing situation of poor families and of those willing to provide relief, especially in the industrial cities, necessitated some reform. The level of social conscience varied with the city and community; the need was not always apparent, and, when it was, finances were insufficient for the expanding poverty and demand.

In England, poorhouses had existed since Elizabethan times but became more widespread after the Poor Law Reforms of 1834. Based on the belief that the real causes of poverty were not to be found in large economic changes but rather in too-generous relief to the poor, the Poor Law Reforms sought to restore the work ethic and public morality by tightening the criteria for aid and by developing prisonlike workhouses as a punishment for those who committed the "crime" of being a pauper. Separation of families, even mothers from their children, into separate workhouses dissolved the family for these paupers. If either the husband or wife were habitually drunk and failed to work, their children might be taken to the workhouse. Indigent mothers of extranuptial children could be taken into the workhouse as a disciplinary measure. They, too, would be separated from their children. The only women likely to get relief outside the workhouse were those who had been widowed or abandoned and were trying to support several young children living at home. Local Poor Law guardians played a paternalistic police role in deciding how families should function and which among them were in the deserving category.

Whenever possible, kith and kin would take in orphans. When a family fell apart, usually from the death of a parent, an older child sometimes went to a workhouse while women relatives took in the baby. As one woman in London explained her decision "to take in her husband's three-year-old orphaned nephew: ... 'When he is older I shall be obliged to let the [Poor Law] Guardians have him; but I can't let a baby like that go where there is no woman to love him, as long as I can find a bit for his mouth.' "[16] The family, the community, and, as a last resort, charity were more desirable and effective than the public institutions in providing for poor families and children.

Destitute orphans and extranuptial children without kin and community had to depend on the kindness of strangers, which often was lacking. They were sent out to baby farmers (nonlactating women who kept infants for a fee) or confined to poorhouses or industrial workshops. Because Poor Law guardians incarcerated nonproviding fathers or indigent mothers separately, children of the indigent had little contact with their siblings and parents. Guardians occasionally opted to take some of the children from a family into the workhouse so the rest of the family could remain in their own houses; families sometimes went along with this expediency. Under the Poor Laws, there was close cooperation between local Poor Law authorities and charitable organizations.

Some parents in Europe and in the United States, when they were ill or out of work and could not feed their children, intended the placement of a child in an almshouse or orphanage as a temporary measure—an option of last resort to hold the rest of the family together in hard times. In the climate of calamities, using almshouses was part of a family's culture of expediencies. This use of almshouses and poorhouses differed little from some mothers' intended use of foundling homes, although the abandoned children were generally infants and those sent to almshouses were older; many were the children of widows. In Ireland, poor Jinny O'D's mother brought her to the William Henry Elliott Home for Waifs and Strays. "[B]oth were in rags and without shelter. Jinny had provided for herself and her mother by selling matches and newspapers on the street. The mother had left her in the home for two months and then removed her, finding that she could not support herself without the child's assistance."[17] Families in every country used similar strategies as they attempted to manage their lives; some sought temporary housing for unmanageable children. Critics charged that families often wanted to shed the financial burden of their children and have the state support them, and those children were not really out of control. A desperate mother might place a child in a workhouse, and the workhouse would pay another foster family to take the child out of the institution. In turn, the foster family would return the child to his or her parents, along with a portion of the money. Few questioned the entitlement of children to food and sustenance through local institutions when their mothers could not provide, although state officials sought to avoid abuses. Generally, however, families tried to avoid institutions.

PUBLIC WELFARE, 1870 TO 1914

During the last decades of the nineteenth century, public welfare institutions and programs expanded, and governments created many new ones, in part to "save the children" while promoting the creation of a republican citizenry based on middle-class domestic models. Authorities not only viewed children as victims of poverty, but they also regarded them as threats to the moral and social order. Social reform became part of state-building projects that enlisted children as potential citizens—future soldiers and workers. The developing social welfare state resulted in a complex interrelationship between new, rationalized, centralized state programs and long-standing local private charities. In all countries, private philanthropies enjoined legislators to provide maternity insurance, maternity leave, publicly supported maternity care, and state subsidies for breast-feeding.

Public authorities perceived that underprivileged families were in a state of crisis, contributing to high infant mortality, and thought the problem could be partially resolved by teaching women how to be better mothers and by protecting infants. However, tensions existed between efforts to keep families together while also providing for the welfare of the children. Differentiating between deserving and undeserving families and children, public authorities made an effort to keep children with their families if there was proper supervision of problematic families. Starting in the late nineteenth century, and lasting well into the twentieth, municipal, state, and philanthropic agencies in all countries established organizations to educate mothers on child care. The aim was to instill useful work habits, ensure good hygiene, and decrease childhood deaths. These organizations included infant and child day care facilities whose goals were to safeguard and educate young future citizens by overseeing the children of working mothers; regular health check-ups at school; examinations for illness and dental health; free milk dispensaries for nurslings; and breakfast milk at school for needy children. They were less concerned about the mothers than with the possibility that deprived children might die.

For example, several German cities installed infant welfare offices, patterned after the French well-baby clinics that began in the 1880s, to teach working-class women the benefits of breast-feeding. Initially, few women visited these offices, but the introduction of "breast-feeding premiums" radically changed this. In 1908, more than eighteen thousand infants were brought to these offices. In England, voluntary societies organized and staffed well-baby clinics. With encouragement from physicians and legislators, they developed programs to educate mothers in methods of efficient and hygienic infant care. The 1908 Children's Act of Great Britain gave the state the responsibility of protecting young children from deprivation by providing for programs such as school meals. In the early twentieth century, the U.S. federal government established the Children's Bureau to collect and disseminate information on child welfare. It lobbied successfully on behalf of the Maternity and Infancy Protection Act (the Sheppard-Towner Act), adopted by Congress in 1921 to improve maternal and children's health.

Russia may have promoted the public upbringing of children more than elsewhere, and such efforts reflected the Russian philosophy that the state could raise children better than poor, uneducated, working mothers. The Russian Society for the Protection of Infants' Lives and Childrearing, incorporating new ideas about infant feeding and child care education, constructed welfare institutions for mothers and children. In 1904, the Union to Combat Child Mortality distributed free cow's milk to infants and children at walk-in clinics while personnel provided advice to mothers on breast-feeding and child care. The Russian Society for the Care of Indigent Children, in which district guardians provided charity to indigent children they found in basement and garret rooms, achieved wide acclaim. In effect, Russian institutions became surrogate mothers that enabled poor women to continue working, but the major goal was protection of the children.

The creation of mothers' pensions in West Europe provided another building block to state involvement in families. Despite the opposition of church authorities, who regarded the payments to unwed mothers as a "subsidy to debauchery," mothers' pensions began first in France in the 1870s and 1880s with programs of aid to single and married mothers, with the goal of saving infants' lives. Portugal developed an equivalent system called a "subsidy of lactation." Regions of Italy almost immediately followed France with similar programs of subsidies to single mothers who nursed their babies. Much of the European legislation for the protection of children and mothers resembled French programs. These began on a municipal level in the 1870s, developed through the 1880s, and became nationally legislated in 1893, 1904, and 1913.[18]

Child-saving efforts, whether by European governments or states across the Atlantic, increased in the 1880s, reaching a crescendo in the 1890s and the first decades of the twentieth century, with amazing similarities. "Save-the-children" efforts were a cornerstone of Progressive Era reforms in the United States, prevention of cruelty to children movements in England, and attention to materially and "morally abandoned" children in France and Italy. Reformers in all countries came to view children as abused, ragged, starving, neglected, and exploited victims, and also as social, economic, moral, racial, and sexual threats. State efforts aimed to produce obedient, disciplined children and adults while imbuing poor homeless children with ideals of virtue in order for them to grow up to be good middle-class citizens. Public policies for these children became part of the national interest to strengthen the families and the nation and improve the children's lives and health; they were intertwined with the growing public hygiene, social purity, and education movements of the time.

The unprecedented immigration to the cities, with many unemployed, spurred save-the-children movements. The enormous numbers and visibility of street children in cities such as New York, Rome, Paris, and London fueled public attitudes that the state should do something to save these children, get them off the street and out of sight, and protect society from them. The plights of urban poverty and diseases leading to the horrifically high mortality of children, combined with burgeoning industrial economies relying on child labor, gave further impetus to save-the-children movements. Initially, such movements broke up families, having faith that state institutions could rear children better than pauper families.

During the last third of the century, reformers and public authorities in the United States and Europe sought to replace the large orphanages and almshouses (or workhouses), which had been warehousing thousands of youths, with family-style "cottages." Progressive Era reformers, as part of their critique of asylums and institutions for children, like their counterparts in Europe, favored the cottage system as a "family-type" surrounding with buildings generally housing fewer than fifty youths. Some of these institutions were public and run by lay officials; most, however, were under the aegis of religious denominations but received public funding. Regardless of state or country, children in these institutions received the minimal necessities of life, but those provisions went along with the requirement of hard work, regimentation, disciplinary action, and a brutal and dehumanizing life. The children rebelled and often tried to run away.

Legislation of 1889 epitomizes child-saving movements in many countries. To defend children from abusive, alcoholic, or criminal parents, the French, British, and German governments enacted almost identical legislation enabling police and state welfare authorities to decide which parents were placing their children in moral danger and then deprive those parents of authority over their children. Police and welfare agents would subsequently remove the children from their parental homes and place them in the custody of the nonoffending parent, with relatives, in foster care, or in institutions such as workhouses or orphanages. In these instances, public authorities entered the private spaces of families, depriving fathers and mothers of parental authority. The French Parliament enacted a law protecting these "morally abandoned" children in 1889. The same year, the British parliament passed the National Society for the Prevention of Cruelty to Children Act, followed by an 1894 act that made cruelty to children a punishable crime. Scottish Poor Law authorities, who had been separating children from abusive or dangerous family situations for decades, continued this process in the interest of protecting the children and imbuing them with sober work habits. In Italy, the 1889 Public Security Law attempted to deal with vagrant and errant youth.[19] Comparable German legislation came about a decade later.

Further legislation for child protection followed in the first decade of the twentieth century. The British Acts of 1904 and 1908 and the French 1904 Strauss Law consolidated many aspects of child welfare from abandoned infants to morally abandoned adolescents, imposing penalties for abuse, neglect, and child endangerment, whether physical or moral. The British 1908 act was also intended to protect youths in reform school, so that "the children grow up ... [to] become useful, serviceable and profitable citizens of this great Empire."[20] Gender made a difference; in all cases, girls needed protection longer than boys did, and the age of consent for sexual relations applied only to girls. A 1901 Italian emigration law punished those who took minor children out of the country to "work in unhealthy occupations;" for girls, that was generally prostitution, and, for boys, it was work in factories. Uniform child protection laws came later to the United States, beginning with Ohio in 1911.[21]

National laws often required implementation from religious or secular philanthropic associations of child savers who were convinced that they knew what was best for the children and the state. Sometimes child-saving organizations ignored parental authority, treating poor children like "waifs and strays" to get them off the streets and into institutions, or out of the institutions and far from the cities, sending them from New York to Kansas, London to Australia, and Paris to Algeria. Some of these children were true orphans or half orphans; others may have had parents who failed to provide for them or were unable to do so. The New York orphan trains are the most infamous of measures sending children out of the cities. Charles Loring Brace and the New York Children's Aid Society (CAS) pioneered the idea that foster care was better and cheaper than providing for the children in institutions. The CAS, a private religious organization, took children, usually Catholic Irish immigrants, from city streets and orphanages of New York and sent them on trains to customarily Protestant homes out West, where the majority were forced to work. Brace and the CAS had severe critics and staunch supporters. By the first decades of the twentieth century, however, the states' child rearing roles expanded, and the power of private agencies, such as Brace's, declined dramatically as state welfare agencies took over many of the responsibilities that religiously based child-saving organizations had borne. The philosophy of state social workers and reformers opposed keeping children in institutions or sending children away from their families. Rather, they favored keeping children with their own families, albeit with "mothers' pensions" and under the supervision of doctors, teachers, judges, and social workers.[22]

PUNISHMENT OF JUVENILES

In all countries, public concern with the potential and actual criminal activity of homeless, vagrant, and begging street children pervaded politics from the 1880s through the first decade of the twentieth century. The problem of juvenile delinquency was complicated because nineteenth-century images of children were contradictory: on the one hand, children were innocent and pure; on the other, they were wicked and needed discipline.

Efforts to punish juvenile delinquents began early in the century, with municipalities and states making vagrancy and begging illegal. The debate focused on what to do with the children picked up off the streets or brought in on criminal charges. At the beginning of the century, juvenile offenders—for offenses as mild as begging and vagrancy to more severe cases of assault and robbery—were generally punished and incarcerated in prisons with adult criminals. Customarily, police seized children wandering the streets and brought them before a magistrate, who might have released them to their parents on their assurance that they would go to school, obtain an apprenticeship, or find employment. The state could also assume custody of vagrant children, whether they were orphans or had families. In France, police would round up vagrant youths on the city streets and bring them to the state-run asylum for abandoned children, which in turn would place them in reformatories or keep them until their parents or guardian came to get them. Although the Napoleonic Penal Code, which applied in Italy as well as France, called for separation of minors from adults in prisons or separate houses of correction for minors, separation did not exist until the 1830s, with the founding of new prisons and agricultural colonies for young children.[23]

Starting around midcentury, reformers campaigned for reform of the juvenile justice system. For example, during the 1850s, Napoleon III in France sought to remove young vagrants and delinquents from the cities and send them to the countryside, which he deemed more beneficial to the reform of youths. In Italy, similar state reforms occurred contemporaneously. In England, the Youthful Offenders Acts of 1854, 1857, 1861, and 1866, recognized juvenile delinquents as separate and different from adults, and even tried to reform potentially delinquent children. These acts, and similar ones in other countries, called for reformatories and industrial workshops for young vagrants aged seven to fourteen in order to change their behavior rather than just punishing them. These acts consequently extended the concept of childhood through the early teen years.[24]

Private philanthropies took the lead in establishing prisons for juvenile delinquents with the intention of reforming troublesome and delinquent boys, but most of these institutions received some state funding and were subject to state inspection. The most famous, and among the first, was Mettray, established in rural France in 1839. Mettray initially received state subventions, although these steadily withered away as the French republican government after 1870 began to erect its own agricultural colonies based upon the Mettray model. Almost all were for boys; juvenile delinquent girls were considered to be prostitutes and incarcerated in separate facilities. Following the principles of Mettray, an archipelago of reformatories for the re-education of juvenile delinquents of all social classes developed in West Europe. These institutions were geared to instill obedience and discipline in poor children in order to reform them into hard-working citizens of the state. Reformers argued that, if they could control children's environment, they could control their character. Like Mettray, most of these re-education reformatories were established by private philanthropies, but they had a close relationship with the state through subventions and by judges sending children to these institutions. Moreover, child welfare laws in each country influenced the existence and function of these reformatories, and some of the children in the institutions were wards of the court—abandoned, orphaned, or taken from their abusive parents after the 1889 laws. Not all reformatories were cottage style; some were huge institutions housing several hundreds of youths, with girls separate from boys. Strict military discipline and regimentation pervaded. Whether cottage or barrack style, the institutions functioned more often as prisons where a fortunate few would learn a trade—for girls it was usually training as domestic servants. Alternatively, emigration societies worked with the courts to ship the youngsters to distant places such as Canada, Australia, and Kansas. Despite the laws and intentions of the courts and increasing numbers of state reformatories, most juvenile delinquents, especially African Americans, served time in jails and prisons.

Adolescent girls and boys received different treatment. Vagrant girls were accused of prostitution; vagrant boys accused of petty theft. Boys were seen as dangerous to property; girls seen as a danger to the public morality. In some states, laws promulgated around 1850 called for state-run penitentiaries for young girls to supplement the church-run institutions (such as the Good Shepherd or Magdalene homes) for delinquent girls or those whom their parents declared unmanageable. Later in the century, social purity campaigners in all countries focused on child prostitution and the sexuality of children, especially of girls. The ostensible goal was to eliminate the prostitution of children and the traffic in young girls, both domestic and foreign. In Britain, in an effort to control prostitution, the 1885 Criminal Law Amendment Act raised the age of consent to sixteen for girls and made it a criminal offense to procure a girl younger than twenty-one years of age for prostitution. The act did not apply to boys, but it outlawed male homosexual activity. A campaign against incest starting in the 1890s resulted in the 1908 Punishment of Incest Act in Britain, which made incest within a certain degree of consanguinity a misdemeanor and incest by a man with a girl younger than thirteen a felony punishable with penal servitude for life.

Around the turn of the century, states established juvenile courts to protect as well as to punish children as part of the attempt to regulate childhood. The Cook County (Illinois) juvenile court, created in 1899, was the first in the United States; by 1903, five other states added juvenile courts.[25] England established them in 1908 and France in 1912. These courts and judges viewed their roles as ordering reform rather than punishment to prevent further crime by severing a child's ties with an injurious, poor, and delinquent family background. Paternal authority was reduced by an interventionist state policy including court-ordered sentences for incarceration and the teaching of good behavior. Judges, as state officials, became patriarchs when the patriarch of the family was absent or could not control his children.

CONCLUSION

By 1900, children were objects of state study and scrutiny in an effort to mold them according to middle-class ideals. States, through their laws and in the persons of police and judiciary, stepped in when they judged the family patriarch to have been abusive or violent to his children, to have neglected or abandoned them, or to be generally unfit. In pursuit of the national interest—which included the establishment of a stable workforce, public health, education, and responsible parenthood—the influence of the state increased to create model citizens. Despite state intervention, however, and what social control theorists have argued were state attempts to colonize the family, most children lived in families, whether conjugal, common law, single-parent, blended, foster, or surrogate. The family remained the ideal environment for children.

CHAPTER EIGHT

Faith and Religion

CHRISTINA DE BELLAIGUE

Religious belief and practice had a considerable influence on the shape and experience of family life and childhood in the West throughout the nineteenth century. The family had been of central concern to Protestants and Catholics since the Reformation. From the 1780s, and throughout the first half of the nineteenth century, the rise of evangelical Protestantism and efforts by the Catholic Church to regain ground following the damage done by the Enlightenment saw religious models of family life becoming increasingly influential. It could be argued, in fact, that the religious revivals of the early nineteenth century were predicated on the reformation of family and home and on the education of the young. The proper conduct of family life, relations between the sexes, and the way children should be raised came to be central concerns of both Protestant and Catholic thought and practice. The sanctity of the home and the holiness of childhood became significant themes in religious literature. Churches of all denominations sought to disseminate their conception of the Christian household and to shore up the family as the key institution of society through their philanthropic and educational initiatives. Sacred rituals framed childhood and family life, and, for many, parenthood and growing up were defined and experienced in spiritual terms. Yet, from the mid-nineteenth century, religious models were declining in importance, and religious practice was becoming less central to family and social life. New, scientific conceptions of childhood began to supplant older models, and states began to take over from religious philanthropy in supporting poor families and in educating the young, emphasizing national concerns over Christian teachings. Looking first at religious models of family and childhood, then at the religious institutions that intervened in the lives of children and families, and finally at religious practice and belief, this chapter will trace the growing importance of religion in family life from the late eighteenth century and the way it was increasingly supplanted over the course of the nineteenth century.

MODELS AND PRESCRIPTIONS, 1800 TO 1900

Religious ideas were central to the idealized conceptions of the domestic realm and the modern family that were gaining influence and shaping middle-class life throughout Britain, North America, and the European continent in the first half of the nineteenth century. Indeed, Leonore Davidoff and Catherine Hall have argued that, in England, the Protestant Evangelical revival was the key factor in the rise of a new domestic ideology, central to the identity and success of a burgeoning professional and commercial middle class. From the mid-eighteenth century, Evangelical thinkers such as William Cowper and Hannah More underlined the importance of the home as a "sanctuary" from the amoral world of capitalist commerce. Across all denominations, the family was presented as the source of virtue and faith, and the home seen as standing at the heart of the project to reform society along new moral lines. Similar ideas informed family life in North America and in Protestant parts of Western Europe. In the United States in the 1840s, Joseph Smith, the founder of the Church of Latter-day Saints, took such arguments to a radical extreme. He argued in favor of polygamy on the grounds that emulating the patriarchal structures of the Old Testament would generate in modern Mormon families a bastion against the depredations of American individualism. Although no more than ten percent to twenty percent of Mormons in fact practiced polygamy, Smith's approach highlights the mutually reinforcing relationship between religion and family at the heart of contemporary responses to social, economic, and cultural change.[1]

One feature of the sanctification of family life in Protestant communities was a new emphasis on private family worship. Since the seventeenth century, fathers had been enjoined to lead their households in daily prayers; renewed emphasis on this responsibility in the nineteenth century saw private family worship increasingly supplanting attendance at daily services outside the home. The theme of the family at prayer or of children praying became a common trope of nineteenth-century genre painting, expressing this sense of the holiness of family life and highlighting the centrality of the family in Christian thought. Similarly, Sunday worship and observance of the Sabbath were recast as familial activities. Religious observance within the family and an emphasis on the sanctity of family life were integral to nineteenth-century domestic ideologies in Protestant Europe and North America.[2]

These idealized conceptions of domesticity and domestic piety depended on gendered distinctions between public and private life and on elaborate constructions of masculinity and femininity. In England and North America, as many historians have noted, the notion that the two sexes occupied "separate spheres"—women's sphere being the private domain of the home and men's being the public world of commerce and politics—was particularly widely disseminated and upheld as the ideal to which all families should aspire. Although in practice these spheres often overlapped and the distinction between the responsibilities of men and women was rarely as clear-cut as the prescriptive literature implied, in the ideal Christian family, it was seen as the particular duty of women—as wives and mothers—to preserve and maintain the sanctity of the home, to ensure that children were brought up as Christians.[3] Departing from early modern ideas about the susceptibility and weakness of women

FIGURE 8.1: *Frank Holl (1845–1888)*, The Lord Gave and the Lord Taketh Away—Blessed Be the Name of the Lord, *1868*. Guildhall Art Gallery, City of London. Oil on canvas. City of London Libraries and Guildhall Art Library.

and building on Reformation notions of women as the "helpmeet" of their husbands, Protestant Evangelical thinkers had contributed to shaping a more positive conception of women's nature. Indeed, women who conformed to these domestic models, devoting themselves to preserving the sanctuary of the home, were held to be morally superior, the guardians of faith and piety, not only within the family, but also in wider society.

If the influence of pious wives and mothers was emphasized in the religious literature as a key to the moralization of society, these images of femininity nevertheless assumed the dependence of women on their fathers, husbands, and sons. Moreover, while the home was conceived of as women's proper sphere, men were far from excluded from it. Indeed, the father was a central figure in the Evangelical conception of the ideal family, and his masculinity depended on fulfilling his religious responsibilities. In the United States, Theodore Dwight's *Father's Book* (1834) encouraged men to oversee the moral and religious life of their household.[4] The head of the household was not only responsible for maintaining a Christian house and, as God's representative, upholding God's law, it was also his responsibility "under God" to provide for the household. In Germany, a direct line of authority was traced from the *Gottesvater* to the *Landesvater* to the *Hausvater*.[5] Protestant Evangelical conceptions of masculinity assumed a direct connection between fathers and God the Father and underlined the role played by men in upholding Christian family life.

In the Catholic world, men were far less prominent in nineteenth-century religious writing on the family. This was partly because of the greater importance of the clergy as mediators between God and the faithful, which meant that the key moments of religious observance and practice took place in public, under the aegis of the church, rather than in the home. However, it also reflected the extent to which piety and religion were regarded as women's domain. The late eighteenth century had seen a decline of men's religiosity in many Catholic countries; in France, it was women who were particularly active to defend the church during the Revolution, a phenomenon that reflected its importance both as a source of spiritual comfort and as a social institution for the female population. In the years after 1815, the church built on this female devotional solidarity, giving women a central role in strategies for the church's recovery. The hope was that fostering the piety of wives and mothers would ensure the Catholic upbringing of future generations and that religion would be central to domestic life. Such strategies were at least partly effective. By the mid-nineteenth century, women made up three-quarters of French practicing Catholics, and female pilgrims far outnumbered their male counterparts.[6]

The women who seemed so loyal to the church were in part responding to the development of a new, more positive conception of femininity within Catholicism. In the first part of the eighteenth century, Catholic writers had emphasized the sinfulness and corruptibility of women and the danger of their capacity for seduction, harking back to the example of Eve and the fall of man. Chastity, and the denial of sexuality, was the only path to virtue for a woman. From the mid-eighteenth century, however, Catholic thinkers began to move away from this rhetoric, arguing that women's virtue might be expressed through motherhood and contending that women were naturally pious. Between 1800 and 1850, a new genre of Catholic advice literature for women proliferated, emphasizing the sanctity of motherhood and holding up the example of the Virgin Mary as the ideal of femininity. Mary was presented above all as a mother, and she was evoked in emotive terms. In 1854, a papal encyclical gave the doctrine of the immaculate conception the status of dogma, further promoting the Marian cult. Inspired by this new emphasis on Mary's maternity, in France, Bishop Dupanloup's *Catéchisme Chrétien* instructed its readers that: "We owe the Holy Virgin a profound respect, because she is the mother of God, a great love and a tender trust, because she is our mother."[7] Increasingly, women were portrayed as the morally superior element in society. *La Donna Cattolica*, published in Italy in 1855, presented women as the source of moral and religious virtue.[8] This reverence for motherhood and belief in the piety of women reflected a decisive shift in Catholic conceptions of femininity. Motherhood now matched—even surpassed—chastity as women's route to virtue and salvation, and the family now equaled the convent as a site of women's piety.

Similarities existed between Protestant and Catholic conceptions of femininity, particularly in the emphasis on women's role in safeguarding religious and moral virtue. Over the course of the century, however, in both Catholic and Protestant societies, the religious element of the notion of women's piety and responsibility for disseminating religious values was gradually diluted. What emerged was a generalized notion of women's virtue and moral superiority and idealized conceptions of motherhood and family less closely tied to the specific beliefs and practices upheld by the various churches. In France, Louis Aimé-Martin's *De l'Education des Mères de Famille, ou de la Civilization du Genre Humain par les Femmes* drew not only on Catholic ideals of femininity but also on eighteenth-century notions of women's capacity for sensitivity, understanding, and civility to argue that women could become the redeemers of humanity. In England, the success of Coventry Patmore's poem extolling the virtues of the "Angel in the House" exemplifies the way in which the notion of women as by nature domestic, virtuous, and morally superior had gained ground beyond Evangelical circles and points to the widespread influence of idealized conceptions of familial domesticity. Indeed, such ideas even influenced the experience of middle-class Jewish families. In traditional rural Jewish communities in East Europe, religious practice was the preserve of the men of the family, and women had little religious status in their own right, often working outside the home to permit the men of the family to devote themselves to religious observance and scholarship. Over the course of the nineteenth century, however, Jewish families in Britain and Germany came to conform to the dominant models of domesticity and piety. In Germany, Jewish housewives differed little from their middle-class Protestant neighbors in their household management and in the way they raised their children. Significantly, the publications advising women on their special responsibilities within the home, which were proliferating in this period, tended not to assume any significant differences of approach between their Protestant, Catholic, and Jewish readers. At the same time, in the urban environment in both England and Germany, as men increasingly worked outside the home and attendance at synagogue lost its centrality to communal life, Jewish women became more central to religious practice. Domestic religious tasks performed by women became more central to the practice of faith and piety, and women increasingly took on the role of preservers of religious identity, reflecting a new belief in their inherent spirituality. In France, efforts to improve the education offered to Jewish girls were fueled by the sense that women played a critical role in maintaining the family's religious identity.[9] As the Jewish experience suggests, Christian models of femininity and domesticity had considerable influence over middle-class families—whatever their faith or economic circumstances—throughout nineteenth-century Europe and North America. It also demonstrates the way in which, by the end of the century, these models had detached themselves from specific theologies and dogmas, and the religious content of middle-class ideals of gender and the family had declined in importance.

A similar pattern of dilution and generalization of religious ideals can be observed in relation to conceptions of childhood. At the beginning of the century, however, the Evangelical revival of the late eighteenth century gave new vigor to Protestant conceptions of the child as inherently weak and sinful, the consequence of belief in original sin. Thus, in Britain in 1799, the *Evangelical Magazine* opined that children were "sinful polluted creatures."[10] The idea that children were sinners by nature led to arguments in favor of strict discipline as the only means to ensure they would learn virtuous behavior and be saved from damnation. Such discipline would be enforced through parental, and particularly paternal, authority. In the United States, the Baptist intellectual and president of Brown University, Francis Wayland, contended that "the *right* of the parent is to *command*; the *duty* of the child is to *obey*. Authority belongs to the one, submission to the other" (emphasis in original).[11] It is, of course, difficult to unpick the relationship between prescription and practice, but such ideas do appear to have influenced the way children were treated by middle-class parents in the first part of the century. Wayland himself once refused to feed his fifteen-month-old child for two days, until the baby's assertive behavior was curbed and he surrendered to his father's will. But strict discipline by no means always involved corporal punishment. On the contrary, the diaries of Evangelical parents of all denominations reveal their hope that their children would learn to understand their sinfulness and to try to master it through self-examination and self-regulation in the Protestant tradition.[12]

In the Catholic world, the sacramental efficacy of baptism meant that original sin was less of a concern in relation to childhood. And by the 1830s, the Evangelical emphasis on sinfulness in children was declining in influence. Rousseauist notions of the naturally innocent child had gained prominence in the eighteenth century and in the nineteenth century contributed to the emergence of a Romantic conception of childhood that emphasized purity and natural candor. This tradition melded with Christian notions of childhood innocence, which now came to the fore in both Protestant and Catholic thought. The result was a kind of sacralization of childhood itself, which owed little to theologies of original sin and instead highlighted passages in the Gospels that pointed to the virtue and hope exemplified by the child. Children were "fresh from the hand of God, living blessings which have drifted down to us from the imperial palace of the love of God."[13] Children, unsullied by experience, were believed to be particularly close to God, even godlike themselves—a view given vivid expression in Thomas Gotch's image of *The Child Enthroned* (1894). In didactic religious literature, children were now more likely to be presented as the redeemers of adult sin rather than as sinful creatures in need of correction.

If, by the 1830s, ideas of the sinfulness of youth were being abandoned with respect to young children, it could be argued that their influence endured longer with respect to ideas about adolescence. Thus, at Rugby School in the 1830s and 1840s, which catered to English boys of the middle and upper classes, Thomas Arnold sought to cultivate what has been described as "Christian manliness," conceived of primarily as a kind of moral adulthood. The system he created at Rugby was predicated on the desire to hasten the transition from sinful youth to virtuous Christian manhood. It would inspire and strengthen a Protestant tradition in education that emphasized the importance

FIGURE 8.2: *Thomas Gotch (1854–1931)*, The Child Enthroned, *1894*. Private collection. Oil on canvas. Bridgeman Art Gallery.

of reflection, self-discipline, and character formation and that influenced the education offered to boys and girls throughout Protestant Europe and North America.[14] However, Arnold's disciples would build on his notion of manliness in a self-conscious attempt to respond to the apparent feminization of religion, developing what has been termed a "muscular Christianity." Authors like Charles Kingsley elaborated a new ideal of youthful masculinity predicated on chivalric notions of honor, valor, and a kind of spiritualized healthiness. This new conception of boyhood was taken up with gusto in middle-class schools and in new genres of fiction and journalism for boys, but, by the end of the century, its secular and imperial connotations were much more heavily emphasized; domesticity, piety, and religious observance were increasingly presented as antimasculine.[15] In the Catholic world, concerns about adolescent sexuality focused on young women and informed the instruction offered to girls. Innocence was prized over understanding and self-reliance, and strict limits were placed on what young women were taught. Rather than the kind of thoughtful devotion expected of young Protestant women, the Catholic Church sought to cultivate a kind of mystical, sensual piety, based on acceptance of the church's teachings. From the 1860s, however, pressures to bring girls' education into line with "modern" and "scientific" principles increasingly undermined this emphasis on female innocence. By the end of the century, in both the Catholic and the Protestant worlds, idealized conceptions of male and female adolescence were much less closely tied to religious models.[16]

INSTITUTIONS

The religious models of masculinity and femininity and prescriptions of family life described above were chiefly derived from and influential among the nineteenth-century middle classes. The rhetorical force of the relationship between religion and family is evident from the use of familial metaphors beyond the home; Methodist converts referred to themselves as "brother" or "sister," and Catholic convents—headed by a mother superior—frequently claimed to model themselves on the family. And both Catholics and Protestants were keen to disseminate their idealized models of the religious family among the working class and to support religious observance and pious behavior. In order to do so, throughout the nineteenth century, churches of all denominations established a range of philanthropic institutions intended to shore up their conception of proper family life and to instruct children in faith and piety.

One of the key institutions of this type in France was the Société de Charité Maternelle. Since the 1780s, these associations of laywomen had provided

poor mothers with money to cover the cost of childbirth. Their objective was
to limit the number of legitimate children in foundling hospitals and to reduce
infant mortality by encouraging breast-feeding. Staffed for the most part by
bourgeois laywomen, the Société reinforced the idea that women were naturally religious and charitable and also shored up idealized conceptions of
family life. Significantly, it was only the "deserving" poor who would receive
assistance, and conformity to religious models of the family was a key factor in
deciding which families were deserving. Thus, a religious marriage ceremony
was required of all the families to be assisted. In Germany, similar functions
were performed by *Rettingshausen,* established by reformed Protestants to rescue the children of failed families. By 1868, 355 such institutions had been
established. Catholic charities built on this precedent, and the 1860s saw the
creation of the Good Shepherdesses or *Gute Hirtinnen,* intended to care for
young women in need.

From midcentury, however, in both Protestant and Catholic countries,
Catholics and Protestants differed, however, in their approach to caring for
abandoned children. In France, Italy, and Spain, institutions were established
by various religious orders (and frequently supported by the state) to care for
illegitimate children and the children of parents who could not provide for
their offspring. In Protestant Europe, on the other hand, the authorities were
permitted to investigate the paternity of abandoned children, and fathers, once
identified, were expected to provide for their offspring. If they were unable
to, the father's parish would step in. The contrast points to a confessional
difference in the conception of men's and women's sexuality. In Catholic countries, it was argued that supporting unwed mothers directly would encourage
sexual license among young women. In Protestant countries, a premium was
placed on children remaining within a familial setting, expectations of paternal responsibility were higher, and welfare was distributed through the male
breadwinner.[17]

From midcentury, however, in both Protestant and Catholic countries,
responsibility for children in need and child protection was increasingly taken
over by nonreligious foundations and the state. For example, in Britain, a series
of acts were passed in 1872, 1897, and 1908 whose effect was to limit wet-
nursing, informal adoption, and infanticide. In 1883, a Liverpool Society for
the Prevention of Cruelty to Children was established and incorporated as the
National Society for the Prevention of Cruelty to Children in 1884.[18] Responsibility for poor children and families was shifting away from private religious
charitable and philanthropic organizations.

A similar pattern of state takeover of church initiatives can be observed in
the field of education. For Catholics and Protestants, schooling had been seen

as an important tool of Christianization and conversion since the Reformation. In Catholic Europe and the Americas, religious orders like the Jesuits and the Ursulines had placed the instruction of youth at the heart of their mission. At the end of the eighteenth century, convent schools and Jesuit colleges had increasingly come under threat, but the first half of the nineteenth century saw a revival of the established teaching sister- and brotherhoods and the emergence of new, highly efficient teaching orders, such as the Sacred Heart. Established in 1800 in Paris, by 1865, the order had established schools for girls throughout Europe and in North and South America.[19]

Institutions like the Sacred Heart served primarily to middle-class families. Christians of all denominations also sought to ensure the Christian education of the children of the working class, and their starting point was often a lack of confidence in the ability of working-class parents and families to provide their children with the religious instruction and proper understanding of family life that they needed. In the Protestant world, early efforts often took the form of Sunday or Sabbath schools. Catering to children from families that relied on their earnings during the week, Sunday schools were a flexible and adaptable form that proved highly effective in reaching working-class children. In the 1830s in England and Wales, there were about one million children attending Sunday schools, rising to two million by 1850. Sabbath schools proved equally successful in the United States, appearing even in pioneer communities such as Central City, Colorado, where three hundred children were attending Baptist, Congregationalist, and Methodist Sabbath schools in 1866. In the rural south, Sabbath schools were established on some plantations, going against the widely held belief that slaves should not be educated. Thus, Anne Clay, a Presbyterian living near Savannah, established a ministry for slaves nearby, where children memorized scripture, sang hymns, and received oral catechism lessons.[20] The appeal of Sunday schools was clearly due in part to the opportunities they offered for learning to read and write for children who would otherwise not have been able to learn. But for those who established them—whether middle-class philanthropists or working-class believers—the primary objective was the dissemination of religious models of behavior and spiritual values.

Religious objectives were also to the fore in the establishment of the weekday elementary schools, which began to spring up all over Europe and North America at the beginning of the century, under the aegis of churches, religious orders, and religious associations. In the Netherlands in 1784, the Society for the General Good, inspired by an active Christianity, was established to extend elementary schooling. In France, the Frères des Ecoles Chrétiennes were responsible for setting up a network of elementary schools, and in Orthodox Russia, by 1807, the schools of the Holy Synod were serving 24,107 children. In Britain, the National Association for the Promotion of the Principles of the Established Church was established in 1811, and denominational rivalry with the British and Foreign Schools Society (founded in 1814 and catering primarily to nonconformists) played a part in fueling the expansion of schooling for the working class.[21]

Throughout Europe, religious associations were taking the first steps toward the creation of networks of elementary schools for the working class. Their successes were soon recognized by national governments, and religious objectives merged with a concern to develop notions of citizenship and to educate the workforce, as governments sought to build on the infrastructure set up by religious organizations. Thus, in Denmark, laws passed in 1814 that established compulsory schooling in rural areas expressed their aim as being "to form them into good, law-abiding people, in accordance with the teachings of the evangelical Christian religion, as well as to bring them the skills and proficiencies which are necessary for them to be useful citizens of the state."[22] Even where states had taken the initiative in developing elementary schooling, religious objectives might still be prominent. In Prussia, where schooling had been compulsory since 1763, Frederick William III intended that his schools should produce good Christians as well as good citizens of the state.

The advantages of religious instruction, which placed heavy emphasis on obedience and order, were clearly apparent to many in positions of authority. And at midcentury, religious educational establishments throughout Europe won additional support in the wake of the 1848 revolutions. Attributing the unrest of that year to the work of unruly secular schoolteachers, the governments of France and the German states lent their support to the schools established by the Catholic Church and Protestant denominations, and to conservative religious curricula. Thus, in Württemberg in 1854, a ministerial decree proclaimed that seminaries for the training of teachers should focus on religious education and practical teaching skills (rather than aspiring to dangerous intellectual instruction), underlining the importance of piety and acceptance of the social status quo.[23]

In the United States, none of the states retained any kind of established church by 1833. The result was that the emerging network of public elementary schools were less clearly denominational than their European counterparts and tended to cultivate a new kind of secular republican morality rather than to emphasize religious teaching.[24] In fact, despite the postrevolutionary reaction, the same trend was evident in Europe from the 1860s on. The second half of the century saw the gradual supplanting of religious elementary schools and often increasingly fierce conflict between church and state over the supply of education. In France, laicization began in the 1880s, and religious instruction in the network of state-funded and -staffed elementary schools was replaced with instruction in *morale laïque*. In Italy, a network of municipal, secular schools was established between 1859 and 1861. In England, the schools of the National Society and the British and Foreign Schools Society were increasingly sidelined as nondenominational board schools multiplied. By the end of the nineteenth century, the religious orientation of elementary instruction had been significantly reduced, and the secular state had largely taken over the education of working-class children.

RELIGION IN PRACTICE

It is clear that church-based philanthropic and educational initiatives ensured that the religious models of family life, central to nineteenth-century conceptions of gender and the family, were widely disseminated as ideals. It is more difficult to trace the ways in which faith and religion shaped experience and identity. However, evidence from folklorists, memoirs, and correspondence clearly suggests that religious rituals and festivals did frame family life and leisure and play a part in defining childhood.

As suggested, nineteenth-century conceptions of domesticity meant the home was considered a sanctuary from the secular world and that religious practices once part of community and public worship were increasingly shifted into the home. Over the course of the century, religious rituals gained prominence in shaping the rhythm of family life. Domestic practices were imbued with religious significance. Thus, dinner—increasingly the main meal in the middle-class household and bookended by the saying of grace—acquired a new significance as the focus of familial conviviality. Among Jewish families, keeping a kosher kitchen had previously been associated only with certain high holy days, but, from the 1830s, it was increasingly practiced as part of everyday family life. For Protestant families in the United States, Sunday acquired new importance as a family day. Sunday schools had placed children at the center of Sunday religious observance, and the association of Sundays with male community activities was weakened. Religious rituals also gave shape to the year. Over the course of the century, Christmas lost its community function and became a family festival, with a range of special foods and practices celebrating the family and home.

Catholic, Jewish, and Protestant ceremonies and rituals were also important markers of stages in the process of growing up, often signaling changes in civil and community status. Infant baptism—especially central for Catholics—marked the child's appearance in the world and cemented their belonging to the family, as increasingly Christian names were chosen that underlined the continuity of the line. In Jewish families, *bris*—or circumcision—was now relocated from the synagogue to the home, underlining that participation in the faith community happened via the family.[25]

For older children in Catholic countries, first communion was an important moment. It was frequently around the time that middle-class children began to prepare for communion that they were first sent to school. In France, it was common for communion (usually prepared between the ages of ten and twelve in bourgeois families) to mark the start of a young girl's formal education.[26] In Catholic communities, over the course of the century, first communion was increasingly associated with the transition into what was becoming known as adolescence, and the increasingly elaborate ceremonies, with the young girls dressed in bridal white, gave visual representation to the emphasis placed on girlhood innocence and purity. For peasant and working-class children in Zeeland (the Netherlands), on the other hand, first communion at age twelve marked the transition from school to work, a shift that also marked the moment when young women began to wear adult dress. Among Jewish families, the rite of passage of the bar mitzvah marked a boy's entry into full and responsible participation in the community; in the nineteenth century, the celebrations that accompanied the ceremony became an occasion for the performance of family, underlining its centrality in spiritual life.[27] For Protestants, the key ceremony was confirmation, which tended to take place around the age of fifteen or sixteen. In the area around Neuchâtel in Switzerland, confirmation signaled a raft of changes in the religious and civil status of the young man or woman and, from the beginning of the century, was increasingly associated with entry to the adult world. Confirmands were now permitted to take communion, to become godparents, to bear witness in court, and to enter the militia. For most, confirmation signaled the end of schooling.[28] For Catholics, Protestants, and Jews, entry into full adulthood was finally confirmed through the marriage ceremony.

Religious rituals, then, marked changes in the religious status of young people and were also used to mark transitions in social and civil status. However, new markers were also emerging that began to have equal or greater importance than these ceremonies and that more clearly marked out contemporary perceptions of the stages of development and the journey toward autonomy. Thus, for middle-class French children, taking the *baccalauréat* or the brevet began to be associated with the transition to adulthood. For those lower down the social scale, conscription to military service was a decisive turning point. In Germany, the *Abitür* came to have the same function for middle-class boys. At the same time, the psychological and medical literature was attempting to define the stages of individual development scientifically, eschewing the traditional cultural markers. By the end of the century, while religious rituals continued to play a part in family life and to hold spiritual and emotional importance for many young people, their wider importance was declining.

As well as giving shape to the process of coming of age, religion also played a part in the social life and leisure of the young. At the end of the eighteenth century, the desire to teach children correct religious principles and values fueled a massive expansion in the literature aimed at children. In France, Catholic girls were presented with readers like *La Pieuse Pensionnaire* (1850) or le *Journal de Marguerite* (1858) and were enjoined to emulate the pious and virtuous girls who peopled them. In the case of the *Journal,* this was more than a passive emulation—readers were intended to follow Marguerite's example and keep a diary, recording their prayers and spiritual progress.[29] In Britain, didactic novels like Mary Sherwood's *The Fairchild Family* (1818), which described how sinful children might learn to be virtuous, sold in their thousands. By the 1830s, the genre had shifted in accordance with changing conceptions of childhood, and Catherine Sinclair's *Holiday House* (1838) was more forgiving of childish naughtiness and inclined to emphasize childish innocence. Children also drew pleasure from adult religious literature. Many nineteenth-century English and U.S. autobiographers recorded how, like the fictional March sisters of *Little Women,* their imagination was fired by John Bunyan's *Pilgrim's Progress;* for working-class readers, who might not have access to many books, the Bible often served as material for learning to read and as a source of stories and adventures. From midcentury, religious writing for children faced stiff competition from the explosion of cheap print: new secular children's periodicals for the middle classes, penny dreadfuls for working-class children. In Britain, the Religious Tract Society (RTS) retaliated by producing the *Boys Own Paper* from 1879, a periodical that included spiritually uplifting—but also exciting—tales and adventures and was selling half a million copies per week by the 1880s. Yet, despite the success of the RTS's publications and others like it, religious authors had clearly lost their dominance in writing for children by the end of the century.[30]

As well sponsoring the pleasures of the imagination, the church and religious calendar also provided opportunities for more active sociability and leisure. As many historians have observed, the church and religious observance was frequently of central importance to working- and middle-class women, providing an important locus for social exchange and entertainment. It performed a similar function for children and young people. In rural societies at the beginning of the century, traditional events like the Ash Wednesday football game between rival parishes common in England, or Saint Catherine's Day dances were social gatherings of considerable importance for young men and women. From midcentury, such traditional—and often rowdy—events were increasingly frowned upon, and more formal social and religious activities were organized. The Young Men's Christian Association was established in 1844 in London (followed by the Young Women's Christian Association in 1866) and spread rapidly. They offered opportunities for rational sociability and sporting activity to young working-class men and women. In Nottingham, from the 1880s, nonconformist, Anglican, and Catholic voluntary workers set up associations for young men and women in the hopes that the safe recreational activities they provided would preserve the young men and women from the dangers of adolescence. In Lyon in the 1860s, middle-class women organized the Month of Mary—a series of feast days to introduce young children to the cult of the Virgin, and, in St. Etienne, *patronages* were established in each parish to provide educational and cultural activities for young people.[31]

Children were not simply passive recipients of such events. The century witnessed an expansion of children's philanthropic activities parallel to the expansion of women's charitable work. In Britain, the Sheffield Juvenile Bible Society, which grew from the efforts of fifteen-year-old Catherine Elliott, may have been the first children's charity in England, and, by the 1840s, the Church Missionary Society's *Juvenile Instructor* was reaching a circulation of up to eighty thousand. In Lyon, in the 1830s, the Société du Saint-Enfant-Jésus, intended to offer support to children in the schools of the Frères des Ecoles Chrétiennes and whose membership was limited to children, had more than three thousand subscribers.[32] Such activities reinforced associations between childhood and Christian virtues and innocence, led to social gatherings and entertainments, and provided children with a rare opportunity to exercise their political and religious voice. By the end of the century, new, secular—or at least less explicitly religious—youth organizations were emerging and challenging the dominance of church associations, but for much of the century, churches of all denominations had been a focal point for the sociability and leisure of both women and children.

BELIEF

Religious rituals and organizations were clearly important elements in the social and cultural life of children and families in the nineteenth century. It is difficult, however, to know how far religious observance, or participation in philanthropic initiatives, reflected sincere belief and faith. Clearly, the church had much to offer beyond devotion and consolation, and the association of religious rituals with secular matters means that it is not always clear that participation in them had spiritual meaning. For example, for Sébastien Commissaire, first communion had little religious significance, and was remembered more for the social embarrassment it occasioned:

> Among Catholics the day of the First Communion is generally a day of celebration; it was not so for me.... All of the other children wore coats of more-or-less fine cloth while I had only a short jacket; their candles were tall and thick, mine was short and thin.... Despite myself, I felt humiliated, I would rather not have been there.

Children were also frequently less malleable than their religious instructors might have supposed. For example, the diary of Mary Lorrain Peters, who attended Grove Hall School in New Haven in the 1830s, records her dispassionate—and guilt-free—observance of the faith of the girls around her bears little relation to the emotionally charged depictions of childish spirituality found in contemporary religious literature.[33]

Yet there is also clear evidence of religious belief among children and their parents. For enslaved children in the United States, religion often provided some consolation when they were faced with family separation; many observers remarked on children taking part in "ring shouts"—ritual prayer dances that were an important religious form for many slaves.[34] Across the denominations, adolescence was also clearly identified with intense religiosity and spiritual feeling. In the United States, the Second Great Awakening saw a particular emphasis being placed on adolescent conversion, and numerous memoirs record powerful experiences of religious awakening, understood as part of the process of growing up. In France, for Catholic girls, the entry into adolescence, often following the powerful moment of first communion, was often associated with religious intensity. At her convent school in Paris in the 1810s, Aurore Dupin (the future George Sand) had a deeply religious phase, briefly considering joining the sisterhood.[35] For Catholic girls, the examples of Bernadette Soubirous, who experienced the vision at Lourdes, and Saint Thérèse of Lisieux offered powerful models of spiritual experience from which many young women drew inspiration. There are also many examples of parents taking their religious responsibilities toward their children very seriously. The correspondence of parents and children in the American West, for example, reveals mothers and fathers attaching sufficient importance to their religious duties that they would find time while traveling on steamboats and wagons to teach children Bible lessons and stories. In England, at the beginning of the century, responses to the death of a child reveal the comfort that some parents found in their faith.[36]

However, the second half of the century also saw an intensification of the masculine shift away from religion. In France, loss of faith was identified by many liberal intellectuals as part of the process of maturation and the point at which sons broke free of their mother's influence and moved to the adult world of manhood.[37] Religious belief was increasingly portrayed as atavistic and condemned as superstition. At the end of the century, modern young women throughout Europe sought to emancipate themselves from the association between faith and femininity. At the same time, analysis of the correspondence of bereaved parents reveals that, by the end of the century, appeals to faith, spiritual consolation, and prayer were no longer dominant in responses to the death of a child; instead, they appeared as just one of a range of possible sources of comfort. Throughout Europe and the United States, by the end of the century, faith and belief had lost their central importance in the experience of family life.

CONCLUSION

Religious models and prescriptions were of central importance to the understanding of family life and childhood in the nineteenth century. They were particularly evident in the ways in which contemporaries understood and disseminated notions of masculinity and femininity. Religious rituals and ceremonies stood at the heart of family life and helped to define child development. Throughout the century, a range of institutions established by churches and religious organizations sought to disseminate these ideals and practices of gender, family, and childhood throughout the wider society, in the process establishing precedents for the development of systems of welfare and education that would eventually be taken over by the nation-state. The second half of the century saw the beginning of this process of institutional secularization and a growing number of challenges to the role of religion in family life. The proliferation of commercial culture and new forms of leisure challenged the near-monopoly of religious organizations over the social and cultural life of children and women; and scientific inquiry promoted new conceptions of childhood development. The decline of religious models and practices should not be exaggerated. At the turn of the century, the vast majority of children in England and France were still being baptized, yet, having been perhaps the defining influence on family life and the experience of childhood at the beginning of the nineteenth century, religion was only one of a range of forces shaping the experiences of young people and their families in 1900.[38]

CHAPTER NINE

Health and Science

RICHARD MECKEL

If we gauge infant and child health during the first decade of life according to the likelihood of contracting a serious disease, acquiring a physical deformity or disability, or dying, then we can state with relative certainty that children in the West were significantly less healthy during the nineteenth century than they are today. Indeed, among the many changes that have transformed childhood in the West over the past two centuries, perhaps the most significant has been a dramatic decrease in the probability of disease, physical incapacitation, or death during the first decade of life. Although data on nineteenth-century levels of disease and incapacitation are rare, what we do have suggests that childhood in that century was far more compromised than it is today by frequent illness, physical discomfort, and disability. Every year uncounted numbers of infants were condemned to lives as partial invalids by congenital deformities and birth trauma. Children who were vision and hearing impaired—from infections or accidents—were common. So too were children whose frames were stunted or twisted from rickets, scoliosis, or tuberculosis or whose hearts had been damaged by bouts with scarlet fever or diphtheria. Also common were children who hobbled around on crutches because of a birth defect, a crippling accident, or because they suffered partial paralysis as a result of poliomyelitis, a disease that began to occur in epidemic form toward the end of the century. Moreover, even those who escaped serious impairment routinely suffered pain and discomfort from a variety of chronic conditions. Among school-aged children, bacterial and parasitic skin infections were close to endemic; discharge from eyes and ear and sinus infections were so unexceptional that they often did not occasion comment; and ongoing mouth and tooth pain from rotting teeth was considered a normal part of childhood. Indeed, records from the periodic dental exams that a number of Western nations began giving school children around the turn of the twentieth century reveal that around eighty percent of those examined had significant dental carries.[1]

Throughout the West, children also faced a significantly higher probability of dying during the nineteenth century than they do today.[2] Although comprehensive mortality records, especially for the first two-thirds of the century, are not abundant, what does exist, along with a half-century of research by historical demographers, allows us to make a number of generalizations about levels and trends. It is probable that in northwestern Europe and North America, roughly 20 percent to 30 percent of all infants born died before they could celebrate their first birthdays and up to 45 percent of all children failed to make it to puberty. In eastern and southern Europe and Central and South America, the rates were considerably higher, with up to 60 percent of all children dying before the age of ten. Today, even in the West's most impoverished and socially disrupted countries, less than 5 percent of all children die in infancy, and less than 7 percent fail to make it to ten. In North America and northern and West Europe, infant mortality has dipped below 0.5 percent and child mortality below 1 percent.[3]

Consonant with this profound improvement in health and survivability, though certainly not the only or even earliest cause of it, has been a dramatic transformation in child health care. Although families, and particularly mothers, continue to be, as they have been for centuries, the primary health care givers of children, their care has been increasingly informed, augmented, and made effective by the proliferation of trained and licensed child health care specialists whose care is situated in institutions and involves medical, surgical, chemotherapeutic, and technological interventions based on biomedical and clinical research. Largely born in hospitals, where the most premature, fragile, or congenitally compromised might spend weeks or months in intensive care units, most twenty-first-century Western children spend their childhoods being periodically examined, occasionally operated upon, and almost always directly or indirectly supervised by professional child health care providers in whose gaze they remain fixed.

INFANTS IN AN INFECTIOUS WORLD

This transformation in child health and health care was part of a long-term *health transition* in the West that has seen life expectancy improve at all ages and infectious disease retreat as the primary killer and disabler of Western humankind.[4] Unlike today, when the young who die do so primarily from congenital problems, degenerative disease, accidents, or violence, the majority of the nineteenth-century young who perished were victims of infectious diseases—either bacterial, viral, or parasitic. For infants, the age group facing the greatest risk of death, a primary danger was infection with a gastroenteric disease. Since at least the early eighteenth century, Western medical observers had commented that infants seemed especially prone to diarrheal diseases and that a particularly virulent strain seemed to proliferate during the warm summer months and carry off large numbers of children in the first year of life. Variously called "summer complaint," "infant thrush," or "disease of the season," it was finally labeled "cholera infantum" by the renowned revolutionary-era American physician, Benjamin Rush, when, in 1877, he published the first systematic description of the disease. As described by Rush and subsequent medical writers, cholera infantum was not only deadly but also frightening to behold. With the onset of the disease, an infant would develop diarrhea that persisted for eight to twelve days. Then it would begin vomiting and, though wracked with thirst, would be unable to retain any liquid. Almost overnight, the infant's body would become emaciated, its belly distended, and its eyes deeply sunk within their sockets. Its skin would lose its resilience and turn ashen and cold. Continuing to vomit and purge, the infant would cry without cessation until it went into convulsions, sank into a coma, and soon after died.[5]

Although the precise cause has never been determined, it seems likely that the disease was bacterial or viral in origin and was probably intensified by malnutrition. One or more strains of *Escherichia coli* bacteria have been suggested as a possible cause, as have bacteria from the *Salmonella* and *Shigella* genera. But it is equally probable that the disease was caused by a virus, perhaps one of the rotaviruses visualized in the 1970s. Whatever the precise cause—and a number may have acted synergistically—infection probably resulted from ingestion of fecal matter containing the pathogen and was transmitted by unclean hands, linen, or bottles or through contaminated milk, water, or food. Moreover, from the clinical descriptions of the disease process, it seems apparent that death resulted from acute electrolytic disturbance and circulatory failure brought about by severe dehydration.[6]

It is difficult to judge whether the summer epidemics of infant gastroenteric disorders increased as the nineteenth century progressed. But it is apparent that they became a prominent feature of urbanization in the West and by all accounts cut a deadly swathe through the urban poor whose ranks proliferated during the century as cities grew dramatically in size and number in both Europe and North America. Indeed, by the second half of the century, summer epidemics of infant gastroenteric disorders had become so commonplace that it was easy for observers of the urban scene to conclude that whatever else cities happened to be, they were for infants, and especially the infants of the urban poor, giant abattoirs in which a large proportion of all those born were slaughtered each summer before they could celebrate their first birthdays. As the *New York Times* editorialized in the summer of 1876, "There is no more depressing feature about our American cities than the annual slaughter of little children of which they are the scene."[7]

Of course, nineteenth-century infants died from many other causes besides gastroenteric diseases. Throughout the century, infectious respiratory diseases, particularly pneumonia, posed a serious threat to infant life, carrying away between 10 percent and 15 percent of all infants who died each year. Additionally, an estimated quarter of all infants who failed to survive their first year did so because of congenital malformations, prematurity, delivery accidents, and other complications of gestation and birth. Yet it was gastroenteric diseases that accounted for the lion's share of nineteenth-century infant deaths, and it was their late-in-the-century decline in incidence, particularly the incidence of the urban summer epidemics, that was hugely instrumental in triggering a contemporaneous decline of infant mortality throughout much of the West. Indeed, the initial late-nineteenth- and early-twentieth-century decline of Western infant mortality would largely be a decline of diarrheal diseases among older infants. It would be several decades before infant mortality from respiratory diseases began a significant decline and over half a century before there was a marked drop in infant deaths from congenital problems.[8]

CHILD DISEASES AND CHILD DEATH

For nineteenth-century children who survived infancy, gastroenteritis continued to represent a threat, but it was one far eclipsed by the threat posed by a gamut of other potentially fatal infectious diseases. In addition to periodic epidemics of cholera and, in the Americas, yellow fever plus the endemic nineteenth-century killer, tuberculosis, that gamut included dangerous respiratory infections like influenza, bronchitis, croup, and pneumonia, as well as the so-called infectious childhood diseases. Of these last, the most deadly to nineteenth-century children were whooping cough, measles, scarlet fever, and diphtheria.

Whooping cough, or pertussis, was an infant's and toddler's disease, particularly dangerous to those younger than two years of age. Infection was bacterial and, in the early stages of the disease, highly transmissible through airborne droplet. Initially showing symptoms of a common cold accompanied by a dry, rasping cough, an infected child would eventually develop a high fever, be seized by paroxysms of coughing and vomiting, and quickly lose weight and strength. If the child survived this middle stage of the disease—and many did not, either because they died from the disease itself or, in their weakened state, contracted a secondary infection like bronchopneumonia—they entered a slow convalescent period that could last several weeks. Although not eliciting the public concern of the more epidemic childhood diseases, whooping cough was almost as deadly, and remained so throughout the century. In mid-nineteenth-century London, only scarlet fever killed more of the young, and in the late-nineteenth-century United States, only diphtheria did.[9]

Measles, another infectious disease that was a major killer of nineteenth-century children, also elicited less public concern than its deadliness should have warranted. This is probably because for children who are well nourished and generally healthy and are robust enough and lucky enough to avoid a number of possible complications, the disease is discomforting but not deadly. However, for the malnourished and for those living in crowded and unsanitary conditions, the disease was often fatal. Not surprisingly, then, the highest rates of measles mortality in the nineteenth century were among the children or the urban, industrial poor and among those living in foundling homes and other congregate institutions. Measles was also more deadly among "virgin populations"; that is, populations that had never or not recently been exposed to the disease. Hence, as had been true in the sixteenth through the eighteenth centuries, epidemics of measles in the nineteenth century that flashed through isolated rural populations or through unexposed indigenous populations, like the Aborigines of Australia, tended to be more fatal than outbreaks that occurred in towns and cities where the disease had become endemic.[10]

If whooping cough and measles did not occasion much public concern, scarlet fever—or "scarlatina," as it was often called—certainly did. In 1860, the British medical journal, the *Lancet,* called it the "most dreaded" of the childhood diseases and noted that both health professionals and parents considered it the deadliest and most communicable of all the infections to which children were vulnerable. Striking equally at all classes, it could and did often ravage families, killing over half of the children and physically impairing those who survived. During the third quarter of the century, when it was at the height of its virulence, it caused some ten thousand deaths per year in England and Wales and was the leading killer of young children throughout Europe and North America.[11]

An acute infectious disease, scarlet fever is caused by Group A beta hemolytic streptococci, the bacteria that also cause strep throat. It is characterized by the sudden onset of swollen glands, a sore throat, and a high fever, followed within a few days by the sandpapery reddish rash that gives the disease its name and is a reaction to the erythrogenic toxins the bacteria release. During convalescence, the affected skin will often peel, a process known as desquamation. In severe cases, if the patient is not treated with antitoxins and/ or antibiotics, the erythrogenic toxins can accumulate and remain circulating in the body, potentially leading to rheumatic fever, kidney disease, and other possibly fatal or disabling complications. Indeed, in the nineteenth century, serious complications were almost as feared as the disease itself and were often represented in fiction depicting family life. For instance, in what may be the saddest moment in the immensely popular 1868 U.S. novel *Little Women,* by Louisa May Alcott, one of the daughters, who seems to be recovering from scarlet fever, develops rheumatic fever and ultimately dies of congestive heart failure. Less serious complications also attended the disease. Perhaps one of the most common in this era before effective chemotherapy was caused by toxins remaining in the body and producing a spasmodic condition of the face and extremities known as Saint Vitus' dance.[12]

Present in Europe and North America as a relatively mild disease in the seventeenth and eighteenth centuries, scarlet fever seems to have mutated into a much more virulent infection in the middle third of the nineteenth century, becoming the source of a series of deadly epidemics that raged through European and North American cities and small towns from the 1850s through the 1890s. Although more deadly to children under six than school-aged children, these epidemics were made visible when they raced through school systems and were greatly feared and talked about throughout Europe and North America as school epidemics. In a much-publicized U.S. example, a scarlet fever epidemic swept through Charleston, South Carolina, in 1881. Health authorities subsequently defined the epidemic as beginning when first one and then several children at a single school presented the telltale symptoms that signal the onset of the disease. Within a few weeks, the disease had spread to children at almost all the schools in the racially segregated system and ultimately claimed the lives of 117 victims while leaving scores of others physically impaired.[13]

Beginning in the late 1880s, scarlet fever seemed to mutate again, gradually evolving into a less virulent form. With that evolution came a drop in child deaths from the disease, a development which, by the turn of the century, was being noted on both sides of the Atlantic. At first it was not clear whether this was a temporary epidemic ebb or a permanent change, but, by the second decade of the twentieth century, most Western health officials could agree with the assessment of Britain's Arthur Newsholme that "Scarlet fever has undoubtedly become a much milder disease. Such terrible cases as I saw in the period of 1881–90 now seldom occur."[14]

Joining and eventually displacing scarlet fever as the most dreaded children's disease of the nineteenth century was diphtheria, an illness caused by a bacillus that usually lodges in the throat, where it can remain for weeks producing little more than minor soreness. In some cases, however, the bacteria multiply and launch an attack on the throat tissue that produces a leathery "pseudomembrane" that can grow thick enough to block the airway and cause death by strangulation. Also deadly is the virulent toxin that the bacteria produce. Causing

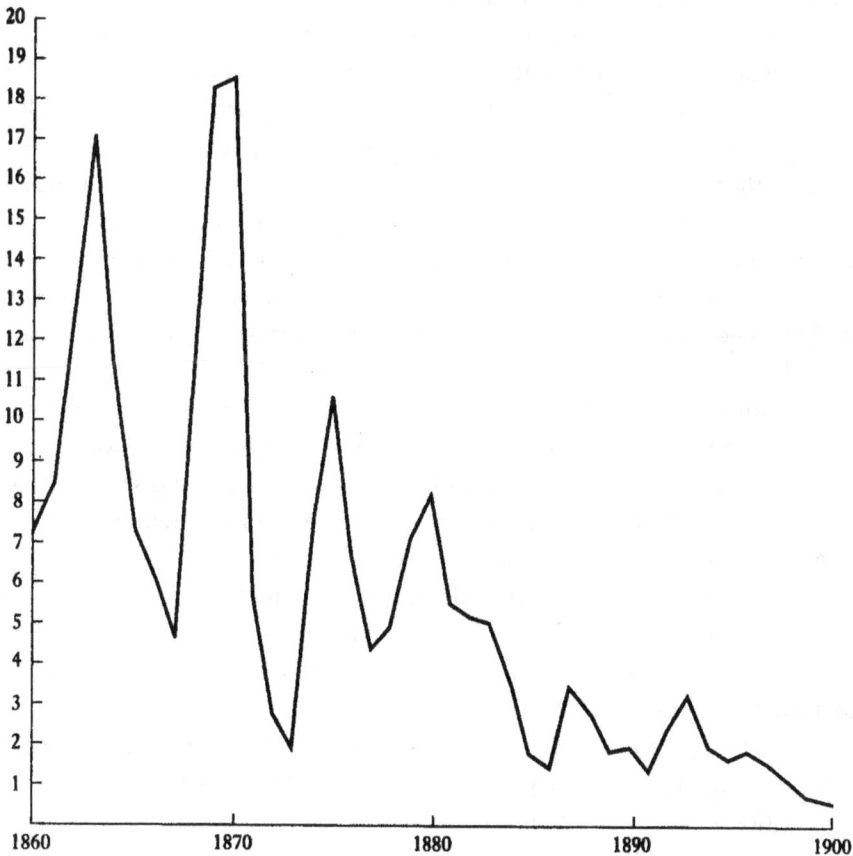

FIGURE 9.1: Scarlet fever deaths in London, 1860–1900, per ten thousand population, from *Epidemic Streets: Infectious Diseases and the Rise of Preventive Medicine,* by Ann Hardy, p. 57 (1993). By permission of Oxford University Press.

high fever, it attacks nerve and muscle tissue, doing damage severe enough to cause death or lifelong incapacitation. Difficult to diagnose because of its various presentations, diphtheria was often confused with septic sore throat and whooping cough or classified as a complication of measles or scarlet fever, even after it was identified as a distinct disease entity in the 1820s.[15]

As was true with scarlet fever, a more virulent and deadly strain of diphtheria seems to have emerged in the middle third of the nineteenth century and was responsible for a number of increasingly severe epidemics in Europe and North America from the late 1850s through the beginning of the twentieth century. With an even higher case fatality rate than scarlet fever, diphtheria came to be greatly feared for the number of child deaths it could cause in a relatively short period. During a few months in 1876, for instance, when it was epidemic in New York City, the disease claimed over one thousand victims, most of whom were children. Indeed, although diphtheria killed people of all ages, by far its most numerous victims were the young. Of the 3,264 people reported as dying from diphtheria in the state of Michigan during the years 1876 through 1879, three thousand or 92 percent were under the age of fifteen.[16]

Diphtheria also provoked considerable fear because its symptomatology and mode of transmission seemingly defied logic, a consequence, some historical epidemiologists suggest, of the simultaneous existence of three types of the diphtheria-causing bacilli, each of which produces different sets of symptoms and complications. Some cases were mild and presented as little more than a sore throat, while others were deadly and showed the full panoply of symptoms. Although increasingly considered a contagious disease, it did not appear to act like one, because its contraction seemingly did not require contact with an infected person or object. Yet neither did it act like a filth disease. Though widely believed to be nurtured by insanitation and transmitted by sewer gas, it often failed to be kept at bay by hygienic measures, whether personal or domestic. It appeared to afflict both the wealthy and the poor and found its way into families devoted to hygiene as often as it did into families where hygiene was a stranger. Indeed, even the most informed and careful parents seemed powerless to protect their children, a point tragically underscored in 1883 when diphtheria claimed the life of seven-year-old Ernst Jacobi, whose father, Abraham, was widely considered one of the Western world's leading authorities on the hygienic prevention of the disease.[17]

The symptomatology and transmission of diphtheria remained in some dispute even after the bacillus causing it was identified in 1883 and laboratory and field techniques were developed in the 1890s to collect and analyze cultures taken from the throats of those suspected of being infected. The increasing use of culturing and laboratory analysis to distinguish the infected and contagious from the noninfected and noncontagious revealed the widespread presence of the bacillus in the throats of those who showed no symptoms of the disease. Nevertheless, during the 1890s, the use of effective detection techniques, combined with development and dissemination of an antitoxin that countered many of the disease's most destructive consequences, and the probable mutation of the disease into a less virulent form seem to have initiated a sharp downward trend in death from the disease that was made permanent by the development of an effective vaccine in the 1920s.

WORMS, BUGS, AND POOR NUTRITION

Less-fatal infectious diseases, often caused by parasites, along with a number of nutritional disorders also compromised the health of nineteenth-century children. In cities, and especially among poor children who shared beds, had less than perfect hygiene, and generally lived on top of each other, head lice infection was near universal. In rural areas, many children sported the telltale circular patch of bumpy skin of the fungi-caused ringworm. In warmer climates, where it was common to go about barefoot, children were often infected with intestinal worms. Some of these, like pinworms, caused itching and discomfort but rarely did serious harm. Others, most notably hookworm, could and did damage the health of large numbers of children, particularly in southern Europe, the U.S. South, and Latin America. Contracted from soil, contaminated food, and even though mother's breast milk, hookworm infection, when it progressed far enough, could cause severe anemia and nutrition-impairing intestinal inflammation. This latter was of especial concern, because the disease was most common among the rural poor, whose nutritional intake was already insufficient. After turn-of-the-century school-child testing showed infestation was widespread in the U.S. South, a Rockefeller campaign was mounted to eradicate the disease through improving local sanitation. In subsequent decades, Rockefeller money also helped fund an international campaign to eliminate the disease in Latin America.[18]

The health of nineteenth-century children was also frequently compromised by nutritional disorders. Among the more common specific nutritional diseases was rickets, a vitamin D deficiency disorder involving a softening of the bones and resulting in increased fractures; bowed legs; knocked knees; and pelvic, spinal, and cranium deformities. Nineteenth-century social reformers frequently described the twisted children of the urban poor and observed that even the healthy ones looked stunted compared to the children of the better-off classes. Their observations had merit. Especially in Europe, urban slums were hives of rachitic children, and, according to anthropomorphic studies done late in the century, urban poor children grew up to be shorter and less robust than their rural or better-off counterparts.[19]

A WORLD OF VARIABLE RISK

While all children in the West were at risk of contracting and dying from these and other diseases, they were not equally so. More than anything else, variation of risk characterized the disease experience of nineteenth-century Western children. There are many reasons for this, but a central one is that, in the infectious world they inhabited, navigating through childhood involved nineteenth-century children in a complex interaction between themselves and their immediate disease environment, an interaction whose outcome was dependent on a number of variables. Children who successfully made it to puberty either avoided exposure, resisted infection, or survived the diseases they contracted. Avoidance of exposure was dependent on how prevalent pathogens were in a child's immediate environment and the likelihood of coming into contact with those who were infected. Resistance was dependent on acquired immunities and general robustness, both of which were dependent on such variables as past exposure, artificial immunization (in the case of smallpox), nutrition, and freedom from other disease. Surviving the disease also heavily depended on general robustness, along with age or level of development and virulence, not only of the disease but of the particular strain of the disease. As was the case with scarlet fever and diphtheria, diseases evolved over time, gaining or losing virulence.

The complexity and variability of the interaction between nineteenth-century children, their nutrition, and their disease environment can be partially illustrated by focusing on a single national setting: that of the United States. Although national-level U.S. vital records do not exist for all but the end of the century, historical demographers, by examining local records, creatively manipulating census data, and employing complementary measures such as stature, have been able to construct a broad outline of health and mortality in nineteenth-century United States that is detailed enough to adumbrate some of the ways that the critical interaction between children's nutrition, physical robustness, and disease environment varied over time, place, and population. For instance, it is probable that the interaction changed significantly during the second quarter of the century as early urbanization, industrialization, and immigration broke down spatial barriers to disease transmission and increased the incidence of infectious disease among U.S. children. That this came at the same time that changes in the production, marketing, and distribution of food were making nutrients less available to children of the lower strata may have contributed to what anthropometric historians have shown was a decline in stature among lower- and middle-class males born in the 1820s, 1830s, and 1840s.[20]

It is also probable that the health and survival of urban infants and children declined significantly over the middle third of the century as the influx of rural Americans and foreign immigrants into the nation's cities dramatically increased insanitation and overcrowding. Evidence suggests that morbidity and mortality was highest among the children of the impoverished newcomers. Yet, as studies of both midcentury Boston and Pittsburgh show, it was not dramatically so.[21] One reason for this is that, in an era before the horse car, both the prosperous and the poor tended to live close to the city core and thus experienced the same general environmental conditions. Another is that, unlike today, higher income did not allow families greater access to effective medical care, because little, if any, such effective medical care existed.

As well as varying over time, the health and survival of nineteenth-century U.S. infants and children varied according to family size, type of community, region, and population group. According to a study based on a national sample of households matched from midcentury census manuscript schedules, children in larger families tended to get sick more frequently and die more often than those in smaller families. This was probably because more children increased the likelihood that disease would be introduced into the family. Similarly, the urban young faced a heightened risk of exposure to potentially fatal disease. In the study sample, infants and children living in larger cities were twice as likely to die as their counterparts in small towns and established rural areas. Region also determined risk, though, surprisingly, despite its concentration of cities and industrial towns, the Northeast was not the least healthy. Rather, as seems to have been true in Canada, South America, and Australia, the least healthy region for infants and children was the frontier—most likely because conditions were primitive, nutrition poor, and sanitation bad. Over 21 percent of children aged one to four died, while another 25 percent to 30 percent died in infancy.[22] Moreover, it was not just the infants and children of settlers for whom the American frontier proved deadly in the middle decades of the nineteenth century. It was also deadly for the young of the indigenous peoples of the plains and western tribes who came in increasing contact with white Americans after 1840. In an ecological disaster replicated in other frontier nations, increasing contact brought disruption and destruction of the tribes' food supplies and exposure to new diseases. As a consequence, in the decades of expanding contact, the often nutritionally compromised indigenous populations were ravaged by a number of epidemics that cut a deadly swathe through their young.[23]

Infancy and childhood were also particularly deadly for another population of U.S. children whose social condition was drastically different than that of most of the young in the West. These were slave children. Although the health and longevity of nineteenth-century adult slaves on the North American continent were far better than that of their counterparts in the Caribbean and compared favorably with that of working-class adults in Europe, the risk of disease and death faced by their children was remarkably high. Indeed, mining the generally detailed vital records kept by slave owners, historians have constructed a picture of slave infancy and childhood that shows it to have been particularly deadly, with thirty-five percent of all those born dying before age one, forty-eight percent before age five, and fifty-seven percent before age fifteen. Why this was so again demonstrates the intersection between nutrition and disease environment that determined the health and survival of nineteenth-century children. Forced to return quickly to work after birth, slave mothers had to substitute artificial or mixed feeding for breast-feeding, which compromised the nutrition of their infants and increased their risk of contracting and dying from gastroenteritis or diarrhea. Moreover, children who survived infancy faced a childhood of poor nutrition and high risk of disease. Slave workers were fed in the fields and received relatively nutritious meals. Not so their children, whose diet seems to have consisted in large part of hominy and fat. As a consequence, slave children were nutritionally disadvantaged and thus less able to resist and survive infectious disease. Plantation records show that slave children were shorter and lighter than their free counterparts and caught up in stature only after they became field workers.[24]

HEALTH CARE IN THE FAMILY
AND BEYOND

If the disease experience of nineteenth-century children varied significantly across time, place, type of locale, race, family size, and a host of other variables, it remained constant in one respect. Their fundamental dependency meant that children who became ill had to be cared for by others. Throughout the century, the vast majority of that care was provided in the home by family members, particularly mothers. But in the latter half of the century, families faced with an acutely ill child would also increasingly call in a family physician or take the child to one of the free-standing dispensaries and children's hospitals that were beginning to be established in urban areas. This turn toward physician-provided care was less the consequence of medicine developing theory and practice distinctly effective in preventing and curing childhood ills than the medical profession casting its gaze on children and assuming for itself a cultural authority that increasingly lent its prescriptions on child health care more weight than popular, folk, and traditional ones.[25]

At the beginning of the nineteenth century, physicians were rarely direct participants in the health care of infants and children. Most women gave birth in the home with the aid of family members, neighbors, and perhaps a midwife. Moreover, in those rare instances when a physician was called to attend, it was almost never expected or desired that he would continue to care for either mother or child. Child health care was a family responsibility, most often directed by mothers who dosed their young with home-prepared nostrums and employed therapies and disease management learned from their mothers or passed down as part of family oral tradition. The literate might also consult carefully preserved family "receipt" or "recipe" books,

FIGURE 9.2: Mrs. Alexander Farmer (1825–1869), *An Anxious Hour*, 1865. Victoria and Albert Museum. Oil on panel. Copyright V & A Images. Throughout the century, mothers were the chief caretakers of sick children.

compilations of formulas and directions jotted down over the years and generations for everything from dressing cuts and burns to curing leather. Toward the middle of the century, such recipe books could also increasingly be purchased, as publishers recognized that there was a market for domestic guidebooks among the expanding literate classes.[26]

Outside of crowded urban areas, most families had herb gardens, and family caregivers drew on tradition and recorded recipes to concoct a wide variety of tonics, elixirs, poultices, and dressings to treat the various illnesses of childhood. In rural France, red poppy mixtures were favored for calming the spasms accompanying whooping cough. In the English countryside, a popular cure for earache was a heated shallot placed in an ear and wrapped with flannel. Almost everywhere, infusion of black alder was employed as a laxative, and laudanum, a resin from rockroses, was used to treat coughs and colds.[27] Such herbal therapies were also often accompanied by resort to prayer or magic. In a world where faith and folk belief held powerful sway, parents regularly prayed to and even bargained with God when a child fell ill, sought the intercession of saints, or employed various magic talismans and potions.

What family caregivers could not find in their gardens or the nearby woods, they purchased from apothecaries and traveling druggists who stocked and sold a large variety of powders, syrups, and ointments. In the second quarter of the century, mass-produced patent medicines also became available. Often alcohol and opiate conflations, they were advertised in the burgeoning collection of popular magazines aimed at women or hawked by individual itinerant salesman at medicine shows. A number of these claimed to cure or help manage most or all of the childhood diseases. Hopper's Elixir, for instance, advertised itself as the safest and most effective remedy for whooping cough and other respiratory diseases, as well as for fever, colds, poor appetite, and all the other common ailments of childhood. Also apparently popular were tonics designed to quiet colicky babies and, in general, to make infants more docile and manageable. Among these were the suggestively named Mother's Helper and Infants Quietness. But the most popular, especially in urban areas, was Godfrey's Cordial, a mixture of opium, sassafras, brandy or rectified spirit, caraway seed, and treacle. A midcentury investigation of infant mortality in Manchester, England, reported that five out of six working-class families used it habitually.[28]

Although family members provided most of the care for children, they did not provide all. Especially in cases of acute illness, or when parents felt incapable of handling an injury or ailment, they would seek the assistance of someone in the community. This might be a midwife or other woman known for her skill in nursing. Or it might be a botanic, empiric, or faith healer. But only rarely and at last resort would it be a regular physician. Early-nineteenth-century parents rarely, if ever, employed physicians to attend their sick children for a variety of reasons, not the least which was the aggressive therapeutics then in vogue. Between the mid-eighteenth and mid-nineteenth centuries, the vast majority of regular physicians in the West favored bold or "heroic" therapeutics that were designed to restore the morbidly animated patient to a healthy state through the use of such aggressively depletive procedures as bloodletting, blistering, and using calomel and emetics to induce purging and vomiting. Most parents considered these procedures too harsh and dangerous for children and acquiesced to their use only if all else failed.[29]

Yet if early-nineteenth-century parents shunned physician's services, they did not shun their counsel. Continuing a trend that had begun in the latter part of the eighteenth century, nineteenth-century Western parents increasingly purchased or consulted an ever-expanding body of physician-authored child health care advice. Much of this advice was contained within general family health guides, like William Buchan's *Domestic Medicine* (1769), a work that went through scores of reprintings and is said to have been only slightly less ubiquitous than the Bible in early-nineteenth-century British and U.S. homes.[30] Advice was also produced by a small but expanding group of physicians, many of them male midwives, who were defining themselves as experts in early infant and child nurture and were producing health guides concerned with the care and feeding of the young. Two prominent examples—both of which went through several reprintings and were frequently paraphrased or excerpted verbatim in almanacs, broadsheets, and cheap pamphlets—were Michael Underwood's *A Treatise on the Diseases of Children, With Directions for the Management of Infants from Birth,* published in London 1784, and Christoph Wilhelm Hufeland's *Guter Rath an Mütter und Kindswärterinnen über die wichtigsten Punkte der physischen Erziehung der Kinder in den ersten Jahren,* which came out in Berlin in 1799. Although books on children's diseases had been produced as early as the sixteenth century, this literature represented a new phenomenon and reflected Western medicine's discovery of children, their bodies, and their ailments. Claiming to be motivated by statistical documentation of high rates of infant and child mortality, prepared for the task by their experiences as staff physicians in recently established foundling hospitals and other congregate child institutions, and inspired by the discovery of the child by social theorists like John Locke and Jean-Jacques Rousseau, European physicians had begun in the mid- and late eighteenth century to bring infants and children under the medical gaze. And in so doing, they laid the foundations not only for modern pediatrics but also for what is now a two hundred and fifty–year tradition of parents consulting physician-authored manuals for everything from information on nutrition and development to assistance in determining whether a fever might be signaling the onset of serious disease.[31]

Through the early decades of the nineteenth century, published research and advice on the diseases and care of infants and children increased significantly and even came to include the fetus in 1827, when Hufeland published a treatise on diseases *in utero*. Yet the care and treatment of infants and children was not yet, as it is today in most Western countries, conceived of as a separate and discrete area of medicine, distinct from obstetrics and the diseases of women. Almost all of the eighteenth- and early-nineteenth-century writers on what came to be known as pediatrics were male midwives whose interest in the care and management of the young was an extension of their interest in the reproductive process. When taught at all in medical schools, the care of the young was almost always covered in courses on obstetric theory and practice. Indeed, prior to the last quarter of the nineteenth century, there were only two Western professorships in pediatrics: one held by Frederick Theodore Berg at the Karolinska Institute in Stockholm and the other held by Abraham Jacobi at New York Medical College. Breaking from obstetrics and establishing a distinct identity was thus necessary for pediatrics to emerge as a specialty. This happened slowly, unevenly, and in some cases only partially, occurring first and most completely in Germany, Austria, the Scandinavian countries, and North America. In France, the separation came in the twentieth century, and, in England, it occurred only partially in that both pediatrics and obstetrics remained part of general practice.

Serving to encourage the separation of pediatrics and obstetrics and bring the health and health problems of infants and children into sharper focus within the nineteenth-century medical gaze was the founding of children's hospitals after 1850. Although the first children's hospital—the Hôpital des Enfants Malades—opened in Paris in 1802, it was not until fifty years later, with the establishment of the Hospital for Sick Children in Great Ormond Street, London, that the rest of the West began to follow suit. Within the next three decades, children's hospitals were opened in major cities in North America and on the Continent. These institutions allowed a small but significant number of physicians to gain considerable clinical experience diagnosing, treating, and managing children; and, more importantly, enabled a new generation of pediatric text writers to base their works on clinical observation of large numbers of patients. Charles West, the eminent English pediatrist who helped found the hospital on Great Ormond Street, used his experiences there in producing the many revisions of his widely used and much-respected *Lectures on the Diseases of Infancy and Childhood*. Similarly, in writing his popular 1869 textbook, *Treatise on the Diseases of Infancy and Childhood*, American Job Lewis Smith (1827–1897) drew heavily on his observations as an attending physician in the children's wards of Bellevue Hospital and as a consulting physician to the New York Infant Hospital.[32]

By the 1880s, enough physicians had begun to consider themselves experts in child health that local and regional pediatric associations were being founded in most Western countries, while in Germany (1883), Russia (1885), and the United States (1888), national organizations were also formed. To a certain extent, the late-nineteenth-century emergence of pediatrics can be understood as the product of a general trend in Western medicine toward specialization and in Western society toward professionalism. But it can also be seen as part of a profound change in Western attitudes toward children. By the end of the century, most Westerners had come to consider children and childhood in developmental terms. What made children distinct from adults, and what determined their capabilities and responses to stimuli, was

FIGURE 9.3: *Hospital for Sick Children*, circa 1856. Wood engraving. An etching of Drs. Charles West and William Jenner examining a child in the great ward of the Great Ormond Street Hospital for Children.

that they were developing organisms. For physicians, this view gave logic to abandoning the long-accepted idea that children's diseases were distinct from adult diseases and replacing it with one that located difference in the developing patient's response to disease. As the eminent Austrian pediatrician Theodore von Escherich explained to a U.S. audience, "If the diseases of childhood show such great difference in their number and in the form of their manifestation, as well as in the course of their termination, this can only be due to the fact that between the growing organism of the child and that of the completely developed adult, great differences exist in the reaction called forth by the disease process variations, which change constantly in the course of childhood."[33]

The developmental concept of children and childhood disease also encouraged other emerging specialties, as well as medicine in general, to look more closely at childhood as the source of adult health problems, thus giving medical imprimatur to both the age-old aphorism "the child is the father to the man" and the Romantic conception of maturation as degeneration. Hence, where early-nineteenth-century alienists had considered insanity an exclusively adult disease, their late-nineteenth-century counterparts, especially those in the emerging specialty of neurology, often found cause in childhood disease, trauma, or damaging behavior, such as masturbation or precocious learning. Similarly, during the last third of the century, many medical researchers, most of whom self-identified with the emerging specialty of ophthalmology, conducted scores of studies of North American and European schoolchildren to demonstrate the thesis that adult myopia began in childhood and was due to overtaxing the immature eyes of the young. Indeed, by the turn of the century, even adult pulmonary tuberculosis was being linked to primary infection during childhood.[34]

The notion that adult health was intimately linked to child health also supported an expansion of nineteenth-century child welfare concern to include the physical as well as the moral health of children. Although organized state and philanthropic child hygiene activity would not truly begin until after 1900, by the end of the century, its guiding convictions were already widely accepted. From the pulpit and podium and in the popular and medical press, social commentators of all stripes warned that urban, industrial society was mounting a devastating assault on child health and that the likely consequence would be the degeneration of future adult populations and national efficiency. Among the better-off classes, that assault was said to be taking the form of pressurized urban schooling and life overtaxing the brain, nerves, and eyes. Among the working and impoverished classes, it was described as devolving from unsanitary surroundings, poor nutrition, and too-early entry into the labor force.[35]

PARENTS AND PHYSICIANS

While physicians were discovering children, parents were discovering physicians, in part because in Europe and North America the number of physicians increased significantly in the latter half of the century. This was true not only in the United States, where resistance to licensing and the proliferation of short-term proprietary medical schools combined to produce a mid- and late-nineteenth-century bumper crop of physicians claiming to be formally trained MDs, but also in various parts of Europe, which saw the loosening of formerly strict licensing rules after midcentury. In Germany and Great Britain, for instance, the number of formally recognized irregular and regular physicians increased dramatically after the passage of midcentury licensing reforms. And even in France, the Netherlands, and other areas where the Napoleonic Code strictly defined the qualifications of a doctor of medicine or surgery, the number of physicians also increased substantially in the second half of the century.[36]

The expanding ranks of physicians made them far more available than they had been in the past to families in small towns and rural areas and in the poorer precincts of cities. The small-town or village doctor, respected for his education; the country physician, mobile in horse and buggy; and the urban dispensary doctor all became familiar figures in the latter half of the century. That familiarity, combined with regular medicine's increasing abandonment of heroic measures and its embrace of at least the trappings of the laboratorial sciences, made late-nineteenth-century families much more likely than their early-nineteenth-century counterparts to call in physicians when their children became ill. That physicians still had no effective medicines to treat such illnesses was of little import. For what they had, or what parents assumed they had, was knowledge of how to manage illness and, more importantly, experience and expertise in reading the signs of the course of an illness. When surviving a childhood illness was still widely understood as making it past the climax of an infection, parents employed physicians to help the child "make it through the night" and to interpret the signs of the child's progress. No one better captured this new role of the physician as child attendant and disease interpreter than did the English painter Luke Fildes in his 1891 popular masterpiece, *The Doctor.* Destined to become one of the icons of modern Western medicine, the painting depicts the interior

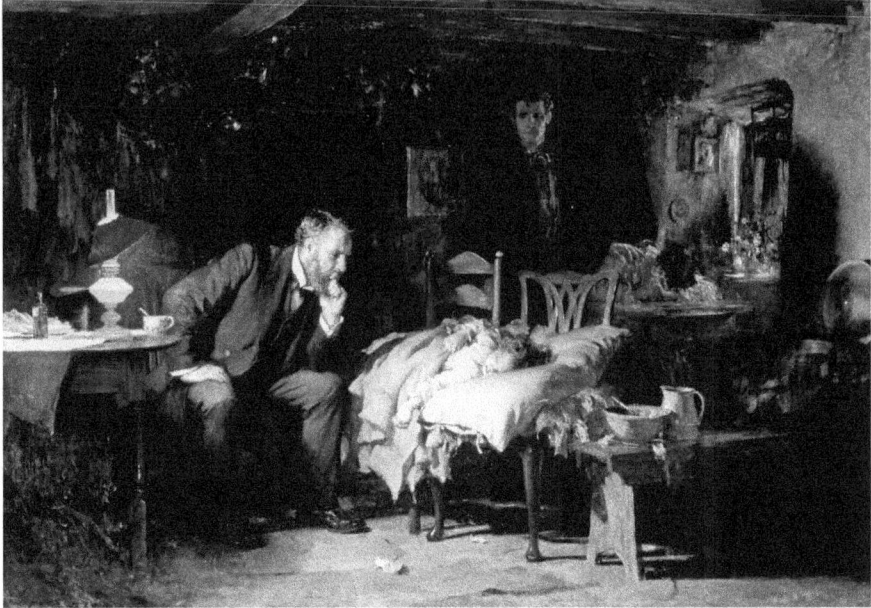

FIGURE 9.4: Luke Fildes (1843–1927), *The Doctor*, 1891. Tate Gallery. Oil on canvas, 65 × 95 in (166 × 242 cm).

of a country cottage, at the center of which is a physician sitting next to a sleeping sick child. It's nighttime or morning before light, and the doctor has the child illuminated with a lamp. He is leaning forward in his chair, intently staring at the child, ready to read the subtlest change in her condition and interpret it for the anxious parents who stand and sit just outside the circle of light.

THE EDGE OF A CENTURY

One would like to think that the child in Fildes's painting survives. Such would be appropriate, for when Fildes painted it, children were not only more likely to see a physician when they became ill, they were more likely to survive their illnesses. These two developments, however, were not causally related—or, to be more accurate, were not *yet* causally related. Although biomedicine, in its contribution to a broad range of public health activities such as identifying and quarantining the sick and purifying urban water supplies, played a significant role in initiating the late-nineteenth-century downward trend of infant and child mortality and morbidity, it had not yet provided medical treatments capable of significantly reducing the likelihood that infancy and childhood would be scarred by disease or ended prematurely by death.

It would not be until the second and third quarters of the twentieth century that physicians would have at their disposal effective fluid and electrolyte therapy to combat acidosis and dehydration in infants; vaccines to provide immunity against traditional killers like pertussis, measles, and polio; sulfonamides and antibiotics to reduce fatalities from bacterial infections; and vitamin and mineral therapies to aid metabolism and combat such childhood scourges as rickets, pellagra, and pernicious anemia. If it was in the nineteenth century that medicine discovered children and child health, it would be in the twentieth century that the beneficial consequences of that discovery would be felt.

CHAPTER TEN

World Contexts

DAVID M. POMFRET

In September 1899 in Hanoi, soon to be anointed capital of "French Indochina," officials at the French High Residency of Tonkin received reports that a child prophet possessing mysterious powers had been discovered in a village in the Vietnamese countryside. Rumors of the child's vast intelligence and miraculous abilities had spread quickly, along with claims that he had been sent from the heavens to become king of Annam. Concern over the growing reputation of the child—a nine-year-old boy named Ly Thanh Long—had led village authorities to banish him, and the boy and his entourage fled to the port town of Haiphong. Here a French agent placed them under discreet surveillance, but just a few days later, as officials in Tonkin scrutinized the agent's reports, the high resident received a request, delivered by an intermediary, that he grant this "sacred, strange, extraordinary child" a personal audience.

Invited to the residence in Hanoi, Ly Thanh Long declared before his bemused interrogators that it was his destiny to become king of Annam and that similarly gifted celestial "brothers" would soon descend from the skies to assume divine leadership of neighboring lands within the French imperial sphere. The impact of these outlandish prophecies was enhanced by the illiterate country child's accompaniment of them with dark mutterings in Chinese. The ability to speak Chinese, which was increasingly rare even among educated Vietnamese by the turn of the century had, according to the boy, been bestowed upon him by the heavens.

The prophecies of the so-called *enfant miraculeux* provoked deep unease among officials, not least for their chilling familiarity. In 1887, just two years after Tonkin had fallen into French hands, another *Ky Dong,* or "miracle child," had emerged from this land. Fluent in Chinese at age eight, the child, believed by those who flocked to visit him to be a reincarnation of the scholar-prophet Nguyên Binh Khiem, had, by age thirteen, emerged at the center of an insurrectionary ferment in the Nam Dinh area. Incredulous French colonial authorities responded by capturing the boy and sending him off to receive a French-style education in Algeria. However, a decade later, in 1897 and only two years before the case of Ly Thanh Long was to come to light, the infamous *Ky Dong* (now in his early twenties and back in Tonkin) began stirring discontent anew in Thai Binh and Yen Thé. The French colonial government took draconian action, sending him into exile in Tahiti. These millenarian maneuverings ensured that rumors of the appearance of a new "sacred child" in the restive outpost of Tonkin were treated with the utmost seriousness.

Although these curious incidents dominated official attention only briefly, the intense interest aroused by the miracle children of Tonkin illuminates powerful and enduring (though little studied) connections between the history of childhood and the history of empire. The significance of such interlinkages resonated well beyond eastern outposts of the rebuilt French empire. They acquired wider significance during a century in which Western imperial expansion transformed relations with the rest of the world—especially after 1870, when a scramble for markets brought large parts of Africa and Asia (including Tonkin, secured by the French in 1885 following a brief war with China) under European rule. As competition for colonies intensified in the 1880s, empire emerged as a key conduit through which non-Western societies encountered and engaged with Western notions of childhood. Children and childhood, moreover, emerged as a core concern in deliberations over how these colonies should be governed.

Focusing mainly upon Britain and France—two European powers with long-standing maritime and imperial traditions and possessing empires that together covered vast areas of the world's land surfaces during this period—this chapter aims to elaborate upon some elements of this rich and complex engagement.

CHILDHOOD AND IDEOLOGIES OF EMPIRE: SUCCESSION AND EMANCIPATION

It is perhaps not surprising that age and empire should have become deeply enmeshed during the nineteenth century, given that a powerful ideology grew up in this period around childhood, which presented it as another new "continent" or frontier to be colonized. Such romantic formulations achieved wide currency in educated circles in Britain during the late eighteenth and early nineteenth centuries, forming part of a complex response to the intellectual ferment of the Enlightenment and to the political tumult ushered in by the French and American Revolutions. As revolutionary upheaval drove European colonial fortunes into temporary decline from roughly 1775 to 1825 (when Britain lost its thirteen colonies, the French lost Haiti, and the Spanish lost America), the mood of introspection that prevailed among political commentators led them to appeal to childhood, as it was contemporaneously reconfigured, in order to articulate a sense of colonial authority in crisis.

In Britain, the world's preeminent imperial power, the setback of losing the American colonies created a climate in which reflections on childhood as a transient, preparatory stage distinct from adulthood, marked by plasticity, took on deeper political significance. An important starting point for such engagements was the series of late-eighteenth-century philosophical studies ascribing childhood and children the status of viable subjects for scientific investigation. These challenged pejorative, counter-Reformation, neo-Augustinian conceptualizations of this life stage as marked by original sin and exalted it instead as evidencing the innate goodness of man.[1] Literary responses to change meanwhile gave expression to powerful assertions of the spiritual qualities of childhood.[2]

Those skeptical about Britain's imperial future drew on portrayals of childhood as a separate, qualitatively different world as a means of questioning the "motherland's" relationship with its colonies and of giving voice to a powerful sense of disillusionment and loss. In his book, *An Inquiry into the Nature and Causes of the Wealth of Nations* (1776), Adam Smith, for example, invoked references to colonies as children to call into question the value of empire for settlement.[3] These themes remained deeply interwoven with discussions of empire in British political circles. Into the 1820s, the radical newspaper, the *Westminster Review,* edited by the anticolonial Jeremy Bentham, harped with some regularity on the theme that, "it is pretty much with colonies as with children."[4] Even as new territories for settlement were acquired, colonizers' early articulations of a nascent sense of national identity continued to inspire a powerful and pervasive sense that such colonies would, like children (and rather unruly and ungrateful ones at that), inevitably go their own way. At a time when global imperialism had yet to be subjected to sophisticated theoretical analysis, then, childhood emerged as a shorthand through which anxieties over empire, and particularly its transience, could be powerfully expressed.

Yet with French continental and colonial ambitions in tatters, the British government contemplated the dawn of an era of commercial and naval dominance, powerfully supported by the advantages of early industrialization. Throughout the century, Britain's imperial reach extended further, over "possessions" in Asia, the Pacific, and Africa (the securing of which was inspired by anticipations of a great Pacific trade for which China would be the hub). The Indian empire, produced by commercial competition between France and Britain and administered by the East India Company until 1858, provided the principal case upon which the British official and political class deliberated over the nature of and justifications for imperial authority.

Solely commercial or strategic justifications for the extension and consolidation of imperial power proved unsatisfactory. The questions remained as to whether the managed exploitation of resources should be accompanied by a paternal genre of governance and whether imperial authority should be legitimated through the conferral of scientific and material progress on subject peoples. The issue of introducing educational and other "improving" institutions came to the fore. In 1813, the Charter Act obliged the East India Company to set aside funds for the education of Indians. During the 1830s, a struggle developed on India's Committee of Public Instruction over whether these funds should be used for the teaching of European science and literature in English. Anglicists, who favored instruction in English, triumphed.

And yet, until the Woods Education Despatch of 1854, restated in 1859 following the imposition of formal Crown control, these tutelary initiatives translated into engagements to "improve" only a narrow stratum of the colony's indigenous elites.[5] Although liberal discourses of empire as improvement proved resilient, the transition to formal colonial rule in India in 1858 ushered in a period marked by declining sympathy for the utilitarian idealism that had inspired these commitments—limited though they were. After education became the province of the government of India, which was answerable to the India Office in London, tentative experiments with the extension of mass vernacular education to the general population lost their impetus. The failure of such schemes was affirmed by the Hunter Commission of 1882.[6]

While anxieties over "paternity" and "succession" continued to inform discussions of whether empire could endure, explicit appeals to the sentimental language of childhood faded from discussions of these possessions. It remained useful, of course, to infantilize subject peoples, through references to them as children. But the radical resonances with which childhood had come to be infused in the first half of the nineteenth century served to devalue it around the middle of the nineteenth century in empire builders' eyes as a paradigm that might be appropriately invoked to affirm imperial relations.

Revolutionaries, radicals, and utopians had built up such interpretive connections from the late eighteenth century, linking childhood to an inspiriting savage innocence. In this form, it came to inform assertions of popular sovereignty and arguments for the abolition of slavery and the extension to Africans of the rights of man. Jean-Jacques Rousseau, notably, in his widely read *Emile* (1762), had ascribed to childhood a key role in the liberation of mankind and presented the condition of childhood and the savagery of "natural man" as mutually interdependent concepts.[7] Other writers, picking up on references to childhood as imbued with a spiritual superiority, inflected this paradigm in radical new directions by emphasizing the links between childhood and society. Advancing abolitionist arguments in his *Observations on the Slave Trade* (1789), the Swedish writer and philosopher Carl Bernhard Wadstrom, for example, referred to Africans as spiritually superior "child peoples." In the same year, the radical William Blake engraved "The Little Black Boy," depicting Africans as spiritualized children deserving of pity.

In the early nineteenth century, writers working in a romantic vein, such as Wordsworth, Lamb, and Coleridge contributed reflections on the "essential child." Though by no means advocates of reform, these writers drew upon a spiritually informed emancipatory ideal of childhood, which Christian reformers and sections of liberal opinion could drawn upon in their (ultimately successful) efforts to galvanize the rising, leisured bourgeoisie into challenging slavery: the British Anti-Slavery society was formed in 1823, and a Slavery Abolition Act followed in 1833. This also informed the growing clamor for the reform of child labor, with the Factory Act of 1833 regulating conditions in textile mills and factories. In 1842, the reports of a royal commission investigated the employment of children, describing "cruel slaving" conditions.

Critiques of imperialism drawn upon the idea of the right of nations to self-determination remained underdeveloped during this period. Nonetheless, through writings such as these, slavery and an exalted childhood threatened to emerge as a mutually galvanic coupling endowed with considerable moral leverage. Readings of colonies and natives as children continued to play through and across a heavily gendered discourse of the East, but advocates of empire building, aware of the potential for such romantic portrayals of childhood to inform internationalist emancipatory projects, were disinclined to extend them to Britain's "second" empire. Willingness to ground colonial rule in explicitly affective, paternal paradigms had begun to fade, even as the

British middle class learned to interpret its imperial ascendancy through the lens of race.

THE NURTURANCE OF "MOTHER FRANCE": CHILDHOOD AND FRENCH COLONIALISM

While the challenges of imperial supremacy prompted British interpretations of empire in austere and unsentimental directions, the political contests driving Britain's continental rivals, and most notably France, toward the acquisition of new colonial outposts in the late nineteenth century encouraged explicit appeals to sentimental ideals of childhood and the modern family. Following the destruction of most of the first French colonial empire, clear demographic, commercial, or political imperatives for empire building had failed to emerge. The subsequent piecemeal acquisition of colonial outposts reflected deep divisions of opinion over the reconstruction of empire. During the first two decades of the Third French Republic's existence, a small but influential colonial lobby, eager to embark upon a rapid program of imperial reconstruction, struggled against conservative dismissals of imperial "adventurism" as irresponsible and colonies as distractions from the emotive quest to recapture Alsace-Lorraine.

With economic justifications for empire alone insufficient to sway a skeptical parliament, enthusiastic deputies linked childhood to the imperial cause. Ideals of civilization, humanity, and progress had long been associated with childhood in emancipatory Republican rhetoric. Republicans committed to a process of rolling back clerical influence at home and predisposed to interpreting their historical-political mission in terms of rescuing children from "backwardness" now extended this perspective to empire in portrayals of colonies and the colonized as children of a nurturing motherland. Among the leading lobbyists for empire was Jules Ferry, who steered a series of reforms secularizing elementary education through parliament and led the campaign for credits necessary to seize Tonkin. A key concern for the French colonial lobby was to fashion a genre of colonialism distinct from both Second Empire precursors and "cold-blooded" (though influential) commercially minded Anglo-Saxon models of empire building. French advocates of empire naturalized imperial bonds through references to childhood. These extended beyond rhetoric alone and were reproduced in the material and visual cultures generated by the colonial presence, in particular, coins, notes, and posters.[8]

Appeals to ideas of childhood malleability permitted colonial theorists to propagate claims that these societies might eventually participate on an

FIGURE 10.1: Honoré Daumier, *La République nourrit ses enfants et les instruit*, 1848.
Musée d'Orsay. This association was also explored in allegorical paintings of *The Republic*,
such as the one submitted in February 1848 by Honoré Daumier, better known at the time
as a popular illustrator, to a competition organized by the Republican government.

equal basis with the French within the same political state while at the same
time deferring this emancipatory "coming of age" to an unspecified moment
in the future. British and Dutch commentators and officials, keen to maintain
the imperial status quo, ventured far more tentatively onto such terrain in the

WHAT WILL HE DO?

The eyes of the world are upon him.—Minneapolis Tribune.

FIGURE 10.2: "What Will He Do? The Eyes of the World Are upon Him," *Minneapolis Tribune,* 1898. Cartoons such as this one articulated the view that the McKinlay administration should add to the United States' overseas colonial empire by portraying the alternative to taking responsibility for extending political tutelage over the Philippines as being akin to throwing a savage child off a cliff.

late nineteenth century. In the United States, by contrast, where elites also struggled with the contradictions of "democratic colonialism," the themes of childhood, savagery, and enslavement featured heavily in popular depictions of Western imperialism as a form of tutelary overlordship.[9]

Lurid reports of children and "child peoples" as victims of indigenous customs equating to slavery reinforced empire builders' claims for colonial rule as a delivery from despotism and savagery. The French Catholic Church, which had a key stake in empire (though one requiring delicate negotiation with a Republican government), played an important role in linking the expansion of French influence with an antislavery rationale. With Germany, France jointly sponsored the West African Conference in Berlin (November 1884 to February 1885). The efforts of Cardinal Charles Lavigerie, who established the *Société Anti-esclavagiste* in 1888, helped to establish France at the forefront of international abolitionist efforts. Advocates of empire drew contrasts between enlightening French rule and what they described as the neglectful tutelage of precolonial elites in outposts such as Tonkin, where a millennium of Chinese overlordship had shaped Vietnamese culture.

This emphasis upon age and emancipation allowed the rigidities of race to be temporarily attenuated in the service of imperial expansionism. However, within French, British, and other European colonial cultures, supple, fluid, and amorphous understandings of childhood as a protected life stage remained deeply interwoven with ideas of Western racial superiority. Assumptions about the contrary dispositions of Europeans and non-Europeans mapped closely to a rational-nonrational dichotomy, which ultimately was used in support of claims for white superiority. As racial theorists regrounded hierarchical relations between European and non-European peoples in biology from midcentury, they referenced childhood, a category of biological inferiority, regularly in their writings. Although ethnographers and anthropologists produced detailed studies of racial "types" to which *indigènes* could be assigned on the basis of their physical appearance and traits, childhood continued to function as a shorthand in writings about colonized peoples, permitting such differences to be subsumed. Those individuals who took up the colonial "vocation" often found such rhetoric reassuring and invoked infantilizing vocabulary as a means of rendering strangeness familiar and reasserting theories of dominance that were repeatedly compromised on a practical level in everyday life.

"TROPICAL" CHILDHOODS: BRITISH VISIONS OF WHITE AND NONWHITE CHILDREN IN EMPIRE

By the late nineteenth century, observers generally agreed that "native childhoods" were characterized by a striking "otherness." Fascinating and unsettling, romanticized and demonized, the children of empire were deemed quite different to those featuring in sentimental contemporary bourgeois renderings of the

European family. As education and labor reform in Europe took children out of the labor market, colonialists identified indigenous children as a rich source of the contrasts essential to their claims for the right to rule as self-evident. These differences, while supposedly essential, remained fragile and required constant reinforcement. The paradigm of profound difference through which Western and non-Western children and childhoods were read remained an enduring feature in the writings of officials, travel writers, and other commentators who appealed, in making such claims, to contemporary scientific research on "tropical" nature.

By the 1830s, European reflections upon the causes of high levels of mortality among colonial troops in the East had helped to create "the tropics" as a specific geographical space with its own history. However, the widely observed tendency of the young to "degenerate" in the tropics also proved integral to dismissals of the possibility of white settlement.[10] Studies by British physicians of the degenerative impact of tropical nature focused upon the bodies of white children, despite the fact that this demographic remained numerically tiny. Mortality was high during the first five years of life among the miniscule cohort of white children resident in tropical contexts. Bringing one's family out to the tropical outposts of empire was regarded as an exercise fraught with danger, if not altogether foolhardy.

By midcentury, pejorative views on the prospects of settlement were in the ascendant in Anglophone scientific circles. However, in the late nineteenth century, rather than inspiring the complete removal of white children from the tropics, these findings coincided with the introduction of larger numbers of bourgeois women and children to Eastern colonies. This development intensified after the opening of the Suez Canal reduced travel times between Europe and Asia in 1869. It proceeded in the 1880s as metropolitan critiques of empire drove a refashioning of colonial governance through which bourgeois norms of respectability—and the recreation of home and family, in particular—came to be more closely linked to demonstrations of white racial authority.

As priorities shifted from expansionism to demonstrations of good governance, the need to evidence the ascendancy of elite sexual and social mores in empire grew more pressing. The tolerance of concubinage correspondingly declined, and the realization of sentimental, modern ideals of the family, to which white children were essential, acquired new significance in colonial contexts. In a certain sense, the lives of those Europeans who aspired toward the realization of this ideal on the edges of empire, and who were often to be found among the ranks of commercial elites and colonial administrators, "turned inward" in the last quarter of the nineteenth century. Accompanying this trend was a tendency for European colonial communities to revolve to a greater extent around white children.

The cult of "true" childhood, as it was coming to be defined, was celebrated enthusiastically within British colonial communities on the edge of empire.[11] Claims for white children's special vulnerability and protected status within the family in some cases drove, or validated, a series of controversial developments in colonial policy. These included, for example, the withdrawal of Europeans from the plains to hill stations in India and other "possessions" in Asia. Segregated as far as possible from subject peoples (other than the servants who staffed elite quarters) in hill stations, elite children embodied hopes that "essential" childhood, ideally situated in nature, achieved wide currency in British cultures of colonialism. Children emerged as consolatory emblems of fixity, not change, and of the *possibility* of the bourgeois family, with all of its attendant connotations of racial authority. The performance of elite childhood within the family and beyond the situated degeneracy of the pestilential tropics acquired considerable import in the late nineteenth century as the maintenance of order and the imperial status quo appeared to be under threat.[12]

If this vision of childhood represented an ideal to which many elite expatriate families aspired, daily life even in colonial environments that were increasingly carefully segregated and controlled continued to present manifold dangers. These dangers ensured that children and childhood remained a source of profound anxiety. Around the domain of not only health but also schooling, language acquisition and basic comportment crystallized fears that children thus displaced would become degenerates, rendered racially inferior and inadequately British on account of their growing up in these "alien" environments.[13]

And yet it is worth remembering that these manifold missteps, and the anxieties they induced, were in themselves productive of British colonialism and the claims for racial authority undergirding it. In particular, they served as markers of difference between rulers and ruled, which had in certain important respects begun to diminish by the end of the nineteenth century as a result of prolonged contact between Western and non-Western societies. Moreover, the tendency of children who grew up in colonies to "pick up the wrong cues" from nonwhite children, servants, and others presented valuable opportunities for redemptive correction.

The core anxieties that played out around and were inspired by (inadequate) performances of elite white childhood in British colonial culture were, meanwhile, permitted and underwritten by the inevitability of these children's

FIGURE 10.3: "Kathleen and Margaret Goodman, Hong Kong, 1904," in Sir William Meigh Goodman, *Reminiscences of a Colonial Judge* (London: Kingsgate, ca. 1907), p. 314. Within British colonial communities during the late nineteenth century, children, such as those of William Goodman, who served as chief justice in Hong Kong, emerged as the focus of and justification for intensive efforts to effect the segregation of white from nonwhite populations.

return to Britain before puberty. Contemporary gender mores ensured that boys' departure from the colonies before the threshold of adolescence was reached was considered crucial if they were to be classed fit to govern. In the meantime, however, the failure of children of both sexes to behave in accordance with bourgeois norms of respectability sustained daily engagements with the nature of colonial authority and ultimately reassured itinerant elites that the emotional sacrifice they were to make in sending their children away was justified.

In this way, even as laboratory science challenged climatological explanations of risk in the late nineteenth century, and as scientific studies produced childhood as a universal condition, white children in the colonies served as representatives of productive points of difference that were perceived to be under threat. As emerging, wealthy native elites acceded to Western living standards and as perceptions of an exotic, toxic Orient faded with improved sanitation and growing familiarity, Western childhood grew more important as a referent of difference upon which racial authority was understood to rest. Colonial elites strove to shore up the exclusivity and particularity of white childhood through studies legitimating misgivings over native education, through legislation designed to prevent the infiltration of European residential areas, and through scientific denials of the possibility of white settlement. Children (to a greater extent than women, whom, it was assumed, did not have to leave the colonies definitively) constituted the ultimate body of proof that prolonged stays in the colonies (still) threatened racial reproduction. While notions of vulnerability were central to this paradigm of difference, children on the edge of empires remained in practice risk takers, accustomed to moving in ways that unsettled adults, across the boundaries between rulers and ruled, which their very presence served to define.

Attempts to realize the ideal white childhood in the tropics underpinned the claims to respectability of a professional European administrator class. They also served to block the alignment of native children with a universalizing paradigm of childhood. Though indigenous children shared many apparent similarities with European children—both, notably, being understood to inhabit savage or uncivilized identities—by the late nineteenth century, the former had come to be linked in British visions of empire with a pestilential nature. They were, as such, irretrievably and fundamentally alien.

Yet in scientific and literary explorations of this gulf, British commentators invoked familiar dichotomous categories of "true" and "other" children. This breach had opened along fault lines of class during the nineteenth century as rapid urbanization transformed Britain, shaping a landscape that relegated nature to the fringes. Native children of empire were, in a manner akin to the poor children of the metropole, examined and judged in the light of bourgeois ideals of childhood generated by the British path to modernity and found to be something other than "truly" childlike.

Contact between colonials and the children of colonized peoples yielded accounts detailing deviancy and degeneracy. Precocious, all-too-serious, impassive, "slavishly" respectful of their parents, these children, commentators asserted, did not look, play, or act like Western children.

Some experts ascribed blame to inadequate parenting or the influence of wider cultural and environmental contexts. This raised the possibility that individual native children might be "retrieved" from their predicament, or "improved." However, the goal of such intervention in colonial childhoods, of the "improvement" sought, was never entirely clear. Nor was it clear that any such articulation of purpose might necessarily serve the interests of colonial overlords. More often, encounters with indigenous children yielded evidence that could be used to affirm the validity of subjugation. Childhoods absent, abbreviated, or otherwise in doubt were allowed to depreciate the currency of reformers' claims that differences between Western and Eastern childhoods should be leveled.[14] Possibilities of "retrieval" were forestalled by accounts highlighting non-Western children as fundamentally alien.

British colonial elites had little to gain by permitting the extension of "true childhood," unmarked by time or place, class or gender, across race. As competition for colonies intensified, indigenous elites were becoming more assertive, and the work of reformers was permitting metropolitan mores to encroach more overtly upon colonial communities. Claims for the fundamental otherness of non-Western childhoods remained integral to efforts to underline and justify the distinctiveness of the colonial situation. Although historians have questioned notions that the right to a "true" or "happy" childhood may have served the interests of European children, it is apparent that the resistance of colonial authorities to the conferral of any similar entitlement upon non-European children was critical not only to permitting the exploitation of these children to continue but also to the maintenance of the skewed power relations that were integral to the exploitative colonial order of things more generally.

And yet, by the late nineteenth century, this position was proving increasingly difficult to defend. The "rescue" of children was assumed to be unlikely and continued to be conceded in the main to religious authorities. "Retrieval," when viewed in terms of induction into confessional communities, attracted little interest or criticism from colonial officials. However, it began to emerge

FIGURE 10.4: "Enfants anmamites," postcard, dated 1901. Vietnamese children were a popular choice of subject for photographers keen to supply the growing metropolitan market for exotic images of the Orient.

as a source of tension as metropolitan commentators made indigenous children a key focus of critiques of the colonial record and as missionaries emphasized childhood as the key realm in which the transformative possibilities of salvation might be realized. Such claims directly challenged interpretations of childhood as evidencing and validating the gulf between white and nonwhite society.

As any relaxation of imperial authority in India and other colonies became unimaginable, the rise of the new field of laboratory-based tropical medicine informed reinterpretations of the native child in pathogenic terms, as a source of disease endangering white communities and, in particular, white children.[15] A new nomenclature also came into being in the service of the desire to deny colonized children the right to be considered childlike. While the children of colonial cities might recall the "guttersnipes" or "street Arabs" of Dickensian London, the redeployment in colonial contexts even of terms such as this negating the category child (which had often been inspired by contact with empire) was resisted. At a moment when poor and abandoned British children were coming to be reinterpreted as a vital national resource and as legitimate objects of pity whose recuperation was to be effected, potentially, through transplantation from British cities to settlement colonies, a new terminology emerged reinforcing the irretrievable otherness of the colonized child. In southern Rhodesia, for example, laboring children were referred to as "picanninies" or "picannins." In the Crown Colony of Hong Kong, meanwhile, officials referred to girls transferred into semiservile status as laboring bond servants using the Chinese term *mui tsai*.[16] More often than not, those working within the ranks of colonial officialdom tended to avoid the use of the term *childhood* when referring to the experiences of young people living under colonial rule.

"COLONIAL AUXILIARIES": FRENCH VISIONS OF CHILDHOOD IN EMPIRE

In 1905, speaking at a festival organized by the Union Amicale des Enfants de la Seine, the leftist Republican deputy, Jules Siegfried, declared that in Indochina the tropical climate was not only "often better than our own," but one that "delicate young people, as those of our society often are, would find beneficial." Siegfried's claim ran counter to the dominant view, from metropoles to colonies, that white children were in mortal danger in the tropics. Stripped of much of their empire in the late eighteenth and early nineteenth centuries, French physicians and hygienists drew heavily upon the lessons of the British and Dutch colonial experience in India and the East Indies when addressing the problems of maintaining the presence of their own nationals in recently acquired African and Asian colonial outposts.[17]

In the late nineteenth century, colonies were often viewed in metropolitan France as places of refuge for the desperate. They were considered spaces of last resort for those fleeing debt, dishonor, and criminal prosecution, with little to lose but their lives. As such, they were by no means considered appropriate places to raise a family respectably. Only at the turn of the twentieth century did the increasing number of white children become sufficiently visible to warrant more than a fleeting reference in writings on colonial cities. In Hanoi, for example, the journalist Jules Lubanski (aka Jean Star) felt able to refer only in 1902 to "sir, madam, baby and *congaï*" as "a symbolic and authentic colonial foursome."[18]

The number of parents who took their children to the colonies with them increased in the last quarter of the nineteenth century. This trend accompanied the shift in outposts such as Hanoi and Saigon from military to civilian government. As priorities shifted from the aggressive accrual of new lands to their exploitation through effective colonial state building, embryonic public spheres emerged in these outposts, informed by aspirations for the demonstration of bourgeois morality. To this the roles of women—conceived of according to contemporary gender mores as guardians of colonial morality—and children were considered central. Thus transplanted, the French family required careful maintenance. Hygiene literature proliferated, offering similar advice on the vexed question of tropical prophylactics to that circulating in other European outposts of empire.

Jules Siegfried's comment nonetheless is suggestive of the fact that optimistic views of the possibility of white tropical settlement were taken seriously within high political circles. It may also be seen as illustrating the enduring influence of environmentalist thinking in French deliberations over colonial childhood. For much of the nineteenth century, France lacked extensive overseas colonies in which the experimental scientific study of exotic species might be pursued. This helped a powerful, state-sponsored science of "acclimatization," in which the relations between organisms and their environment emerged as the subject of study, to flourish. The network of scientists committed to such research was profoundly influenced by the ideas of Geoffroy Saint-Hilaire and Jean-Baptiste Lamarck. Geographers and hygienists who embraced Lamarckian and neo-Lamarckian ideas of environmental adaptation exerted considerable influence upon those in the vanguard of the small, diverse, and energetic French colonial lobby groups. Even as detailed racial typologies were set down and as racialists such as Paul Broca, Charles Naudin, and André Sanson attacked environmentalist interpretations of risk, the tendency to foreground climatological perceptions of endangerment remained remarkably persistent in Francophone scientific circles and in colonial contexts, where it continued to inform questions of white settlement.[19]

Rather than viewing tropical nature as fundamentally alien, French geographers and hygienists advanced views of tropical nature as part of a continuum, its species being linked to variants in Europe and thus like those at home, capable of being managed rather than merely exhibited (as the British tended to assume).[20] This view sustained hopes that the adaptation of animals to the environment might be managed within the newly reconstructed empire. Such hopes were far less well developed within the (more amateurish) British acclimatization movement, whose adherents tended to view their work not in terms of transformative experimentation but as a more limited process of redistributing fixed species throughout imperial networks.[21]

Political circumstances further emboldened those convinced that the scientific management of acclimatization might ultimately permit French children to be rendered more robust in the tropics, rather than simply degenerate. The Prussian victory of 1870 and the struggle to consolidate Republicanism brought to the forefront of political contest an emphasis upon childhood, not as separate from society but as linked intrinsically with it and ideally subject to early responsibilities.[22] The political significance of childhood had been augmented during the Revolutionary period and was given new momentum in the late nineteenth century by the extension of the franchise and the Republican drive to secularize French society. The decontextualization of children, or the ascription to them of some ideal duty of residing in nature, gained relatively little purchase in metropolitan France (which remained predominantly rural in contrast to Britain, which had passed the point of urban-rural equipoise at midcentury). As a divided French bourgeoisie disputed the nation's path to modernity, childhood was ushered to the fore in visions of an imperial future that did not turn upon stasis but rather the possibility of radical transformation.

In these circumstances, greater willingness emerged to interpret colonial childhood as part of a dialectic linked to and shaped by the tropical context rather than ideally decontexualized and floating free of it. Although consensus never emerged on the viability of tropical settlement, in contrast to those British colonial administrators who worked "experts'" findings on native childhood into justifications for segregation, French administrators, selected for their Republican sympathies, paid lip service to childhood as a realm in which harmonious and egalitarian relations between individual "cells" of the "organism" of empire might be realized.[23] A stronger sense that the fate of the nation was at stake inspired a greater readiness to consider the potential of tropical acclimatization. Despite, or because of, the well-known attendant risks, notions of the French planter-entrepreneur as the ideal colonial serving the *mère patrie* and raising robust children in the tropics retained a surprising degree of support across the ideological divide at the turn of the century. Even hardheaded colonial publicists could not resist indulging in fantasies of superior rising generations, made stronger by exposure to tropical nature. When Joseph Chailley-Bert helped to found a "feminine emigration society" in 1897, an underlying aim of this initiative was the production of empire families rooted in the Tonkin soil.[24] Although regular trips to hill stations and returns to the *métropole* emerged as essential aspects of the French colonial childhood, the permanent removal of French children from the tropics before adolescence did not emerge as axiomatic to the same extent in elite French colonial cultures as it did in their British equivalent.

The concomitant of this engagement with the tropics was a much greater readiness in French colonial circles to draw non-European children within romantic rather than pestilential frames of reference. In this vein, for example, Jules Boissière, describing street scenes in Hanoi in the late 1890s, invoked a well-worn trope of colonial literature to describe a cartload of Chinese children as "the prettiest bouquet in the world." Claims for children living under colonial rule as irretrievably base and corrupt met with powerful counterclaims presenting them as perfectly happy and free in nature. Imaginings of such vigorous children, "adopted" by France, as less vulnerable to disease than their European counterparts, exerted a powerful attraction, especially at a moment when the rapid spread of eugenic thought was inspiring anxious commentary about the quality of the rising generation at home.[25] "Purple pigs," as colonial writers often affectionately described native children in Indochina, emerged as emblems of a healthy excrescence and reassuring abundance.[26]

Such views were by no means uncontested, but they were often sustained by hostile readings of the native family as a forcing ground for a tradition condemned as debased. Decades after the colonial conquest, writers continued to cast the family and its traditions as a kind of microcosm of precolonial societal enslavement, wherein children became habituated to "passive obedience which touches on servility." Children were identified as victims of their own culture and as viable targets for rescue and reform. Under the tutelage of "mother France," it was assumed that a kind of transformation from servility to enlightenment would occur. The native child continued to fulfill an important role in liberal narratives of progress and improvement, and French observers were far more likely than their British counterparts to catch in the childlike peoples of empire either a retrospective glimpse of the modern adult self or the contemporary youth of modern France.

"MYTH AND MIRACLE": THE STRANGE CASE OF THE *ENFANTS MERVEILLEUX* OF TONKIN

While British observers' tendencies to doubt the childhoods of colonized children allowed them to either dismiss child prodigies or to present them as ciphers of a wider cultural perversity and racial inferiority, French commentators found such brusque dismissals altogether less satisfactory. Considered outgrowths of a nature with which colonialists perceived themselves to be inextricably entangled, commentators continued to claim that such children might beneficially be drawn within the subaltern norm. It was precisely such convictions that prompted the colonial officials who came face to face with the Ky Dong in 1887 to neither dismiss nor banish him but to ensure that he received a French education. It was assumed that the outcome of this process would inevitably be the child's acknowledgment of the superiority of French culture. If the "natural genius" over which French guardianship now extended could be won to the French cause, rendered interpretable and refined through the conferral of rational and scientific knowledge, the tantalizing prospect emerged that the mass education of children under colonial rule might in time rejuvenate a metropole widely criticized by this time as ossified, stultifying, and overcivilized.

Unfortunately for those who found such ideas attractive, the case of the Ky Dong ultimately served to undermine enthusiasm for liberal experiments with the education of indigenous children. The problem was that the boy returned to his homeland not as an exponent of French culture but as a determined adversary of the European presence. For colonial theorists inspired by what they saw as British and Dutch imperial success, this outcome reaffirmed perceptions that the French genre of colonialism was overly sentimental, affective, tutelary, and insufficiently distant and supervisory and hence would ultimately fail. This reevaluation brought into question the nature and extent of the commitment of the colonial state to young *indigènes*. In 1904, Baille, president of the Commission de réforme de l'enseignement en Indochine, captured the prevailing mood when he advised that efforts to educate indigenous children would, "simply develop in the Annamite [the French colonial term for the Vietnamese] a hollow and pedantic vanity which will lead him to spurn his race without endowing him with the ability to raise himself to our level." To underline this point, Baille cited the case of the infamous Ky Dong, who "spoke French fluently and had acquired our *brevets*" but had still proceeded to foment revolutionary agitation in Tonkin. A scaling back of enthusiasm for tutelary commitments to the wards of empire was well under way, and the "childlike" mentality of native adults was allowed to serve as justification for it.

In these changed circumstances, the emergence of the "new Ky Dong," Ly Thanh Long, in 1899, failed to inspire calls for the boy's conversion to Frenchness. However, at a time when the long tradition of resistance to French colonial policy among Confucian scholars appeared to be reviving around this iconic rural child, dexterously manipulating Chinese characters, the alarming persistence of older pedagogies appeared all too evident. Coupled with the retreat from assimilationist claims, this phenomenon seemed to underline the fragility and shallowness of French influence in the region. If miraculous children, impassive and serene, emerging with disturbing regularity from the rural milieu, embodied extremes of an abiding nature, the relinquishment of modernizing, tutelary claims toward them undermined an important argument for empire more generally. It also raised the specter of native childhoods lost to stasis, the supernatural and alternative political loyalties.

Though miracle children were by definition outside the norm of childhood, they could be read as an exaggerated vision of the potential of nature harnessed. As arbiters of a kind of natural law, their presence raised questions as to how this kind of authority could be allowed to coexist with that upheld by the colonial state. Such children represented implacable tradition, in the face of which a modernization consisting of bridges, roads, and mailboxes could be made to look rather prosaic and transitory. It was becoming abundantly clear that, if the construction of empire had been in part inspired by a "conviction with metaphysical, even mystical implications," then appeals to childhood could no longer easily be marshaled in the service of such certainties.[27]

Ultimately, French officials in turn-of-the-century Tonkin agreed on the need to return Ly Thanh Long to the native milieu. For this to occur, however, it was necessary that his claims to genius, and his claims to the authority of tradition, be denied. In late December 1899, after exposing the troubling case of Ly Thanh Long to extensive and careful scrutiny, could Charles Prêtre, head of the office of native affairs in Hanoi, finally reassure himself and high officials that the boy's alleged powers were nothing more than an elaborate hoax.[28] Charles Prêtre's meticulous, "rational," and "scientific" investigation proved, accordingly, that the boy was not a mystic but was, rather, a charlatan carefully tutored by an older brother to deliver his enthralling performances. Through this process of demystification, Ly Thanh Long was reduced, in

Prêtre's words, to little more than a "capricious, willful [and] badly raised" child.

Relief at such an outcome, however, was short lived. This was not only because the boy's transformation from magus to delinquent, whose misdeeds might be attributed to inadequate parenting, revived as-yet-unanswered questions concerning the limits of imperial responsibility for the protection of indigenous children against their own culture. Uncoupling the rising generations of empire from a trajectory that, it had been assumed, would deliver them into fully modern childhoods also exposed the moral and political danger that this category posed to an overlordship revealed to be coercive and exploitative. The role of a disaffected Vietnamese former lower-ranking member of the colonial civil service in the murky case of Ly Thanh Long suggested to official investigators that educated sections of Vietnamese society were now willing and able to exploit the contradictions of colonial childhood and to make children the focus of concerted efforts to challenge French hegemony.

Critics of colonialism had much to gain by binding childhood into these challenges. The vast majority of children in Indochina, as in other colonies, continued to labor rather than learn under European rule, often in dangerous, poorly regulated conditions. The lives of real children could be used to evidence the impoverishment of the tutelary ideal and to expose the shallowness of appeals to a rhetoric of emancipation centering upon childhood. In the following half century, on the basis of such contrasts and contradictions, childhood was to become a dangerously destabilizing force, and indeed a cause célèbre with the potential to inform powerful critiques of European imperialism, colonialism, and of empires ultimately destined to be overthrown and outlived by those whose childhoods they had transformed.

CONCLUSION

Western ideas about childhood emerging from late-eighteenth-century reassessments became enmeshed during the nineteenth century with debates about relations between the West and the wider world. Representations of children living under colonial rule and characterizations of colonized peoples as children were used to naturalize Western dominance and were, in many respects, fundamentally constitutive of empire. Bourgeois ideas about childhood, transplanted into colonial contexts by itinerant European elites, proved integral to the ways that empires were conceptualized and run.

When mapped onto colonized peoples, however, Western models of childhood—associated by some with emancipatory potential and possibilities of a more general social, cultural, and political "coming of age"—emerged as a point of ambiguity and tension. As the nineteenth century drew to a close, this tension ensured that childhood could no longer as easily be used to underpin European ambitions for further expansion. Childhood emerged instead as a focus for indigenous elites' and metropolitan reformers' intense criticisms of the colonial record. Across empires, childhood became a cultural battleground that critics were sometimes able to use to translate local incidents beyond their immediate confines into full-blown imperial crises.

British and Dutch exponents of empire, keen on preserving the status quo, remained wary of the implications of invoking sentimental age-related interpretations of the imperial bond as a kind of modern kinship, but in other colonial cultures—notably those of France and the United States—these kinds of links continued to play an important role in late-nineteenth-century efforts to construct or reconstruct empire. In the early twentieth century, even as claims to oversee colonies in accordance with the demands of trusteeship reinvigorated engagements with paternal paradigms of empire, colonial governments continued in practice to resist reformers' attempts to level differences between Western and non-Western childhoods. They also persisted in restricting the extension of sentimental versions of the modern bourgeois family beyond expatriate enclaves, citing the need to leave local custom undisturbed where possible.

Despite the numerous similarities between children in Europe and Asia, Europeans who upheld assumptions that modern Western childhood should be protected and nonlaboring interpreted non-European children as emblems of the fundamental difference between their respective cultures. This engagement ensured that, even as the Age of Empire drew to a close, far from being rigidly distinct and separate, colonial childhoods and their metropolitan equivalents had become, to an unprecedented extent, mutually constitutive and indissolubly intertwined.

NOTES

Introduction

I would like to thank Olena Heywood for her support in the editing of this volume.

1. Chancellor 1970: 127–128; Heywood 2007: 254.
2. Fass 2007: 44.
3. Ariès 1962; Sommerville 1982: 97.
4. Cunningham 2005: 58; Richardson 1994: 9.
5. Stearns 2006: 6–7, 55; Fass and Mason 2000: 2; Gillis 1996: 72.
6. Zelizer 1985: 3–15, 57–72.
7. Davin, 1999, 27–29; Kelly 2007: 16.
8. Fass and Mason, 2000: 5–6; Mintz 2004: 152.
9. Finkelstein 1985: 111.
10. Stearns 2006: 60.
11. Jenks 1996; James, Jenks, and Prout 1998.
12. Sommerville 1982: 88–97.
13. Garlitz 1966; Wordsworth 1985: 51; Lloyd 1992: 102.
14. Rosenblum 1988: 23; Johnson 2006: 112.
15. Hendrick 1997: 12; Kelly 2007: 59–60.
16. Richardson 1994: 8–25; Heywood 2007: 48–49.
17. Richardson 1994: 12, 42–43; Fletcher 2008: 6–8.
18. Wylie 1964: 121.
19. Zelizer 1985: 11.
20. Rahikainen 2004.
21. Sjöberg 1997.
22. Bolin-Hort 1989: 208–237.
23. Fletcher 2008; Mension-Rigau 1990.
24. Finkelstein 1985: 111–112.
25. Bowen 1981.

26. Heywood 2007: 227.
27. Stearns 2006: 57.
28. Ariès 1962: 397; Fletcher 2008; Richardson 1994: 5.

Chapter 1

1. Mintz and Kellogg 1988: xiv–xv.
2. Sommerville 1982: 150.
3. Illick 2002: 60; Mintz and Kellogg 1988: 51; Hendrick 1997: 18; Laslett 1972: 138–142.
4. McLaren 1990: 178–207; Coontz 2005: 162.
5. Heywood 2007: 112–113.
6. Mitterauer and Sieder 1982: 58–61; Mintz and Kellogg 1988: 46.
7. Gillis 1996: 66–80, 89–92, 101–104.
8. Coontz 2005: 191–195.
9. Shammas 2002: 124.
10. Mintz and Kellogg 1988: 56.
11. Crossick and Gerhard-Haupt 1995: 87–89, 100–101.
12. Macleod 1998: 47–48, 65.
13. Heywood 2007: 2.
14. Reinier 1996: xi–xii.
15. Zelizer 1985.
16. Heywood 2001: 59; Hendrick 1997: 18–21.
17. Heywood 2001: 77–80.
18. Heywood 2001: 72.
19. Heywood 2001: 55.
20. Greven 1977.
21. Cunningham 2005: 89.
22. Mintz and Kellogg 1988: 89.
23. Jordan 1993: 21; Cunningham 2005: 153; Shammas 2002: 153.

Chapter 2

1. Holt n.d.
2. Hobsbawm 1999: 58–60.
3. Hirsch 1978: 53.
4. Heywood 2007: 129, 132.
5. Strange 1982: 3.
6. Mintz 2004: 137–138; Hirsch 1978: 73, 77; Zelizer 1985: 241, n. 44.
7. "First Annual Report" [1854] 1971: 4, 6; Spann 1981: 70.
8. Heywood 2007: 110.
9. Brace [1880] 1967: 145.
10. Klapper 2006: 88.
11. Holt 1992: 12–13.

12. "Children in the Garden" 1869: 151.
13. Holt 1992: 12; Stowe 1934: 99.
14. Holt 1992: 12–13.
15. Child [1831] 1972: 3.
16. Holt 1992: 13–14; Mintz and Kellogg 1988: 84–85; "Health and Beauty" 1849: 370.
17. Belchem 1990: 37, 129–130; Davin 1996: 199.
18. Farge and Revel 1991: 93–95; Holt 1992: 45; Bagnall 1980.
19. Morrison and Zabusky 1993: 68.
20. Klapper 2006: 17, 113.
21. Driscoll 1943: 335–336.
22. Wrigley 1988: 121.
23. Holt 2003: 21; Davin 1996: 31.
24. Hampsten 1991: 70–71.
25. West 1989: 13.
26. O'Kieffe 1960: 180.
27. Turk 1989: 156–158.
28. Holt 2003: 36.
29. Kleberg 1898: 299.
30. Waugh n.d.: 26–27.
31. West 1992: 40.
32. Siceloff 1964: 184–185.
33. Holt 2003: 96–97.
34. Mintz and Kellogg 1988: 85.
35. Zelizer 1985: 75–77; Horn 1974: 83, 85.
36. Katz 1971: 52–53, 62.
37. West 1989: 150–151.

Chapter 3

1. Berg 1993; Mendels 1972.
2. De Vries 1994: 110–115.
3. Traugott 1993: 107.
4. Allen 1994; Clark 1999; Crafts 1985; Harley 1993.
5. Hindman 2002: 248–290.
6. Tilly and Scott 1978: 12.
7. Tullos 1989: 57–58.
8. Wrigley and Schofield 1981: 563–595.
9. Berg and Hudson 1992; Lavalette 1999; Rahikainen 2004.
10. Pinchbeck 1930: 234.
11. Bolin-Hort 1989; Pollard 1965; Von Tunzelmann 1981.
12. Hammond and Hammond 1937: 20.
13. Tuttle 1999: 107–108.
14. Tuttle 1999: 30.
15. Heywood 1988: 102; Weissbach 1989: 16.

16. Goldin and Sokoloff 1982: 773.
17. Hindman 2002: 153.
18. Ure 1835: 301.
19. Davies 1811; Gaskell 1833.
20. Leifchild 1853: 151.
21. Weissbach 1989: 20–38.
22. Hindman 2002: 48–58.
23. Horrell and Humphries 1995; Lavalette 1999; Tuttle 1999.
24. Alfred [Samuel Kydd] 1857: 101; House of Commons Papers 1842 [380] XV: 55.
25. Heywood 1988: 128–139.
26. Trattner 1970: 11–12.
27. Tuttle 1998: 74.
28. Valenze 1995: 91.
29. Rendall 1990: chap. 1.
30. Lindert and Williamson 1983.
31. Brown 1990.
32. Horrell and Humphries 1992: 855.
33. Mokyr 1999: 123.
34. De Vries 1994: 259.

Chapter 4

1. Zeiher 2001.
2. Zinnecker 1990.
3. Calvert 1992; Tressell 1914; Cunningham 2007; Cross 1997; Pollock 1983; Adams and Gossage 2008.
4. Behnken and Jonker 1990.
5. Foucault 1979.
6. For example, Markus 1993; de Coninck-Smith 2000; Châtelet 1999.
7. Burke and Grosvenor 2008 and 2007.
8. Heywood 1988; Sjöberg 1997.
9. Weber 1967: 449–450; Mintz 2004: chap. 8.
10. Nasaw 1985; de Coninck-Smith 1997.
11. Burke and Grosvenor 2008: 41–50.
12. Châtelet 1999: 64.
13. Burke and Grosvenor 2008: 28, 63.
14. Burke and Grosvenor 2008: 40–41.
15. Markus 1993: chap. 3.
16. Châtelet 1999: 84–87.
17. Gutman 2004; de Coninck-Smith 1989.
18. Kristenson 2005: 217.
19. Châtelet 1999: 53.
20. Davin 1996: 124–129; Stang Dahl 1978: 133.
21. Seaborne and Lowe 1977: 29.
22. Davin 1996: 67.

23. de Coninck-Smith 1990.
24. Wagner 1981: 53; Mintz 2004: 158.
25. Stang Dahl 1978; Mintz 2004: chap. 8; Thuen 2002.
26. Thuen 2002: 205–214.
27. Smith 2009.
28. Thuen 2002: 213.
29. Stang Dahl 1978: 72.
30. Foucault 1979: 293.
31. Jablonka 2000 and 2005.
32. Nasaw 1985: 22; Christensen 1961: 96; de Coninck-Smith 1990.
33. Nasaw 1985: 33.
34. Nasaw 1985: 34; Behnken and Jonker 1990: 192–194; Brembeck 1988: 83–88.
35. Weber-Kellermann 1979; Mergen 1992.
36. http://www.pladstilosalle.dk/lidtarbejde/landet3/index.html, accessed July 24, 2008; Nielsen 1927.
37. Mintz 2004: 170; Waites 2005: 68–69.
38. Weber-Kellermann, 1991.
39. Calvert 1992: 143; kid size exhibition (the chair was included in the exhibition but is not in the catalog).
40. Behnke and Jonker 1990: 180.
41. Van Slyck 2007.
42. Benjamin 1992: 73–74; Heywood 2007: 188.
43. de Coninck-Smith 1999.
44. Behnken and Jonker 1990: 182–188.
45. Gutman and de Coninck-Smith 2008: 4.

Chapter 5

1. Sandin 1986; Popkewitz 1997; Cunningham 1991; Mintz 2004.
2. Maynes 1985: 33–61, 133–153; Miller 1998: 143–248; Green 1990.
3. Soysal and Strang 1989: 277–288; Green 1990.
4. Maynes 1985: 33–60; Sandin 1986: 141–226; Green 1990: 111–307; Kaestle 1973.
5. Maynes 1985: 33–60; Sandin 1986: 141–226; Green 1990: 111–307; Kaestle 1973.
6. Green 1990: 76–110.
7. Pomfret 2004: 1439–1475; Miller 1998: 130–142.
8. Miller 1998: 134–149; Maynes 1985: 33–60.
9. Miller 1998: 164–167; Sandin 1986: 175–226.
10. Maynes 1985: 33–45; Miller 1998: 149–152; Heywood 1988: 84–93; Sandin 1986: 227–261.
11. Sandin 1986: 175–226.
12. Sandin 1986: 175–195; Maynes 1985: 33–60.
13. Maynes 1985: 83–102; Green 1990: 111–307; Miller 1998: 200–226.
14. Maynes 1985: 83–102; Miller 1998: 200–226; Green 1990: 208–307.

15. Heywood 1988: 49–91; Maynes 1985: 83–102.
16. Maynes 1985: 83–102; Mintz 2004.
17. Heywood 1988: 49–91; Sjöberg 1996.
18. Heywood 1988: 61–93.
19. Maynes 1985: 83–102; Heywood 1988: 61–93; Sjöberg 1996.
20. Heywood 1988: 82–93; Cunningham 1991: 97–163.
21. Sandin 1986: 227–261.
22. Maynes 1985: 61–81.
23. Green 1990: 208–307; Sandin 1986: 175–226; Maynes 1985: 103–151.
24. Maynes 1985: 61–151; Miller 1998; 183–220.
25. Maynes 1985: 61–151; Miller 1998: 183–220; Green 1990.
26. Miller 1998: 149–171; Maynes 1985: 150.
27. Miller 1998: 149–171; Maynes 1985: 150.
28. Sandin and Novoa 2005.
29. Tyack 1974; Miller 1998; Maynes 1985.
30. Maynes 1985: 83–103; Miller 1998: 143–171.
31. Cunningham 1991: 50–96; Sandin 1997: 17–46; Bolin-Hort 1989; Heywood 1988.
32. Kaestle and Vinovsky 1980; Maynes 1985: 133–151.
33. Sandin 1997: 17–46; Sjöberg 1996; Cunningham 1991: 97–163.
34. Miller 1998: 221–273; Maynes 1985: 83–102.
35. Miller 1998: 221–273; Maynes 1985: 83–102; Fass 1989; Lassonde 2005; Ryan 2005: 66–95.
36. Maynes 1985; Miller 1998: 248–289.
37. Stenkula 1879.
38. Cunningham 1991: 191–217; Miller 1998: 248–289; Hendrick 1997; Sundkvist 1994; Lökke 1990.
39. Cunningham 1991: 191–217; Hendrick 1997; Sundkvist 1994; Lökke 1990; Sandin 1997; Coninck-Smith 2000; Zelizer 1985; Cavallo 1981; Platt 1978.
40. Cunningham 1991: 191–217; Sundkvist 1994; Sandin 1997; Coninck-Smith 2000; Zelizer 1985.

Chapter 6

1. Thornton 2005: 63.
2. Ching 1988: 13–15, 374–377, 390–391, 397–399, 404–405, 414, 419–420, 430–434, 441–443, 451, 453, 459, 467, 469.
3. On Chinese families, see Cartier 1996: 216–241; Baker 1979; Wolf and Huang 1980.
4. Heywood 2001: 48–60; *Enciclopedia italiana* 1930–1934: vol. 6, 393–394; *Enciclopaedia Judaica* 2007: vol. 3, 720–721.
5. *Encyclopædia Britannica* 1910: vol. 3, 990–991.
6. Burguière and Lebrun 1996: 11–94; Kertzer and Barbagli 2002: ix–xxvii; Livi Bacci 2000; Knodel 1988: 542–549. For infanticide, see Heywood 2001: 73–77; Rose 1986.

7. Bardet 1997: 245–261.
8. Heywood 2001: 77–82.
9. Cunningham 2005: 95–96.
10. Ipsen 2006: 45, 151. The calculation of percentages is a rough one based on Coale-Demeny life table south, level eleven (female life expectancy = forty-five) and a 1901 Italian population of forty-three and a half million (Coale and Demeny 1983: 389; Rothenbacher 2002: 441, 448).
11. Van de Walle 1986: 201–233; Livi Bacci 2000: 112–116, 147–151; Bardet 1997; Vallin 1991: 38–67 (54 for French figures); Wolf 2001: 3; Sussman 1982 (104 for Lyon); Heywood 2001: 63–69.
12. Livi Bacci 2000: 140–147; Razzell 1994: 150–172; Schofield and Reher 1991: 1–17.
13. Livi Bacci 2000: 130.
14. Wines 1880.
15. Heywood 1988; Heywood 2001: 129–144; Ipsen 1996: 85–122; Nardinelli 1990.
16. Burguière and Lebrun 1996: 39–45; Brettell 2002: 229–247; Laslett 1965: 14–15, 91.
17. Darroch 2001.
18. Cunningham 2005: 15.
19. Cunningham 2005: 119–122, 157–161.
20. Burguière and Lebrun 1996: 11–94.
21. Ehmer 2002: 282–321; Coontz 2005: 161–195; Encyclopædia Britannica 1911: vol. 17, 753–759; Kevles 1985: 96–112.
22. Knodel 1988: 185–244; Rose 1986.
23. Livi Bacci 2000: 151–157; Kertzer and Barbagli 2002: xxiii–xxviii; Klein 2004: 37–144.
24. Livi Bacci 2000: 116–122, 126–127, 158–163; Moch 1992: 102–160; Brettell 2002.
25. Livi Bacci 2000: 135.
26. Estimates based, respectively, on life table south level four and life table north level fifteen: Coale and Demeny 1983: 385, 163; Swedish infant mortality rate taken from Rothenbacher 2002: 659.
27. Klein 2004: 101–106, 113–118.
28. Encyclopædia Britannica 1910: vol. 4, 823–824; vol. 7, 403–407; Enciclopedia italiana 1934: vol. 23, 890; Enciclopaedia Judaica 2007: vol. 4, 291–294.

Chapter 7

1. Fuchs 2005: 5, 11–16.
2. Mintz 2004: 167.
3. Marten 1998: 122.
4. Clement 1997: 28; King 1995: 142–148.
5. Donzelot 1997: 94–96, 125, 163, 171; Stansell 1986: 214–216.
6. Mintz 2004: 163; Grossberg 1985: 19, 29, 141.
7. Stansell 1986: 214; Grossberg 1985: 234, 237–238.

8. Fuchs 2008: 249–250.
9. Grossberg 1985: 247.
10. Grossberg 1985: 196; Fuchs 2008: 42–46, 112–113, 139.
11. Allen 1991: 142–154; Fuchs 2008: 141.
12. Grossberg 1985: 271–272.
13. Sigle, Kertzer, and White 2000: 326–340; Fuchs 2005: 46–47, 206–209.
14. Gouda 1995: 81–82; Fuchs 1992: 222–225; Fuchs 1984: 102.
15. Miller 2008: 125, 162, 194–195.
16. Ross 1993: 134.
17. Fuchs 2005: 223–228; Luddy 1995: 71.
18. Fuchs 2005: 212–217.
19. Behlmer 1982: 159; Hendrick 1994: 53–56; Fuchs 2008: 207–208; Ipsen 2006: 134–141.
20. Hendrick 1994: 126; Hendrick 2003: 86.
21. Ipsen 2006: 53; Mintz 2004: 173.
22. Mintz 2004: 179; Donzelot 1997: 92–95.
23. Ipsen 2006: 123–164.
24. Hendrick 1994: 27.
25. Hendrick 2003: 84; Cmiel 1995: 54.

Chapter 8

1. Davidoff and Hall 2002; Mintz and Kellogg 1988: 64.
2. Davidoff and Hall 2002: 331; Gillis 1996: 72–74.
3. Kerber 1988; Vickery 1993.
4. Frank 1998: 28.
5. Maynes, 2002: 202.
6. de Giorgio 1993: 169.
7. Mills 1995: 103; Smith 1981.
8. Maynes 2002: 209.
9. Kaplan 1991; Burman 1987: 43; Reagin 2001: 65; Berkovitz 1989: 234–235.
10. Cunningham 2005: 66.
11. Wayland 1836: 347.
12. McLoughlin 1985: 95.
13. Garlitz 1966: 642.
14. Newsome 1961; Honey 1977.
15. Newsome 1961: 210–228.
16. Houbre 2000.
17. Adams 1999: 65–86; Fuchs 2002: 169.
18. Hendrick 1997: 41–42; Heywood 2001: 77.
19. Rogers 2005: 227–252.
20. Sutherland 1990: 126; Reinier 1982: 72–73; West 1983: 161; King 1995: 81.
21. Cunningham 2005: 123; Alston 1969: 12.
22. Cunningham 2005: 123.
23. Cunningham 2005: 123; Green 2001: 209.

24. Sommerville 1982: 91, 97.
25. Bellaigue 2007: 154.
26. Stokvis 1993: 82.
27. Gillis 1996: 72.
28. Heywood 2007: 77; Caspard 2003: 173–183.
29. Lejeune 1993.
30. Springhall 1986: 130.
31. Seeley 1998; Pomfret 2001.
32. Prochaska 1978: 104; Stanley 1994; Pelissier 2003: 480.
33. Maynes 1995: 106–110; Reinier 1996: 92.
34. King 1995: 80.
35. Kett 1971; Cosnier 2001: 145–147.
36. West 1983; Lerner 1997: 16.
37. Seeley 1998.
38. Heywood 2001: 55.

Chapter 9

1. Termin 1914: 167–173.
2. Alter 1997: 95–101; Hill 1995: 37–50; Meckel 2004: 9–13; Oris, Derosas, and Breschi 2004: 359–398.
3. Bacci 2000: table 53; United Nations 2007: tables A18 and A19.
4. Riley 2001: 32–47.
5. Cone 1979: 44–45; Trousseau 1857: 74–76.
6. Rudolph 1982: 552, 615–616, 924.
7. *New York Times* 1876: 4.
8. Preston and Haines 1991: 4–5; Meckel 2004: 14–20.
9. Hardy 1993: 9–14, 81; Cone 1979: 114–115; Preston and Haines 1991: 4–5.
10. Wohl 1983: 18; Cone 1979: 115; Kociumbus 1997: 9.
11. Wohl 1983: 129; Hardy 1993: 57.
12. Dowling 1977: 58–59; Hardy 1993: 16, 57–59.
13. Wohl 1983: 128–129; Hardy 1993: 56–59; Horlbeck 1881: 291–292.
14. Newsholme 1935: 180.
15. Dowling 1977: 18–21; Carmichael 1993: 680–683; Hammonds 1999: 16.
16. Carmichael 1993: 680–683; Baker 1880: 111.
17. Hardy 1983: 81–86; Hammonds 1999: 21, 29.
18. Ettling 1993: 784–788.
19. Hardy 1993: 20, 284–285; Wohl 1983: 56–57.
20. Komlos and Baten 2004: 199–200.
21. Meckel 1990: 28; Davis 1993: 149–150.
22. Steckel 1988: 337–342.
23. Sundstrom 1997: 310–315.
24. Steckel 2000: 449–453.
25. Golden 2004: 70–77.
26. Rosenberg 2003: 5–6, 15, n. 9.

27. Heywood 2007: 183; Horn 1974: 170–171.
28. Horn 1997: 130; Wohl 1983: 34–35.
29. Golden 2004: 71.
30. Rosenberg 2003: 2–3.
31. Cone 1979: 60–62; Spree 1992: 317–324.
32. Meckel 1990: 45–46; Cone 1979: 99–103.
33. Escherich 1905: 58.
34. Jones 2004: 44–48; Meckel 2002: 188–195; Meckel 1996: 92–94.
35. Jordon 1993: 7; Meckel 1990: 102–104.
36. Porter 1999: 352–356.

Chapter 10

1. Heywood 2007: 46–47.
2. Plotz 2001: 1–40.
3. Smith 1904: book 4, chap. 7.2–3.
4. Chamberlain 1999: 64.
5. Bearce 1961; Whitehead 2005: 319.
6. Allender 2007: 47–50; Bagalopalan, 2002: 26–28; Sen 2002.
7. Rousseau 2003: 187; Yousef 2001: 252.
8. Cady 1954; Edwards 2002.
9. Go 2003: 182, 205–206.
10. Curtin 1989: 108–109; Osborne 2000: 135; Anderson 1992.
11. Platt 1923: 63.
12. Kennedy 1996: 117–146.
13. Stoler 2002.
14. Sen 2005: 63–65.
15. Anderson 1995.
16. Grier 2006: 6–7; Pomfret 2008: 186–188.
17. Osborne 1994: 86.
18. Star 1902: 69.
19. Jennings 2006: 15.
20. Osborne 1994: 89.
21. Anderson 1992.
22. Pomfret 2004.
23. Schneider 2002: 31.
24. Ha 2005: 205–206.
25. Schneider 2002: 45.
26. Jennings 2006; Ackerman 1996: 1088.
27. Wesseling 1997: 68.
28. Research for this chapter was generously supported by a Research Grants Council/ Competitive Earmarked Research Grant (HKU7455/05H). This account is based on Centre d'Archives Outre-mer, Aix-en-Provence, RSTNF F68 56362 "Dossier de l'affaire de l'enfant dit 'merveilleux,'" November–December 1899.

BIBLIOGRAPHY

Ackerman, Evelyn B. 1996. "The intellectual odyssey of a French colonial physician: Jules Regnault and Far Eastern medicine." *French Historical Studies* 19: 1083–1102.

Adams, Annemarie, and Peter Gossage. 2008. "Sick children and the thresholds of domesticity: The Dawson-Harrington families at home." In *Designing modern childhoods: History, space, and the material culture of children,* eds. Marta Gutman and Ning de Coninck-Smith. New Brunswick, NJ: Rutgers University Press.

Adams, Christine. 1999. "Constructing mothers and families: The Society for Maternal Charity of Bordeaux, 1805–1860." *French Historical Studies* 22: 65–86.

Ågren, Maria, and Amy Louise Erickson, eds. 2005. *The marital economy in Scandinavia and Britain, 1400–1900.* Aldershot: Ashgate.

Alfred [Samuel Kydd]. 1857. *The history of the factory movement.* London: Simpkin, Marshall.

Allen, Ann Taylor. 1991. *Feminism and motherhood in Germany, 1800–1914.* New Brunswick, NJ: Rutgers University Press.

Allen, Robert. 1994. "Agriculture during the Industrial Revolution, 1700–1850." In *The economic history of Britain since 1700,* Vol. 1, 2nd ed., eds. Roderick Floud and Donald McCloskey. Cambridge: Cambridge University Press.

Allender, Tim. 2007. "Surrendering a colonial dominion: Educating North India, 1854–1890." *History of Education* 31: 45–63.

Alston, Patrick L. 1969. *Education and the state in tsarist Russia.* Stanford, CA: Stanford University Press.

Alter, George. 1997. "Infant mortality in the United States and Canada." In *Infant and child mortality in the past,* eds. Alain Bideau, Bertrand Desjardins, and Hector Perez Brignoli. Oxford: Oxford University Press.

Anderson, Warwick. 1992. "Climates of opinion: Acclimatisation in nineteenth-century France and England." *Victorian Studies* 35: 135–157.

Anderson, Warwick. 1995. "Excremental colonialism: Public health and the poetics of pollution." *Critical Inquiry* 21: 640–669.

Ariès, Philippe. 1962. *Centuries of childhood.* Harmondsworth: Penguin.

Atkins, Anne. 2001. *We grew up together: Brothers and sisters in nineteenth-century America.* Urbana: University of Illinois Press.

Bagalopalan, Sarada. 2002. "Constructing indigenous childhoods: Colonialism, vocational education and the working child." *Childhood* 9(1): 19–34.

Bagnall, Kenneth. 1980. *The little immigrants: The orphans who came to Canada.* Toronto: Macmillan.

Baker, Henry B. 1880. "The relations of schools to diphtheria and to similar diseases." *American Public Health Association, Reports and Papers* 6: 107–123.

Baker, Hugh D. R. 1979. *Chinese family and kinship.* New York: Columbia University Press.

Bardet, J. -P. et al. 1997. "The death of foundlings: A tragedy in two acts." In *Infant and child mortality in the past,* eds. Alain Bideau et al. Oxford: Clarendon Press.

Bearce, G. D. 1961. *British attitudes toward India, 1784–1858.* Oxford: Oxford University Press.

Behlmer, George. 1982. *Child abuse and moral reform in England, 1870–1908.* Stanford, CA: Stanford University Press.

Behnken, Imbke, and Agnes Jonker. 1990. "Strassenkinder in Wiesbaden und Leiden: Historische Etnographie und interkulturelle Vergleich." In *Stadtgesellschaft und Kindheit im Process der Zivilisation,* ed. Imbke Behnken. Opladen: Leske und Budrich.

Belchem, John. 1990. *Industrialization and the working class: The English experience, 1750–1900.* Hants: Scolar Press.

Bellaigue, Christina de. 2007. *Educating women: Schooling and identity in England and France, 1800–1870.* Oxford: Oxford University Press.

Benjamin, Walter. 1992. *Barndom i Berlin omkring år 1900.* Copenhagen: Rævens Sorte Bibliotek.

Berg, Maxine. 1993. "Small producer capitalism in eighteenth century England." *Business History* 35: 17–39.

Berg, Maxine, and Pat Hudson. 1992. "Rehabilitating the Industrial Revolution." *Economic History Review,* 2nd series, 45: 25–50.

Berkovitz, Jay R. 1989. *The shaping of Jewish identity in nineteenth-century France.* Detroit: Wayne State University Press.

Bolin-Hort, Per. 1989. *Work, family and the state: Child labour and the organization of production in the British cotton industry, 1780–1920.* Lund: Lund University Press.

Bowen, James. 1981. *A history of Western education.* Vol. 3. London: Methuen.

Brace, Charles Loring. [1880] 1967. *The dangerous classes of New York and twenty years' work among them.* Glen Ridge, NJ: Patterson Smith.

Brembeck, Helene. 1988. *Arbetarstadsdelarnas barn: Rapport från projektet "Klass och metvetande."* University of Gothenburg, Department of Ethnology.

Brettell, Caroline. 2002. "Migration." In *The history of the European family*. Vol. 2, *Family life in the long nineteenth century, 1789–1913*, eds. David Kertzer and Marzio Barbagli. New Haven, CT: Yale University Press.

Brown, John. 1990. "The condition of England and the standard of living: Cotton textiles in the northwest, 1806–1850." *Journal of Economic History* 50: 591–615.

Buettner, Elizabeth. 2004. *Empire families: Britons and late imperial India*. Oxford: Oxford University Press.

Burguière, André, and François Lebrun. 1996. "The one hundred and one families of Europe." In *A history of the family*. Vol. 2, *The impact of modernity*, eds. André Burguière et al. Cambridge, MA: Belknap Press.

Burke, Catherine, and Ian Grosvenor. 2007. "Designed spaces. Disciplined bodies: E. R. Robson's grand architectural tour." In *Cultuuroverdracht als pedagogisch motief*, eds. G. Timmerman, N. Baker, and J. Dekker. Gronningen: Reaktion Books.

Burke, Catherine, and Ian Grosvenor. 2008. *School*. London: Reaktion Books.

Burman, R. 1987. "Women in Jewish religious life: Manchester 1880–1930." In *Disciplines of faith: Studies in religion, politics and patriarchy*, eds. J. Obelkevich, L. Roper, and R. Samuel. London: Routledge.

Cady, J. F. 1954. *The roots of French imperialism in Eastern Asia*. Ithaca, NY: Cornell University Press.

Calvert, Karin. 1992. *Children in the house: The material culture of early childhood, 1600–1900*. Boston: Northeastern University Press.

Carmichael, Ann G. 1993. "Diphtheria." In *The Cambridge world history of human disease*, ed. Kenneth F. Kiple. Cambridge: Cambridge University Press.

Cartier, Michel. 1996. "The long march of the Chinese family." In *A history of the family*. Vol. 2, *The impact of modernity*, eds. André Burguière et al. Cambridge, MA: Belknap Press.

Caspard, Pierre, 2003. "Les trois âges de la première communion en Suisse," In *Lorsque l'Enfant Grandit: Entre Dépendance et Autonomie*, eds. Jean-Noël Luc et al. Paris: Presses de l'Université de Paris-Sorbonne.

Cavallo, Dominick. 1981. *Muscles and morals: Organized playgrounds and urban reform, 1880–1920*. Philadelphia: University of Pennsylvania Press.

Chamberlain, Muriel. 1999. *Decolonisation: The fall of the European empires*. 2nd ed. Oxford: Blackwell.

Chancellor, Valerie E. 1970. *History for their masters*. Bath: Adams and Dart.

Châtelet, Anne-Marie. 1999. *La naissance de l'architecture scolaire: Les écoles élémentaires parisiennes de 1870 à 1914*. Paris: Honoré Champion.

Child, Mrs. Lydia. [1831] 1972. *The mother's book*. New York: Arno Press and New York Times.

"Children in the garden." 1869. *Tilton's Journal of Horticulture and Florists' Companion* 6(9): 151.

Ching, Frank. 1988. *Ancestors: 900 years in the life of a Chinese family*. New York: William Morrow.

Christensen, Christian. 1961. *En rabarberdreng vokser op*. Copenhagen: Hans Reitzels forlag.

Clark, Gregory. 1999. "Too much revolution: Agriculture in the Industrial Revolution, 1700–1860." In *The British Industrial Revolution: An economic perspective,* ed. Joel Mokyr. Boulder, CO: Westview Press.

Clement, Priscilla Ferguson. 1997. *Growing pains: Children in the Industrial Age, 1850–1890.* New York: Twayne.

Cmiel, Kenneth. 1995. *A home of another kind: One Chicago orphanage and the tangle of child welfare.* Chicago: University of Chicago Press.

Coale, Ansley, and Paul Demeny. 1983. *Regional model life tables and stable populations.* New York: Academic Press.

Coe, Richard N. 1984. *When the grass was taller: Autobiography and the experience of childhood.* New Haven, CT, and London: Yale University Press.

Cone, Thomas E. 1979. *History of American pediatrics.* Boston: Little, Brown.

Coontz, Stephanie. 2005. *Marriage, a history: From obedience to intimacy, or how love conquered marriage.* New York: Viking.

Cosnier, Colette. 2001. *Le Silence des Filles: De l'Aiguille à la Plume.* Paris: Fayard.

Crafts, N.F.R. 1985. *British economic growth during the Industrial Revolution.* New York: Oxford University Press.

Cross, Gary. 1997. *Kid's stuff: Toys and the changing world of American childhood.* Cambridge, MA: Harvard University Press.

Crossick, Geoffrey, and Gerhard-Haupt, Heinz. 1995. *The petite bourgeoisie in Europe, 1780–1914.* London: Routledge.

Cunningham, Hugh. 2007. "Childhood and happiness in Britain." In *Stories for children/histories of childhood.* Vol. 1, *Civilisation,* eds. Rosie Findlay and Sébastien Salbayre. Tours: Presses Universitaires François Rabelais.

Cunningham, Hugh. 2005. *Children and childhood in Western society since 1500.* 2nd ed. New York and London: Pearson Longman.

Cunningham, Hugh. 1991. *The children of the poor: Representations of childhood since the seventeenth century.* Oxford: Blackwell.

Cunningham, Hugh. 1990. "The employment and unemployment of children in England, c. 1680–1851." *Past and Present* 126: 115–150.

Curtin, Philip D. 1989. *Death by migration: Europe's encounter with the tropical world in the nineteenth century.* Cambridge: Cambridge University Press.

Darroch, Gordon. 2001. "Home and away: Patterns of residence, schooling and work among children and never married young adults, Canada, 1871 and 1901." *Journal of Family History* 26: 220–250.

Davidoff, Leonore, and Catherine Hall. 2002. *Family fortunes: Men and women of the English middle class.* London: Routledge.

Davies, David. 1811. *A new historical and descriptive view of Derbyshire.* Belper: S. Mason.

Davin, Anna. 1996. *Growing up poor: Home, school and street in London 1870–1914.* London: Rivers Oram Press.

Davin, Anna. 1999. "What is a child?" In *Childhood in question,* eds. Anthony Fletcher and Stephen Hussey. Manchester: Manchester University Press.

Davis, Eric Leiff. 1993. "The era of the common child: Egalitarian death in antebellum America." *Mid-America* 75: 135–163.

de Coninck-Smith, Ning. 2000. *For barnets skyld: Byen, skolen og barndommen 1880–1914*. Copenhagen: Gyldendal.

de Coninck-Smith, Ning. 1999. ' "He wishes nothing but good for the children, but knew that many had been harmed by it': Film censorship in Denmark 1896–1922." In *Childhood—old age: Equals or opposites?* eds. Jørgen Povlsen, Signe Mellemgaard, and Ning de Coninck-Smith. Odense: Odense University Press.

de Coninck-Smith, Ning. 1990. "Legepladser og byudvikling i København 1830–1930." In *At lære og være—i hvilke rammer?* eds. Ellen Nørgaard and Ning de Coninck-Smith. Vejle: Kroghs Forlag.

de Coninck-Smith, Ning. 1997. "The struggle for the child's time—at all times: School and children's work in town and country in Denmark from 1900 to the 1960s." In *Industrious children: Work and childhood in the Nordic countries 1850–1990*, eds. Ning de Coninck-Smith, Bengt Sandin, and Ellen Schrumpf. Odense: Odense University Press.

de Coninck-Smith, Ning. 1989. *Vor Lærdoms Bygning: Folkeskolens bygninger 1814–1940*. Report no. 2. Copenhagen: Planstyrelsen.

Donzelot, Jacques. [1977] 1997. *The policing of families*. Translated by Robert Hurley. Baltimore: Johns Hopkins University Press.

Dowling, Harry F. 1977. *Fighting infection: Conquests of the twentieth century*. Cambridge, MA: Harvard University Press.

Driscoll, Charles B. 1943. *Kansas Irish*. New York: Macmillan.

Edwards, Penny. 2002. "Propagender: Marianne, Joan of Arc and the export of French gender ideology to colonial Cambodia (1863–1954)." In *Promoting the colonial idea: Propaganda and visions of empire in France*, eds. Tony Chafer and Amanda Sackur. London: Palgrave.

Ehmer, Joseph. 2002. "Marriage." In *The history of the European family*. Vol. 2, *Family life in the long nineteenth century, 1789–1913*, eds. David Kertzer and Marzio Barbagli. New Haven, CT: Yale University Press.

Enciclopedia italiana. 1930–1934. Rome: Istituto Treccani.

Enciclopaedia Judaica. 2007. 2nd ed. Detroit: Macmillan Reference USA.

Encyclopædia Britannica. 1910–1922. 11th ed. New York: Encyclopædia Britannica.

Escherich, Theodore von. 1905. "The foundation and aims of modern pediatrics." *American Medicine* 9: 51–75.

Ettling, John. 1993. "Hookworm." In *The Cambridge world history of human disease*, ed. Kenneth F. Kiple. Cambridge: Cambridge University Press.

Eves, Richard. 2006. " 'Black and white, a significant contrast': Race, humanism and missionary photography in the Pacific." *Ethnic and Racial Studies* 29: 725–748.

Farge, Arlette, and Jacques Revel. 1991. *The vanishing children of Paris: Rumor and politics before the French Revolution*. Translated by Claudia Miéville. Cambridge, MA: Harvard University Press.

Fass, Paula S. 2007. "Childhood and globalization." In *Stories for children/histories of childhood*. Vol. 1. *Civilisation*, eds. Rosie Findlay and Sébastien Salbayre. Tours: Presses Universitaires François Rabelais.

Fass, Paula S. 1989. *Outside in: Minorities and the transformation of American education*. New York: Oxford University Press.

Fass, Paula, S., and Mary Ann Mason, eds. 2000. *Childhood in America*. New York: New York University Press.

Finkelstein, Barbara. 1985. "Casting networks of good influence: The reconstruction of childhood in the United States, 1790–1870." In *American childhood*, eds. J. M. Hawes and N. R. Hiner. Westport, CT: Greenwood Press.

"First annual report." [1854] 1971. In *Annual reports of the Children's Aid Society, Nos. 1–10, Feb. 1854–Feb. 1863*. New York: Arno Press and New York Times.

Fischer-Tiné, Harald, and Michael Mann, eds. 2004. *Colonialism as civilizing mission: Cultural ideology in British India*. London: Wimbledon.

Fletcher, Anthony. 2008. *Growing up in England: The experience of childhood, 1600–1914*. New Haven, CT: Yale University Press.

Foucault, Michel. 1979. *Discipline and punish: The birth of the prison*. New York: Vintage Books.

Frank, Stephen. 1998. *Life with father: Parenthood and masculinity in the nineteenth-century American North*. Baltimore: Johns Hopkins University Press.

Freedman, Russell. 1994. *Kids at work: Lewis Hine and the crusade against child labor*. New York: Clarion Books.

Frijhoff, Wilhelm. 1993. "Enfants Saints, Enfants Prodiges: l'Expérience Religieuse au Passage de l'Enfance à l'Age Adulte." *Paedagogica Historica* 29(1): 53–76.

Fuchs, Rachel G. 1984. *Abandoned children: Foundlings and child welfare in nineteenth-century France*. Albany: State University of New York Press.

Fuchs, Rachel G. 2003. *Child welfare: Historical dimensions, contemporary debate*. Bristol: Polity Press.

Fuchs, Rachel G. 2002. "Private Charity and Public Welfare." In *Family life in the long nineteenth century, 1789–1913*, eds. D. I. Kertzer and M. Barbagli. New Haven, CT: Yale University Press.

Fuchs, Rachel G. 2008. *Contested paternity: Constructing families in modern France*. Baltimore: Johns Hopkins University Press.

Fuchs, Rachel G. 2005. *Gender and poverty in nineteenth-century Europe*. Cambridge: Cambridge University Press.

Fuchs, Rachel G. 1992. *Poor and pregnant in Paris: Strategies for survival in the nineteenth century*. New Brunswick, NJ: Rutgers University Press.

Garlitz, Barbara. 1966. "The immortality ode: Its cultural progeny." *Studies in English Literature, 1500–1900* 6: 639–649.

Gaskell, Peter. 1833. *The manufacturing population of England*. S. l.: Baldwin and Craddock.

Gillis, John R. 2008. "Epilogue: The islanding of children: Reshaping the mythical landscapes of childhood." In *Designing modern childhoods: History, space, and the material culture of children*, eds. Marta Gutman and Ning de Coninck-Smith. New Brunswick, NJ: Rutgers University Press.

Gillis, John R. 1996. *A world of their own making: Myth, ritual, and the quest for family values*. New York: Basic Books.

Giorgio, Michaela de. 1991. "La Bonne Catholique." In *Histoire des Femmes en Occident*. Vol. 4. *Le XIXe siècle*, eds. M. Perrot and G. Fraisse. Paris: Plon.

Go, Julian. 2003. "The chains of empire: State building and 'political education' in Puerto Rico and the Philippines." In *The American colonial state in the Philippines: Global perspectives,* eds. Julian Go and Anne L. Foster. Durham, NC: Duke University Press.

Golden, Janet. 2004. "Children's health: Caregivers and sites of care." In *Children and youth in sickness and health,* eds. Janet Golden, Richard A. Meckel, and Heather Munro Prescott. Westport, CT: Greenwood Press.

Goldin, Claudia, and Ken Sokoloff. 1982. "Women, children and industrialization in the early republic: Evidence from the manufacturing censuses." *Journal of Economic History* 42: 741–774.

Gouda, Frances. 1995. *Poverty and political culture: The rhetoric of social welfare in the Netherlands and France, 1815–1854.* New York: Rowman & Littlefield.

Green, Abigail. 2001. *Fatherlands: State-building and nationhood in nineteenth-century Germany.* Cambridge: Cambridge University Press.

Green, Andy. 1990. *Education and state formation: The rise of education systems in England, France and the USA.* Basingstoke: Macmillan.

Grenby, Matthew. 2003. "Politicizing the nursery: British children's literature and the French Revolution." *The Lion and the Unicorn* 27: 1–26.

Greven, Philip. 1977. *The Protestant temperament: Patterns of child-rearing, religious experience, and the self in early America.* New York: Alfred A. Knopf.

Grier, Beverly Carolease. 2006. *Invisible hands: Child labour and the state in colonial Zimbabwe.* London: Heinemann.

Grossberg, Michael. 1985. *Governing the hearth: Law and the family in nineteenth-century America.* Chapel Hill: University of North Carolina Press.

Gutman, Marta. 2004. "School buildings and architecture: United States." In *Encyclopedia of children and childhood.* Vol. 3, ed. Paula S. Fass. New York: Macmillan Reference.

Gutman, Marta, and Ning de Coninck-Smith, eds. 2008. *Designing modern childhoods: History, space, and the material culture of children.* New Brunswick, NJ: Rutgers University Press.

Ha, Marie-Paule. 2005. "'La Femme Française aux Colonies': Promoting colonial female emigration at the turn of the century." *French Colonial History* 6: 205–224.

Hammond, J. L., and Barbara Hammond. 1937. *The town labourer.* New York: Doubleday Anchor.

Hammonds, Evelynn Maxine. 1999. *Childhood's deadly scourge: The campaign to control diphtheria in New York City, 1880–1930.* Baltimore: Johns Hopkins University Press.

Hampsten, Elizabeth. 1991. *Settlers' children: Growing up on the Great Plains.* Norman: University of Oklahoma Press.

Hardy, Anne. 1993. *The epidemic streets: Infectious disease and the rise of preventive medicine.* Oxford: Clarendon Press.

Harley, Knick. 1993. "Reassessing the Industrial Revolution: A macro view." In *The British Industrial Revolution: An economic assessment,* ed. Joel Mokyr. Boulder, CO: Westview Press.

Hartwell, R. M. 1971. *The Industrial Revolution and economic growth*. London: Methuen.

"Health and beauty." 1849. *Godey's Magazine and Lady's Book* 38(5): 370. kid size. 1997. *The material world of childhood*. Skira editore/Vitra Design Museum.

Hendrick, Harry. 1994. *Child welfare: England, 1872–1989*. London and New York: Routledge.

Hendrick, Harry. 2003. *Child welfare: Historical dimensions, contemporary debate*. Bristol: Polity Press.

Hendrick, Harry. 1997. *Children, childhood and English society, 1880–1990*. Cambridge: Cambridge University Press.

Heywood, Colin. 1988. *Childhood in nineteenth century France: Work, health and education among the 'classes populaires.'* Cambridge: Cambridge University Press.

Heywood, Colin. 2007. *Growing up in France: From the ancien régime to the third republic*. Cambridge: Cambridge University Press.

Heywood, Colin. 2001. *A history of childhood: Children and childhood in the West from medieval to modern times*. Cambridge: Polity.

Hill, Kenneth. 1995. "The decline of childhood mortality." In *The state of humanity*, ed. Julian Simon. Oxford: Blackwell.

Hindman, Hugh. 2002. *Child labor: An American history*. New York: M. E. Sharpe.

Hirsch, Susan E. 1978. *Roots of the American working class: The industrialization of crafts in Newark, 1800–1860*. Philadelphia: University of Pennsylvania Press.

Hobsbawm, Eric J. 1999. *Industry and empire: The birth of the Industrial Revolution*. New York: New Press.

Hobsbawm, Eric J. 1964. *Labouring men*. New York: Anchor Books.

Holt, Marilyn Irvin. 2003. *Children of the western plains: The nineteenth-century experience*. Chicago: Ivan R. Dee.

Holt, Marilyn Irvin. n.d. Holt genealogy. Typescript, in the possession of the author.

Holt, Marilyn Irvin. 1992. *The orphan trains: Placing out in America*. Lincoln: University of Nebraska Press.

Honey, J. R. de S. 1977. *Tom Brown's universe: The development of the Victorian public school*. London: Millington.

Horlbeck, H. B. 1881. "Scarlet fever as it affected the white and colored races, comparatively, in Charlestown, S.C., during the spring and summer of 1881." *American Public Health Association: Reports and Papers* 7: 291–292.

Horn, Pamela. 1974. *The Victorian country child*. Kineton, England: Roundwood Press.

Horn, Pamela. 1997. *The Victorian town child*. New York: New York University Press.

Horrell, Sara, and Jane Humphries. 1995. "The exploitation of little children: Child labor and the family economy in the Industrial Revolution." *Explorations in Economic History* 32: 485–516.

Horrell, Sara, and Jane Humphries. 1992. "Old questions, new data, and alternative perspectives: Families' living standards in the Industrial Revolution." *Journal of Economic History* 52: 849–880.

Horrell, Sara, and Jane Humphries. 1995. "Women's labor force participation and the transition to the male-breadwinner family, 1790–1865." *Economic History Review* 48: 89–117.

Houbre, Gabrielle. 2000. "Demoiselles Catholiques et 'Misses' Protestantes: Deux Modèles Educatifs Antagonistes au XIXe Siècle." *Bulletin de la Société de l'Histoire du Protestantisme Français* 146: 49–68.

House of Commons Papers. 1842 [380] XV *Children's employment (mines).*

Hunter, Jane. 2002. *How young ladies became girls: The Victorian origins of American girlhood.* New Haven, CT: Yale University Press.

Illick, Joseph E. 2002. *American childhoods.* Philadelphia: University of Pennsylvania Press.

Innes, Joanna. 1998. "State, church and voluntarism in European welfare, 1690–1850." In *Charity, philanthropy, and reform: From the 1690s to 1850,* eds. Hugh Cunningham and Joanna Innes. New York: St. Martin's Press.

Ipsen, Carl. 2006. *Italy in the age of Pinocchio: Children and danger in the liberal era.* New York: Palgrave.

Jablonka, Ivan. 2000. "Un discours philanthropique dans la France du XIXe Siècle: la rééducation des jeunes délinquants dans les colonies agricoles pénitentiaires." *Revue d'histoire moderne et contemporaine* 47: 131–147.

Jablonka, Ivan. 2005. "L'éducation des jeunes détenus à Mettray et dans les colonies agricoles pénitentiaires françaises (1830–1900)." In *Éduquer et punir: La colonie agricole et pénitentiaire de Mettray (1839–1937),* eds. Luc Forlivesi, Georges-François Pottier, and Sophie Chassat. Paris: PUR.

James, Allison, Chris Jenks, and Alan Prout. 1998. *Theorizing childhood.* Cambridge: Polity.

Jenks, Chris. 1996. *Childhood.* London: Routledge.

Jennings, Eric. 2006. *Curing the colonisers: Hydrotherapy, climatology and French colonial spas.* Durham, NC: Duke University Press.

Johnson, Dorothy. 2006. "Engaging identity: Portraits of children in late eighteenth-century European art." In *Fashioning childhood in the eighteenth century,* ed. Anja Müller. Aldershot: Ashgate.

Jones, Kathleen. 2004. "A sound mind for the child's body: The mental health of children and youth." In *Children and youth in sickness and health,* eds. Janet Golden, Richard A. Meckel, and Heather Munro Prescott. Westport, CT: Greenwood Press.

Jordan, Thomas E. 1993. *The degeneracy crisis and Victorian youth.* Albany: State University of New York Press.

Kaestle, Carl F. 1973. *The evolution of an urban school system: New York City, 1750–1850.* Cambridge, MA: Harvard University Press.

Kaestle, Carl F., and Maris A. Vinovskis. 1980. *Education and social change in nineteenth-century Massachusetts.* Cambridge: Cambridge University Press.

Kaplan, Marion. 1991. *The making of the Jewish middle class: Women, family and identity in imperial Germany.* Oxford: Oxford University Press.

Katz, Sanford N. 1971. *When parents fail: The law's response to family breakdown.* Boston: Beacon Press.

Kelly, Catriona. 2007. *Children's world: Growing up in Russia, 1890–1991*. New Haven, CT: Yale University Press.

Kennedy, Dane. 1996. *The magic mountains: Hill stations and the British Raj*. Delhi: Oxford University Press.

Kerber, Linda. 1988. "Separate spheres, female worlds, woman's place: The rhetoric of women's history." *Journal of American History* 75: 9–39.

Kertzer, David, and Marzio Barbagli, eds. 2002. *The history of the European family.* Vol. 2. *Family life in the long nineteenth century, 1789–1913*. New Haven, CT: Yale University Press.

Kett, Joseph F. 1971. "Adolescence and youth in nineteenth-century America." *Journal of Interdisciplinary History* 2: 283–298.

Kevles, Daniel. 1985. *In the name of eugenics: Genetics and the uses of human heredity*. New York: Knopf.

King, Wilma. 1995. *Stolen childhood: Slave youth in nineteenth-century America*. Bloomington: Indiana University Press.

Klapper, Melissa R. 2006. *Small strangers: The experience of immigrant children in America, 1880–1925*. Chicago: Ivan R. Dee.

Kleberg, Rosa. 1898. "Some of my early experiences in Texas." Translated by Rudolph Kleberg Jr. *Quarterly of the Texas State Historical Association* 1: 298–308.

Klein, Herbert S. 2004. *A population history of the United States*. Cambridge: Cambridge University Press.

Knodel, John. 1988. *Demographic behavior in the past: A study of fourteen German village populations in the eighteenth and nineteenth centuries*. Cambridge: Cambridge University Press.

Kociumbus, Jan. 1997. *Australian childhood: A history*. St. Leonards: Allen & Unwin.

Komlos, Jon, and Jorg Baten. 2004. "Looking backward and looking forward: Anthropometric research and the development of social science history." *Social Science History* 28: 191–210.

Kristenson, Hjördis. 2005. *Skolhuset: Idé och form*. Lund: Bokförlaget Signum.

Laslett, Peter. 1965. *The world we have lost—Further explored*. London: Methuen.

Laslett, Peter, ed. 1972. *Household and family in past time*. Cambridge: Cambridge University Press.

Lassonde, Stephan. 2005. *Learning to forget: Schooling and family life in New Haven's working class, 1870–1940*. New Haven, CT: Yale University Press.

Lavalette, Michael, ed. 1999. *A thing of the past? Child labour in Britain in the nineteenth and twentieth centuries*. New York: St. Martin's Press.

Leifchild, J. R. 1853. *Our coal and our coal pits*. London: Longman, Brown, Green, and Longmans.

Lejeune, Philippe. 1993. *Le Moi des Demoiselles: Enquête sur le Journal de Jeune Fille*. Paris: Editions du Seuil.

Lerner, Laurence. 1997. *Angels and absences: Child deaths in the nineteenth century*. London: Vanderbilt University Press.

Lindenmeyr, Adele. 1996. *Poverty is not a vice: Charity, society, and the state in imperial Russia*. Princeton, NJ: Princeton University Press.

Lindert, Peter, and Jeffrey Williamson. 1983. "English workers' living standards during the Industrial Revolution: A new look." *Economic History Review* 36: 1–25.

Livi Bacci, Massimo. 2000. *The population of Europe*. Oxford: Blackwell.

Lloyd, Rosemary. 1992. *The land of lost content: Children and childhood in nineteenth-century French literature*. Cambridge: Cambridge University Press.

Löfgren, Orvar, and Jonas Frykman. 1987. *Culture builders: A historical anthropology of middle-class life*. New Brunswick, NJ: Rutgers University Press.

Løkke, Anne. 1990. *Vildfarende børn: om forsømte og kriminelle børn mellem filantropiog stat 1880–1920*. Holte: SocPol.

Luc, Jean-Noël et al., eds. 2003. *Lorsque l'Enfant Grandit: Entre Dépendance et Autonomie*. Paris: Presses de l'Université de Paris-Sorbonne.

Luddy, Maria. 1995. *Women and philanthropy in nineteenth-century Ireland*. Cambridge: Cambridge University Press.

Macleod, David I. 1998. *The age of the child: Children in America, 1890–1920*. New York: Twayne.

Markus, Thomas A. 1993. *Buildings and power: Freedom and control in the origins of modern building types*. London: Routledge.

Marten, James Alan. 1998. *The children's civil war*. Chapel Hill: University of North Carolina Press.

Martin, Mary Claire. 2004. "Relationships human and divine: Retribution and repentance in children's lives, 1740–1870." *Studies in Church History* 40: 253–265.

Martinson, Floyd M. 1992. *Growing up in Norway, 800–1900*. Carbondale: Southern Illinois University Press.

Maynes, Mary Jo. 2002. "Class cultures and images of proper family life." In *Family life in the long nineteenth century, 1789–1913,* eds. D. I. Kertzer and M. Barbagli. New Haven, CT: Yale University Press.

Maynes, Mary Jo. 1985. *Schooling in Western Europe: A social history*. Albany: State University of New York Press.

Maynes, Mary Jo. 1995. *Taking the hard road: Life course in French and German workers' autobiographies in the era of industrialization*. London: University of North Carolina Press.

McLaren, Angus. 1990. *A history of contraception: From antiquity to the present day*. Oxford: Basil Blackwell.

McLoughlin, William G. 1985. "Evangelical child rearing in the age of Jackson." In *Growing up in America*, eds. N. R. Hiner and J. M. Hawes. Champaign: University of Illinois Press.

Meckel, Richard A. 2002. "Going to school, getting sick: The social and medical construction of 'school diseases' in the late 19th century." In *Formative years: Children's health in America, 1880–2000*, eds. Alexandra Minna Stern and Howard Markel. Ann Arbor: University of Michigan Press.

Meckel, Richard A. 2004. "Levels and trends of death and disease in childhood, 1620 to the present." In *Children and youth in sickness and health*, eds. Janet Golden, Richard A. Meckel, and Heather Munro Prescott. Westport, CT: Greenwood Press.

Meckel, Richard A. 1996. "Open-air schools and the tuberculous child in early 20th century America." *Archives of Pediatric and Adolescent Medicine* 150: 91–96.

Meckel, Richard A. 1990. *Save the babies: American public health reform and the prevention of infant mortality 1850–1929*. Baltimore: Johns Hopkins University Press.

Mendels, Franklin. 1972. "Proto-industrialization: The first phase of the industrialization process." *Journal of Economic History* 32: 241–261.

Mension-Rigau, Eric. 1990. *L'Enfance au chateau: l'éducation familiale des élites françaises au vingtième siècle*. Paris: Rivages.

Mergen, Bernard. 1992. "Made, brought, and stolen: Toys and culture of childhood." In *Small worlds: Children and adolescents in America, 1850–1950*, eds. Elliot West and Paula Petrik. Lawrence: University Press of Kansas.

Miller, Julie. 2008. *Abandoned: Foundlings in nineteenth-century New York City*. New York: New York University Press.

Miller, Pavla. 1998. *Transformations of patriarchy in the West, 1500–1900*. Bloomington: Indiana University Press.

Mills, Hazel. 1995. "Women and Catholicism in provincial France." PhD thesis, University of Oxford.

Mintz, Steve. 2004. *Huck's raft: A history of American childhood*. Cambridge, MA: Harvard University Press.

Mintz, Steve, and Susan Kellogg. 1988. *Domestic revolutions: A social history of American family life*. New York: Free Press.

Mitterauer, Michael, and Reinhard Sieder. 1982. *The European family: Patriarchy to partnership from the Middle Ages to the present*. Chicago: University of Chicago Press.

Moch, Leslie Page. 1992. "The history of migration and fertility decline: The view from the road." In *The European experience of declining fertility: The quiet revolution*, eds. John Gillis et al. Cambridge: Blackwell.

Mokyr, Joel, ed. 1999. *The British Industrial Revolution: An economic perspective*. Boulder, CO: Westview Press.

Morrison, Joan, and Charlotte Fox Zabusky, eds. 1993. *American mosaic: The immigrant experience in the words of those who lived it*. Pittsburgh: University of Pittsburgh Press.

Myers, John E. 2006. *Child protection in America: Past, present, and future*. New York: Oxford University Press.

Nardinelli, Clark. 1990. *Child labor and the Industrial Revolution*. Bloomington: Indiana University Press.

Nasaw, David. 1985. *Children of the city: At work and at play*. New York: Oxford University Press.

Newsholme, Arthur. 1935. *Fifty years in public health: A personal narrative with comments*. London: Allen & Unwin.

Newsome, David. 1961. *Godliness and good learning: Four studies on a Victorian ideal*. London: John Murray.

New York Times, July 19, 1876.

Nielsen, Carl. 1927. *Min fynske Barndom*. Copenhagen: Martin.

O'Kieffe, Charley. 1960. *Western story: The recollections of Charley O'Kieffe, 1884–1898*. Lincoln: University of Nebraska Press.

Oris, Michael, Renzo Derosas, and Marco Breschi. 2004. "Infant and child mortality." In *Life under pressure: Mortality and living standards in Europe and Asia, 1700–1900*, eds. Tommy Bengtsson et al. Cambridge, MA: MIT Press.

Osborne, Michael A. 2000. "Acclimatizing the world: A history of the paradigmatic colonial science." *Osiris* 2nd series, 15, *Nature and Empire: Science and the Colonial Enterprise.*

Osborne, Michael A. 1994. *Nature, the exotic, and the science of French colonialism.* Bloomington: Indiana University Press.

Pellissier, Catherine. 2003. "Loisirs et sociabilités juvéniles au sein du patriciat lyonnais (1848–1914)." In *Lorsque l'Enfant Grandit: Entre Dépendance et Autonomie*, eds. Jean-Noël Luc et al. Paris: Presses de l'Université de Paris-Sorbonne.

Pinchbeck, Ivy. 1930. *Women workers and the Industrial Revolution, 1750–1800.* London: George Routledge and Sons.

Platt, Anthony M. 1978. *The child savers: The invention of delinquency.* 2nd ed. Chicago: Chicago University Press.

Platt, Kate. 1923. *The home and health in India and tropical colonies.* London: Baillière, Tindall and Cox.

Plotz, Judith. 2001. *Romanticism and the vocation of childhood.* New York: Palgrave.

Pollard, Sidney. 1965. *The genesis of modern management: A study of the Industrial Revolution in Great Britain.* London: Edward Arnold.

Pollock, Linda. 1983. *Forgotten children: Parent-child relations from 1500 to 1900.* Cambridge: Cambridge University Press.

Pomfret, David. 2008. "Child slavery in British and French Far-Eastern colonies, 1880–1945." *Past and Present* 201: 175–213.

Pomfret, David. 2001. "Representations of adolescence in the modern city: Voluntary provision and work in Nottingham and Saint-Etienne, 1890–1914." *Journal of Family History* 26(4): 455–479.

Pomfret, David. 2004. *Young people and the European city: Age relations in Nottingham and Saint-Etienne.* Aldershot: Ashgate.

Popkewitz, Thomas S. 1997. "Educational sciences and the normalizations of the teacher and the child: Some historical notes on current USA pedagogical reforms." In *Teachers, curriculum and policy*, eds. I. Nilsson and L. Lundahl. Umeå, Sweden: Umeå University Press.

Porter, Roy. 1999. *The greatest benefit to mankind: A medical history of humanity.* New York: W.W. Norton.

Preston, Samuel H., and Michael R. Haines. 1991. *Fatal years: Child mortality in late nineteenth-century America.* Princeton, NJ: Princeton University Press.

Prochaska, Frank. 1978. "Little vessels: Children in the nineteenth-century English missionary movement." *Journal of Imperial and Commonwealth History* 6(2): 103–118.

Rahikainen, Marjatta. 2004. *Centuries of child labour: European experiences from the seventeenth to the twentieth century.* Aldershot: Ashgate.

Rahikainen, Marjatta. 2001. "Children and 'the right to factory work': Child labour legislation in nineteenth-century Finland." *Scandinavian Economic History Review* 49: 41–62.

Razzell, Peter. 1994. "A critique of 'An Interpretation of the Modern Rise of Population.'" In *Essays in English population history*, ed. Peter Razzell. London: Caliban.

Reagin, Nancy. 2001. "The imagined *Hausfrau*: National identity, domesticity and colonialism in imperial Germany." *Journal of Modern History* 73: 54–86.

Reinier, Jacqueline S. 1996. *From virtue to character: American childhood, 1775–1850.* New York: Twayne.

Rendall, Jane. 1990. *Woman in industrializing society: England 1750–1880.* Oxford: Basil Blackwell.

Richardson, Alan. 1994. *Literature, education, and romanticism.* Cambridge: Cambridge University Press.

Riley, James C. 2001. *Rising life expectancy: A global history.* Cambridge: Cambridge University Press.

Rogers, Rebecca. 2005. *From the salon to the schoolroom: Educating bourgeois girls in nineteenth-century France.* University Park: Pennsylvania State University Press.

Rose, Lionel. 1986. *The massacre of the innocents: Infanticide in Britain, 1800–1939.* London: Routledge & Kegan Paul.

Rosenberg, Charles E. 2003. "Health in the home." In *Right living: An Anglo-American tradition of self-help medicine and hygiene,* ed. Charles E. Rosenberg. Baltimore: Johns Hopkins University Press.

Rosenblum, Robert. 1988. *The romantic child.* London: Thames and Hudson.

Ross, Ellen. 1993. *Love and toil: Motherhood in outcast London, 1870–1918.* New York: Oxford University Press.

Rothenbacher, Franz. 2002. *The European population, 1850–1945.* Houndsmills: Palgrave.

Rousseau, Jean-Jacques. 2003 [1762]. *Emile: Or treatise on education.* New York: Prometheus.

Rudolph, Abraham M., ed. 1982. *Pediatrics.* 17th ed. Norwalk, CT: Appleton-Century-Crofts.

Ryan, Patrick. 2005. "A case study in the cultural origins of a superpower: Liberal individualism, American nationalism, and the rise of high school life—A study of Cleveland's Central and East Technical High Schools, 1890–1918." *History of Education Quarterly* 45: 66–95.

Sandin, Bengt. 1986. *Hemmet, gatan, fabriken eller skolan: folkundervisning och barnuppfostran i svenska städer 1600–1850.* Dissertation, Lund University.

Sandin, Bengt. 1997. "'In the large factory towns': Child labour legislation, child labour and school compulsion." In *Industrious children: Work and childhood in the Nordic countries, 1850–1990,* eds. Ning de Coninck-Smith, Bengt Sandin, and Ellen Schrumpf. Odense: Odense University Press.

Sandin, Bengt, and Antonia Novoa. 2005. "Mechanism of inclusion or exclusion?" International Congress of Historical Sciences (2005). 20th International Congress of Historical Sciences, University of New South Wales, Sydney, Australia. Sydney: International Committee of Historical Sciences.

Schneider, William H. 2002. *Quality and quantity: The quest for biological regeneration in twentieth-century France.* Cambridge: Cambridge University Press.

Schofield, R., and D. Reher. 1991. "The decline of mortality in Europe." In *The decline of mortality in Europe,* eds. R. Schofield et al. Oxford: Clarendon Press.

Schwartz, Marie Jenkins. 2000. *Born in bondage: Growing up enslaved in the antebellum South.* Cambridge, MA: Harvard University Press.

Seaborne, Malcolm, and Roy Lowe. 1977. *The English school: Its architecture and organization.* Vol. 2. *1870–1970.* London: Routledge and Kegan Paul.

Seeley, Paul. 1998. "'O Sainte Mère': Liberalism and the socialization of Catholic men in nineteenth-century France." *Journal of Modern History* 70(4): 862–891.

Sen, Sadatru. 2005. *Colonial childhoods: The juvenile periphery of India, 1850–1945.* London: Anthem.

Sen, Sadatru. 2002. "The savage family: Colonialism and female infanticide in nineteenth century India." *Journal of Women's History* 14: 53–79.

Shammas, Carole. 2002. *A history of household government in America.* Charlottesville: University of Virginia Press.

Siceloff, David G. 1964. *Boy settler in the Cherokee strip.* Caldwell, ID: Caxton Printers.

Sigle, Wendy, David Kertzer, and Michael White. 2000. "Abandoned children and their transition to adulthood in nineteenth-century Italy." *Journal of Family History* 25: 326–340.

Sjöberg, Mats. 1996. *Att säkra framtidens skördar: barndom, skola och arbete i agrar miljö: Bolstad pastorat 1860–1930.* Dissertation, Linköping University.

Sjöberg, Mats. 1997. "Working rural children: Herding, child labour and childhood in the Swedish rural environment 1850–1950." In *Industrious children: Work and childhood in the Nordic countries 1850–1990,* eds. Ning de Coninck-Smith, Bengt Sandin, and Ellen Schrumpf. Odense: Odense University Press.

Smelser, Neil. 1959. *Social change in the Industrial Revolution.* Chicago: University of Chicago Press.

Smith, Adam. 1904. *An inquiry into the nature and causes of the wealth of nations.* 5th ed. Edited by Edwin Cannan. London: Methuen.

Smith, Bonnie, G. 1981. *Ladies of the leisure class: The bourgeoises of northern France in the nineteenth century.* Princeton, NJ: Princeton University Press.

Smith, Mark K. 2009. *Johann Heinrich Pestalozzi.* Available at: http://www.infed.org/thinkers/et-pest.htm. Accessed July 22, 2008.

Sommerville, C. John. 1982. *The rise and fall of childhood.* Beverly Hills, CA: Sage.

Soysal, Y., and D. Strang. 1989. "Construction of the first mass education systems in nineteenth-century Europe." *Sociology of Education* 62: 277–288.

Spann, Edward K. 1981. *The new metropolis: New York City, 1840–1857.* New York: Columbia University Press.

Spree, Richard. 1992. "Shaping the child's personality: Medical advice on child-rearing from the late eighteenth to the early twentieth century in Germany." *Social History of Medicine* 5: 317–335.

Springhall, John. 1986. *Coming of age: Adolescence in Britain, 1860–1960.* Dublin: Gill and Macmillan.

Stang Dahl, Tove. 1978. *Barnevern og samfunnsvern: Om stat, vitenskap og profesioner under barnevernets opkomst i Norge.* Oslo: Pax forlag.

Stanley, Brian. 1994. "'Missionary regiments for Immanuel's service': Juvenile missionary organization in English Sunday schools, 1841–1865." *Studies in Church History* 31: 391–403.

Stansell, Christine. 1986. *City of women: Sex and class in New York, 1789–1860.* New York: Knopf.

Star, Jean [Jules Clément Ladislas Lubanski]. 1902. *Tonkinades*. Paris: Calman-Lévy.

Stearns, Peter N. 2006. *Childhood in world history*. New York: Routledge.

Steckel, Richard H. 2000. "The African American population of the United States, 1790–1920." In *A population history of North America*, eds. Michael R. Haines and Richard H. Steckel. Cambridge: Cambridge University Press.

Steckel, Richard H. 1988. "The health and welfare of women and children 1850–1860." *Journal of Economic History* 48: 333–345.

Stenkula, Anders, 1879. *Om folkskolor och barnhem: Anteckningar under en resa.* Lund: C.W.K. Gleerup.

Stoler, Ann Laura. 2002. *Carnal knowledge and imperial power: Race and the intimate in colonial rule.* Berkeley: University of California Press.

Stokvis, Pieter, R. D. 1993. "From child to adult: Transition rites in the Netherlands, c. 1800–1914." *Paedagogica Historica* 24(1): 77–92.

Stowe, Lyman Beecher. 1934. *Saints, sinners, and Beechers*. Indianapolis, IN: Bobbs-Merrill.

Strange, K. H. 1982. *The climbing boys: A study of sweeps' apprentices, 1773–1875.* London: Allison & Busby.

Sundkvist, Maria. 1994. *De vanartade barnen: mötet mellan barn, föräldrar och Norrköpings barnavårdsnämnd 1903–1925.* Dissertation, Linköping University.

Sundstrom, Linea. 1997. "Smallpox used them up: References to epidemic disease in northern plains winter counts." *Ethnohistory* 44: 305–343.

Sussman, George D. 1982. *Selling mothers' milk: The wet-nursing business in France, 1715–1914.* Urbana: University of Illinois Press.

Sutherland, Gillian. 1990. "Education." In *Cambridge social history of Britain, 1750–1950*. Vol. 3, ed. F.M.L. Thompson. Cambridge: Cambridge University Press.

Termin, Lewis M. 1914. *The hygiene of the school child*. Boston: Houghton Mifflin.

Thompson, E. P. 1966. *The making of the English working class*. New York: Vintage Books.

Thornton, Arland. 2005. *Reading history sideways: The fallacy and enduring impact of the developmental paradigm on family life.* Chicago: University of Chicago Press.

Thuen, Harald. 2002. *I foreldrenes sted: Barneredningens oppdragelsesdiskurs 1820–1900. Eksemplelet Toftes Gave.* Oslo: Pax forlag.

Tilly, Louise A., and J. W. Scott. 1978. *Women, work and family.* New York: Holt, Rinehart and Winston.

Tosh, John. 1999. *A man's place: Masculinity and the middle-class home in Victorian England.* New Haven, CT: Yale University Press.

Trattner, Walter L. 1970. *Crusade for the children: A history of the National Child Labor Committee and child labor reform in America.* Chicago: Quadrangle.

Traugott, Mark, ed. 1993. *The French worker: Autobiographies from the early industrial era.* Berkeley: University of California Press.

Tressell, Robert. 1914. *The ragged trousered philanthropists.* S. I. Richards.

Trousseau, M. 1857. "A few words on cholera infantum." *Boston Medical and Surgical Journal* 60: 74–76.

Tullos, Allen. 1989. *Habits of industry: White culture and the transformation of the Carolina Piedmont.* Chapel Hill: University of North Carolina Press.

Turk, Eleanor L. 1989. "Selling the heartland: Agents, agencies, press and policies in promoting German emigration to Kansas in the nineteenth century." *Kansas History* 12: 150–159.

Tuttle, Carolyn. 1999. *Hard at work in factories and mines: The economics of child labor during the British Industrial Revolution.* Boulder, CO: Westview Press.

Tuttle, Carolyn. 1998. "A revival of the pessimist view: Child labor and the Industrial Revolution." *Research in Economic History* 18: 53–82.

Tyack, David B. 1974. *The one best system: A history of American urban education.* Cambridge, MA: Harvard University Press.

United Nations, Department of Economic and Social Affairs, Population Division. 2007. *World population prospects: The 2006 revision.* New York: United Nations.

Ure, Andrew. 1835. *The philosophy of manufactures.* London: Chas. Knight.

Valenze, Deborah. 1995. *The first industrial women.* Oxford: Oxford University Press.

Vallin, Jacques. 1991. "Mortality in Europe from 1720 to 1914: Long-term trends and changes in patterns by age and sex." In *The decline of mortality in Europe,* eds. R. Schofield et al. Oxford: Clarendon Press.

Van de Walle, Francine. 1986. "Infant mortality and the European demographic transition." In *The decline of fertility in Europe,* eds. Ansley Coale and Susan Cotts Watkins. Princeton, NJ: Princeton University Press.

Van Slyck, Abigail A. 2007. "Playing houses: Social class, scale, and separation in Victorian America." Paper delivered to the Society for the History of Childhood and Youth Conference, Norrköping, Sweden.

Vickery, Amanda. 1993. "Golden Age to separate spheres?: A review of the categories and chronology of English women's history." *Historical Journal* 36: 383–414.

Von Tunzelmann, G. N. 1981. "Technical progress during the Industrial Revolution." In *The economic history of Britain since 1700.* Vol. 1. *1700–1860,* eds. Roderick Floud and Donald McCloskey. Cambridge: Cambridge University Press.

Vries, Jan de. 1994. "The Industrial Revolution and the industrious revolution." *Journal of Economic History* 54: 249–270.

Wagner, Gillian. 1981. "Education and the destitute child after 1870." In *Childhood, youth and education in the late nineteenth century,* ed. John Hurt. London: History of Education Society.

Waites, Matthew. 2005. *The age of consent: Young people, sexuality and citizenship.* Basingstoke: Palgrave Macmillan.

Waugh, Frank Albert. n.d. "Pioneering in Kansas." Reminiscence. Library, Kansas State Historical Society, Topeka.

Wayland, Francis. 1836. *Elements of moral science.* Boston: Gould, Kendall and Lincoln.

Weber, Adna Ferrin. 1967. *The growth of cities in the nineteenth century: A study in statistics.* Ithaca, NY: Cornell University Press.

Weber-Kellermann, Ingeborg. 1991. *Die Kinderstube.* Frankfurt am Main: Insel Verlag.

Weber-Kellermann, Ingeborg. 1979. *Die Kindheit: Kleidung und Wohnen, Arbeit und Spiel: eine Kulturgeschichte.* Frankfurt am Main: Insel Verlag.

Weissbach, Lee Shai. 1989. *Child labor reform in nineteenth-century France: Assuring the future harvest.* Baton Rouge and London: Louisiana State University Press.

Wesseling, H. L. 1997. *Imperialism and colonialism: Essays on the history of European expansion.* Westport, CT: Greenwood Press.

West, Elliott. 1992. "Children on the plains frontier." In *Small wonders: Children and adolescents in America, 1850–1950,* eds. Elliott West and Paula Petrik. Lawrence: University Press of Kansas.

West, Elliott. 1989. *Growing up with the country: Childhood on the far western frontier.* Albuquerque: University of New Mexico Press.

West, Elliott. 1983. "Heathens and angels: Childhood in the Rocky Mountain mining towns." *Western Historical Quarterly* 14(2): 145–164.

Whitehead, Clive. 2005. "The historiography of British imperial education policy, Part I: India." *History of Education* 34: 315–329.

Wines, E. C. 1880. *The state of children and of child saving institutions in the civilized world.* Cambridge: Cambridge University Press.

Wohl, Anthony S. 1983. *Endangered lives: Public health in Victorian England.* Cambridge, MA: Harvard University Press.

Wolf, Arthur P., and Chieh-shan Huang. 1980. *Marriage and adoption in China, 1845–1945.* Stanford, CA: Stanford University Press.

Wolf, Jacqueline. 2001. *Don't kill your baby.* Columbus: Ohio University Press.

Wordsworth, William. 1985. *The two-part prelude.* Edited by Jonathan Wordsworth. Cambridge: Cambridge University Press.

Wrigley, E. A. 1988. *Continuity, chance and change: The character of the Industrial Revolution in England.* Cambridge: Cambridge University Press.

Wrigley, E. A., and R. S. Schofield. 1981. *The population history of England 1541–1871: A reconstitution.* Cambridge, MA: Harvard University Press.

Wylie, Laurence. 1964. *Village in the Vaucluse.* 2nd ed. Cambridge, MA: Harvard University Press.

Yousef, Nancy. 2001. "Savage or solitary? The wild child and Rousseau's man of nature." *Journal of the History of Ideas* 62: 245–263.

Zeiher, Helga. 2001. "Children's islands in space and time: The impact of spatial differentiation on children's ways of shaping social life." In *Childhood in Europe: Approaches-trends-findings,* eds. Manuela du Bois-Reymond, Heinz Sünker, and Heinz-Hermann Krüger. New York: Peter Lang.

Zelizer, Viviana A. 1985. *Pricing the priceless child: The changing social value of children.* New York: Basic Books.

Zinnecker, Jürgen. 1990. "Von Strassenkind zum verhäuslichten Kind: Kindheitsgeschichte im Process der Zivilisation." In *Stadtgesellschaft und Kindheit im Process der Zivilisation,* ed. Imbke Behnken. Opladen: Leske und Budrich.

CONTRIBUTORS

Christina de Bellaigue is fellow, tutor, and university lecturer in history at Exeter College, Oxford. Her first book, *Educating Women: Schooling and Identity in England and France, 1800–1867* was published in 2007. She is currently working on a comparative study of ideas and experiences of adolescence in nineteenth-century France and England.

Ning de Coninck-Smith is professor in the Danish School of Education/Aarhus University. Her many publications include (as co-editor) *Industrious Children: Work and Childhood in the Nordic Countries 1850–1990* (1997) and *For barnets skyld: Byen, skolen og barndommen 1880–1914* (2000). She is currently working on projects concerning schooling for life in Denmark and housing for Danish children over the past 275 years.

Rachel G. Fuchs is the Distinguished Foundation Professor of History at Arizona State University. She is the author of six books, including *Poor and Pregnant in Paris: Strategies for Survival in the Nineteenth Century* (1992), *Gender and Poverty in Nineteenth-Century Europe* (2005), and *Contested Paternity: Constructing Families in Modern France* (2008).

Colin Heywood is professor of modern French history at the University of Nottingham. His publications on the history of childhood include *Childhood in Nineteenth Century France* (1988), *A History of Childhood* (2001), and *Growing Up in Modern France* (2007). He is currently working on a history of childhood and youth in modern Europe.

Marilyn Irvin Holt has been on staff at the Illinois State Historical Library and the Kansas State Historical Society. She has been a consultant for PBS television documentaries and served on the adjunct faculty at the University of Kansas and Emporia State University. Her book publications include *The Orphan Trains: Placing Out in America* and *Children of the Western Plains: The Nineteenth-Century Experience*. Her current research focuses on government policy and child-related issues in post-World War II United States.

Carl Ipsen is a historian of modern Italy. His major publications include *Dictating Demography: The Problem of Population in Fascist Italy* (1996) and *Italy in the Age of Pinocchio: Children and Danger in the Liberal Era* (2006). He studied at the University of California, Berkeley, and teaches at the University of Indiana.

James Marten is professor and chair of the History Department at Marquette University in Milwaukee, Wisconsin, where he teaches courses on children's history and on the era of the American Civil War. He is author or editor of more than a dozen books, including *Children and Youth in a New Nation* (2009); *Children in Colonial America* (2006); *Childhood and Child Welfare in the Progressive Era: A Brief History with Documents* (2004); *Children and War: A Historical Anthology* (2002); and *The Children's Civil War* (1998). He is founding secretary-treasurer of the Society for the History of Children and Youth and currently serves as president of the Society of Civil War Historians.

Richard Meckel is associate professor of American civilization at Brown University. He is the author of *Save the Babies: American Public Health Reform and the Prevention of Infant Mortality 1850–1929* (1990) and co-editor of *Children and Youth in Sickness and Health* (2004). He is currently studying a century and a half of (largely unrealized) plans to use the public school system to improve the health of U.S. youth.

David M. Pomfret is an associate professor of modern European history at the University of Hong Kong. He has published widely on the history of childhood and youth in Europe and European empires, including *Young People and the European City: Age Relations in Nottingham and Saint-Etienne* (2004), and on age more generally as a category of historical analysis. He is currently completing a monograph on the comparative history of childhood and youth in British and French colonies.

Bengt Sandin is a professor of child studies at the University of Linköping in Sweden. He is presently the head of the Department of Child Studies. His publications include work on early modern urban childhood and education, child labor, normalization of childhood, and changing conceptions of children and childhood in the modern welfare state. He is currently writing on the history of child psychiatry in Sweden and engaged in a project about welfare, child murder, abortion, and fetal identity.

Carolyn Tuttle is the Betty Jane Schultz Hollender Professor of Economics at Lake Forest College, where she has taught for twenty-five years. Her publications include a book entitled *Hard at Work in Factories and Mines: The Economics of Child Labor in Great Britain* (1999). She has several publications on child labor in encyclopedias and a chapter entitled "Why Countries Use Child Labor to Industrialize" in the book *Child Labour's Global Past: 1500–2000* (2010). In 2004, she finished field research in Mexico, interviewing six hundred *maquiladora* workers along the border. Using this data, she recently completed a book manuscript entitled *American Factories in Mexico: Liberation or Exploitation?*

INDEX

www.ingramcontent.com/pod-product-compliance
Lightning Source LLC
Chambersburg PA
CBHW081432270326
41932CB00019B/3174